Also by Peter Gethers

FICTION

The Dandy

Getting Blue

Ask Bob

WRITTEN AS RUSSELL ANDREWS

Gideon

Icarus

Aphrodite

Midas

Hades

NONFICTION

The Cat Who Went to Paris

A Cat Abroad

The Cat Who'll Live Forever

THEATER

Old Jews Telling Jokes
(cocreated with Daniel Okrent)

A Bed and a Chair: Sondheim/Marsalis
(cocreated with Jack Viertel and John Doyle)

MY MOTHER'S KITCHEN

My Mother's
Kitchen

————

Breakfast, Lunch, Dinner, and
the Meaning of Life

Peter Gethers

Henry Holt and Company New York

Henry Holt and Company
Publishers since 1866
175 Fifth Avenue
New York, New York 10010
www.henryholt.com

Henry Holt® and ® are registered trademarks of
Macmillan Publishing Group, LLC.

Library of Congress Cataloging-in-Publication Data

Names: Gethers, Peter, author.
Title: My mother's kitchen : breakfast, lunch, dinner, and the meaning of life /
    Peter Gethers.
Description: First edition. | New York : Henry Holt and Company, [2017] |
    Includes bibliographical references.
Identifiers: LCCN 2016042322| ISBN 9780805093308 (hardcover) |
    ISBN 9781250120656 (electronic book)
Subjects: LCSH: Gethers, Judy. | Gethers, Peter—Family. | Food writers—United
    States—Biography. | Cooks—United States—Biography. | Authors—United
    States—Biography. | Cooking.
Classification: LCC TX649.G48 G48 2017 | DDC 641.59092 [B]—dc23
LC record available at https://lccn.loc.gov/2016042322

Our books may be purchased in bulk for promotional, educational, or busi-
ness use. Please contact your local bookseller or the Macmillan Corporate and
Premium Sales Department at (800) 221-7945, extension 5442, or by e-mail at
MacmillanSpecialMarkets@macmillan.com.

First Edition 2017

Designed by Kelly S. Too

Printed in the United States of America

1 3 5 7 9 10 8 6 4 2

To Judy Gethers

And to the women who made her life (and mine!) easier,
better, and filled with love over the past ten years:
Jennifer Morris, Janet Bennett Scott, Karlene Phillips,
Beth Lefft, Laurie Eagle, and Janis Donnaud.

To the men who did the same:
Alan Tivoli and Dr. Mark Lachs.

And to Steven Gethers,
a supporting character in this
book but a lead in real life.

When nothing else subsists from the past . . . the smell and taste of things remain poised, a long time, like souls . . . bearing resiliently, on tiny and almost impalpable drops of their essence, the immense edifice of memory.

—Marcel Proust

MY MOTHER'S KITCHEN

PART ONE

AMUSE-BOUCHE

There is no sincerer love than the love of food.

—George Bernard Shaw

CHAPTER ONE

I have two distinct images of my mother that I will always carry with me.

One is from Christmas 2007, when she was eighty-five years old. On October 5 of that year, she suffered a massive stroke that hit the absolute center of her brain. In the hospital, the next afternoon, a doctor in the ER told me it was likely she would have locked-in syndrome—she would not be able to speak or move ever again.

On October 7, the day after this dire diagnosis, my mother laughed. I walked into her room, saw her gray hair soaked with sweat and plastered against the top of her head, her skin a kind of faded yellow-green, the color of a fish out of the water for too long, the bright hues disappearing at the speed of life, and my first words were: "Lookin' good, Mom." Her eyes rolled in mock annoyance, her lips curled into a "Don't be such a smartass" expression, and she barked out a hoarse chuckle. An hour or so after that, she crooked the index finger of her left hand—the right one was curled up in a rigid fist against her body—motioning me to come closer. "A lot of shit," she managed to whisper.

The day after that, she began physical and speech therapy.

Several days later, she was moved to a rehabilitation center where she didn't just have to learn how to walk and talk again, the therapists had to teach her how to swallow and eat and drink. Their prediction: she would never be able to go home.

On December 18, five weeks or so after she entered the facility, I managed to take her out of the rehab center in a wheelchair, with the help of my lifelong friend Paul Eagle. I probably should say "*barely* managed to" because it was as if two of the Three Stooges had been put in charge of this maneuver, and unfortunately we were Larry and Curly; we didn't even have Moe's mental dexterity. Forget about getting her in and out of the chair and in and out of the car, we couldn't even figure out how to fold the wheelchair and stick it in the trunk. My mother marveled at our ineptitude the entire way, but somehow we moved her from West 110th Street to West 84th Street so she could attend an annual Christmas party thrown by our close friends, Kathleen Moloney and Dominick Abel. My mom hadn't missed one of their seasonal bashes since she'd moved to New York over a decade earlier.

She would not allow me to wheel her into the party—she refused to enter like that. She insisted on walking in, which, with some assistance, is exactly what she did. She had dinner, participated in the evening's conversation (she mostly listened; I don't want to make her sound like some kind of superhero), and took some pleasure in being the center of attention. Toward the end of the evening, Dominick ceremoniously brought out his glorious special dessert, which he makes every year for the party, a mound of croquembouche: pastry cream–stuffed profiteroles piled high into a cone-like mound and linked with crunchy strands of caramel. My mother was the only other person I knew who ever made them (every Halloween, while most kids got Snickers and jelly beans from the neighbors, my mom made croquembouche, and that's what she passed out to the small ghosts and princesses and aliens who knocked on her apartment door). As Dominick approached with the tray, my mom took one of the doughy balls very carefully with her left hand—her right hand and most of her right side were basically still useless at this point—and bit into it. I remember the look on her face as the taste resonated, and I watched her lick a dab of the custard that had settled on her upper lip. Our eyes met and, although she didn't utter a word, I knew what she was saying to me: *This is why I refused to die.*

The other is from the late 1970s, a couple of years after another life-changing event. At the age of fifty-three she had taken her first-ever real job, a low-level one, in a fancy Los Angeles restaurant. I knew that she was quite suddenly immersed in a whole new understanding of and appreciation for food, chefs, and cooking, but I had yet to see any manifestation of that.

I was in L.A. on my first business trip there from New York and, not secure enough to trust that my company would actually fork out the dough to pay for a hotel room, I was reduced to staying with my parents. They lived in a beautiful 1920s Spanish-style house above Mulholland Drive, with a glittering airplane view of the San Fernando Valley. Coming straight from the airport, I pulled my Rent-a-Wreck car into their driveway and, small canvas suitcase in hand, went through the gate that led to the patio off the garage, then through the side door that opened into the kitchen. I stepped inside to see my mother, her back to me, preparing something on the well-worn tiled counter that snaked around most of the room. I'm not sure what she was making, but it was something substantial and weighty: an onion, perhaps, or carrots or potatoes. She was chopping, the way a real chef does, slicing down rapidly and efficiently with the knife in her right hand, effortlessly guiding the blade with her left, making sure the sharp edge could only come up against her knuckles and not cut into her skin. She didn't immediately notice that I was there, so for several moments I was able to watch her closely. Displaying a remarkable sense of ease and comfort, she was at peace while she chopped. But there was also something more than that: she was in total command of this small and immediate world. Her movements showed a supreme confidence, a subtle but sublime control of her actions.

I had never seen this sort of satisfaction emanating from my mother before and I realized, for the first time, that I had never quite understood her. There were layers I had missed and a depth that had been kept hidden from me. My father was the dominant personality in our family: he was the public success, the one with the large ego, and our gregarious link to the outside world. But I had never observed this kind of quiet confidence in my father. He always seemed to be shadowed by doubt and, just beneath the surface, was clearly engaged in some sort of internal struggle.

After a few moments, my mother heard me, or maybe just sensed my presence, turned, and smiled. She put down her knife, wiped her hands instinctively on her apron, and kissed me on the cheek to say hello.

Moments later, my father came downstairs to greet me with his usual effusiveness and edgy affection. I went up to my old room to shower, change, and unpack, my dad headed back to his electric typewriter to continue working, and my mom continued preparing dinner. Even though I was now a bit of an outsider in their world, even though we were all well aware that my return was brief and temporary, life for the rest of that afternoon and evening was as it always had been.

Except I knew that, somehow, it really wasn't.

It is never easy to find comfort.

Not the kind that is lasting and true. Not the kind that confronts reality head-on rather than seeking to disguise it.

Faith is not comfort as far as I'm concerned. Faith is all about *hoping* to find comfort. I prefer something that will do me some good in the here and now. But the world does not seem to be designed that way. At least for most people.

My mom has most definitely never been most people.

In the early fall of 2014 I got a phone call from my mother, who had recently turned ninety-two. I could tell from her tone that she wanted to discuss something a bit more serious than the oversalted soup her aide had made or the tasteless tomatoes bought at the supermarket.

After her stroke in 2007, my mom couldn't cook anymore—a genuine lessening of the quality of her life since cooking was a true and valued personal pleasure, not just a professional one. But her superb palate was unchanged. Her ability to distinguish between good and not-so-good food was probably more important to her than at any point in her life. So not long after her stoke, I arranged to have a young chef, a lovely woman named Jenny Cheng who had recently graduated from cooking school in New York, spend one day a week cooking for my mom. Jenny soon realized that my mother was more than just a passive diner; her knowledge of food was extensive and she loved to pass that knowledge on. So before long, in addition to cooking, Jenny also started going through the many cookbooks on my mom's bookshelves and *talking* to my mother about food and recipes and technique, about flavors and taste.

My mother, quite aphasic after the stroke, had dismissed the idea of speech lessons and group speech classes from the very beginning of her home recovery process; she found them condescending for some reason, plus she didn't love displaying her handicap in public. But discussing food with Jenny engaged and energized her and she realized she still had the ability to teach (and to make the food Jenny was preparing a lot better, taking back some of the control she had lost). Talking about her meals—critiquing what she had just eaten, going through recipes to figure out what she would eat the following week, telling stories about her various food-related experiences, reexploring recipes from the cookbooks she'd written over the years—was more than just an important element in her recovery, it was critical to maintaining her daily appreciation of life.

In time, Jenny had a baby and she was replaced by another terrific woman (and cook), Joyce Huang, who eventually also moved on, replaced by yet another wonderful woman and chef, Cynthia Tomasini. They are all passionate about what they do, and they value the time they have spent talking food with my mother; they learned as they worked. For my mom, these three women became a link to the outside world as well as to a much younger generation, a connection she valued as much as the delicious food they prepared for her.

On the phone that evening, my mother seemed subdued. Sensing that something was bothering her, I went over to her apartment—the apartment the doctors said she would never return to but where she is living comfortably with several wonderful live-in companions (thank you, long-term health care insurance!). Post-stroke, it is difficult for my mother to walk without someone holding her and guiding her. She needs help showering and with all bodily functions. Her hearing is pretty much gone. And it's difficult for her to read and focus on anything much longer than a *New York Times* article. But what frustrates her the most is that her aphasia makes it difficult for her to have lengthy or substantive conversations. Her memory is perfect, she forgets nothing, and there is zero hint of any dementia, but it's an aggravating and sometimes torturous process for her to recall certain words, particularly nouns and proper names. She will struggle, for instance, to come up with the name of the restaurant she ate in the night before or what kind of cuisine they serve, but she'll tell you exactly where it is located, including the cross streets. She'll also tell you precisely what she thought of the food.

On this night, we were having an impromptu dinner of Joyce's leftovers when my mother made it clear that she was determined to say something, no matter the struggle. And she did. It was arduous and exhausting work for her, but she managed to say something she had never said to me before.

"I think . . . it's . . . too hard."

"What's too hard?" I asked.

A long silence and then: "Life."

"Really?"

I was shocked. My mother has had at least four different cancers and two strokes. When she was forty, she was given a 5 percent chance of living twelve more months due to a melanoma. When she was in her early seventies, she had her first stroke while in a tent, on safari in Africa. With the right side of her body partially paralyzed, she walked several miles, took a boat across a river, got to an airport so she could take a plane to London, spent the night at a hotel there, and then flew back to New York—I swear this is true!—at which point she called me to say she must have eaten some bad giraffe meat or something because she couldn't move her right arm or leg. As I repeated her symptoms aloud, my longtime girlfriend, Janis Donnaud, was frantically mouthing the words, "She had a stroke! We have to get her to the hospital!" Which is what we did, and she spent several weeks there until she recovered fully.

But with all of that, she had never—not once, not ever—hinted that her life was anything but enjoyable.

I was certain my mom hadn't heard me so I repeated, louder: "Really? You think your life is too hard?"

She nodded. And also made a face at me to show she knew I was talking too loud, because she hates any reference to her poor hearing and refuses to acknowledge the need for hearing aids, even though she is pretty much deaf as a stone. The only words she ever seems to hear clearly are those I mutter quietly, the ones she's not supposed to hear.

"As in too hard to keep going?" I asked.

She shrugged. The shrug said: *It's possible.*

"What's so hard about it?" I asked. "Can you tell me?"

She nodded. "It's hard."

"I know. But what in particular?"

"Hard . . . for you."

"For me? What do you mean?"

"Hard for you . . . to . . . take care of me."

I couldn't help it. I had to laugh. A few days earlier one of her air conditioners had sputtered and quit working—not a good thing during a summer heat wave—and I'd quickly purchased her a new one, arranging to have it delivered and installed. My mom doesn't like that I have to handle many of her day-to-day problems—a new air conditioner, talking to the cable company when her TV goes out, scheduling her physical therapy—and it drives her crazy that I often don't let her pay for whatever needs to be done. Of course, not everything goes off without a hitch, especially in Manhattan, and there was a screwup with the air conditioner delivery—my mother had gone out for a walk (actually, she went out for a wheel, as in wheelchair, but she likes to call it a walk) during the allotted delivery time. I'd gotten aggravated that I had to rearrange the service call and I guess hadn't disguised my aggravation too well.

"So," I said, "you're talking about being ready to die because I had to buy you an air conditioner and got pissed off that you weren't here when the guys delivered it?"

"Yes," she said.

"I promise," I told her, "your being alive is not too hard on me. In fact, I actually like it."

She nodded, accepting the information.

"So other than being hard on me, you still like your life?"

"Yes," she said.

She then took a bite of the duck breast that Joyce had made for her.

"How's the duck?" I asked.

"Delicious," my mom said. And suddenly all traces of her aphasia were gone. "Very well cooked. Better today at room temperature. Outside crisp but moist inside. Maybe too much salt."

And there it was again. The same quiet confidence and discernment, the comfort that comes with knowledge, the calm that comes with understanding something from the inside.

Many months after my mother had her stroke, her doctor, a

brilliant gerontologist, Mark Lachs, said something that astonished me and yet wasn't really a surprise. "There's something very
odd about your mother's recovery," he said. "She never went through
a period where she got depressed or angry. Everyone whose life
changes the way hers has—she needs a constant companion, she's
lost most of her self-sufficiency, her aphasia, everything is a struggle—gets angry or depressed. I tried to put her on an antidepres-
sant, which is normal for people in her position, but she refused.
And I spent a lot of time talking to her about it. She's not in denial,
not in any way. She just seems to accept what happened and has
refused to buckle under to it. She's decided to do the best she can
and be happy with what she's got rather than worry about what
she's lost. I've never actually seen anything like it."

I didn't understand how she'd become that person. I don't
remember her being like that when I was a child. No one else was
like that in my family. Not my dad, who got a huge amount of pleasure from so many things but was, at heart, angry and disappointed
with a good chunk of what life had dealt him and frustrated by
the compromises he'd chosen to make. Certainly not my brother,
who is, as near as I can tell, unhappy to his core. My father's side
of the family could hardly be called happy-go-lucky. It would be
hard to even label many of his relatives as sane. None of my
mother's sisters or brothers came even close to the kind of honor-
able and intelligent equanimity with which she goes through life.
Nor do any of their children.

In some ways I come closest, I suppose. But it still isn't all that
close. I get a huge amount of pleasure out of life but also understand melancholy and fury and frustration. I am capable of pun-
ishing myself with regret over poor choices and missed opportunities
and just plain screwups, can seethe over the injustices I perceive in
the world, all too often struggle against the inevitable future, rage
against narrow-minded thinking and people who shrink away from
knowledge and facts, and feel defeated by the things I am unable to
affect and change. I can also be brought to a near-murderous fury,

especially when talking to Verizon representatives or pondering our insane gun culture, or reading about female genital mutilation in Africa or having to live through James Dolan's reign over the Knicks, making the odds approximately a billion to one that I will ever see another championship banner in the Garden in my lifetime.

I wondered how my mother could be so damn accepting, wondered if I could ever be like that. If I really *wanted* to be like that. The fact is, I have always kind of liked my anger and thought I had it contained just enough so it worked in my favor. But now I was intrigued: What would life be like if I found that kind of peace? That kind of comfort? And I began to wonder how the hell one could achieve it.

I am not in any way a spiritual person. I never accepted that inner peace could come from something I basically think of as make-believe. I also never saw much difference between worshipping dead religious figures of yore, be it Jesus, Mohammed, or Joseph Smith, and worshipping circus clowns or balloon sculptures. They all have the same degree of believability as far as I'm concerned. I don't understand patriotic fervor, either, which seems to be the other thing that grounds people and links them together. I'm not quite able to grasp the whole concept of thinking you're better than someone else because of the geographical location in which you were born.

Narrowing things down, I also never thought that contentment could truly come from other people—from relationships or children or family. I think that to have a good relationship, one has to bring a certain amount of confidence and stability *to* that relationship, not hope to just make a withdrawal. Love and relationships and all that good stuff could build upon a foundation of happiness, but, for me, they could not create that foundation.

That pretty much exhausted my perceived channels to attain some kind of spiritual peace. I didn't really know what the other choices were.

I looked at my mother across her dining table as she took another bite of Joyce's duck, abandoning the whole hard-to-handle fork thing and taking the last piece in her good hand and putting it into her mouth. Chewing firmly, a small piece of the duck hanging from the corner of her mouth, she smiled without bothering to look up at me. "Yes," she said, ending the conversation about the air conditioner and how hard things were for her or for me. "I still like my life."

I wondered: How did she get to be who she is?

I LEFT MY mother's apartment and for several days afterward I found myself obsessing more and more about the idea of family: What is it? Why do we either cling to our natural one or create new ones? What actually holds a family together or splits it apart?

Why does it seem to be the one thing in the world that, for better or worse, winds up defining who we are and how we respond to the world around us?

And perhaps most important: What is it about family that seems to be our main source of comfort—or the main reason we can't find any?

At some point during my grappling and pondering, I realized that, going back generations, there was one thing that unquestionably dominated my family dynamic in a bizarre variety of ways: food.

My mother's family owned a legendary Jewish dairy restaurant on the Lower East Side of New York City called Ratner's. Started by my grandfather in the early 1900s, the restaurant had a huge influence on my family's identity and on so many of our complicated family relationships—I know it had a profound effect on my mother as she was growing up. It shaped her—and later my—understanding of human nature.

In her fifties, my mother went to work at another legendary restaurant, this one in Los Angeles, Ma Maison. That move changed and reshaped her own life to a substantial degree, and it changed the lives of many others, especially those of her husband and her two children. It raised our level of sophistication, it broadened our views, it introduced us to a universe of people who possessed previously unknown skills and talents and even genius. It also, as she grew and evolved, caused a fairly seismic shift in the family dynamic and the roles we all eventually played going forward.

My father, who never in his life cooked a meal, as far as I know, loved to eat and drink. He also delighted in going to restaurants: he relished the fuss made over him as a regular customer and he got a thrill talking about wine to the sommeliers. Most of all he loved to use food and wine as a way to celebrate and to share. That has had a huge impact on the way I see life—and the way I perceive people who either share or don't share.

So, at my instigation, my nonagenarian mother and I began to talk about food in a more in-depth way than we had probably ever discussed anything other than our immediate family.

I knew that food and the preparation of food were essential to my mother's sense of well-being, but I realized that I didn't know the actual foods that were important to her. I decided that was something important to *me*. So that's where we began. I pressed her for specifics. It took some time, due to her aphasia, but over many meals—in and out of her kitchen—and a decent amount of wine, beer, and vodka, she eventually came up with a list.

We started with dessert and although she had something in mind, it was rough sledding. She struggled to come up with the name of even one special sweet. I asked pointed and focused questions, as one does with aphasic people, to try to narrow things down.

"Is it chocolate?" I asked.

"No."

"Another flavor? Vanilla or coffee?"

"No."

"A cake?"

"Yes, a cake." Then, "No . . . not a cake. Like a cake."

"A pie?"

"A pie." Then, "Kind of."

"Kind of a pie?"

She nodded.

"Fruit?"

She nodded again. It seemed like we were getting close. "Fruit."

"Apple?"

"No."

I went through a list of every possible pie fruit I could think of until I couldn't even come up with the name of another fruit except for breadfruit, which I'm reasonably sure isn't actually fruit. I even included, in my promptings, lychees and pomegranates, both of which I refuse to even acknowledge as actual foods. None of them bore fruit, as far as an answer. So I changed tack.

"Is it American?" I said. "Something you first ate here or in Europe?"

"Europe. Ate it . . . in Europe."

"France?"

"France . . . Paris."

"Is it a tarte tatin?"

"No."

"Really? A kind of fruit pie you ate in Paris and it's not tarte tatin?"

"No."

"Are you sure it's not apples?"

"No . . . I mean yes . . . I'm sure."

"And it's not lemons?"

"No."

I started going through my fruit list again. "Raspberries? A raspberry tart?"

"No."

"Pears?"

"No!" For some reason my mention of pears, the second time around, seemed to annoy her, as if it was a ridiculous choice.

"I think it's a tarte tatin, Mom."

"It isn't."

"Okay," I said. "I know you'll think of it. When you do, tell your companion so she'll remember to tell me. Or you just call me."

I went home soon after that exchange. Three hours later, she called me. When I picked up the phone, I heard:

"I thought of it."

"Great. What is it?"

"Tarte tatin."

I did my best not to laugh. "That's the dessert you like the most?"

"Yes," she said.

"I'm glad you thought of it. I never would have come up with the name on my own."

Eventually, over time, we came up with her complete fantasy menu. We did it by meal, breakfast, lunch, and dinner, because that's the way my mother tends to think: in total meals rather than just individual dishes. She thinks of food the way Sinatra, in the fifties, and the Beatles, in the sixties, took the concept of albums to a different level: they became whole entities, not just compilations of songs. As we went over the possible foods—and there were many—I did my best to narrow them down. The ones that made the final cut were selected not just because they are delicious but because they have emotional resonance for her. Each dish on the menu is in some way deeply meaningful to my mom.

When the list was complete, I didn't know quite what to do with it. I wasn't sure there was anything *to* do with it. But it was knowledge—some insight into my mom—and I was glad to have it.

And then one evening we started talking about a lot of things: my father, families in general, *our* family in particular, relationships, love, disappointment, pleasure, getting older, changes.

"Why did you like cooking so much?" I asked her. " 'Cause it made other people so happy?"

"No," she said, surprising me. "Well, partly . . . but . . . not really . . . about that."

"Then what?"

"I like making other people happy. But . . . more about . . . me."

She was silent for a while after that, but I waited. I could tell more was coming. That's one of the interesting things about dealing with people who have lost some aspect of themselves that the rest of us take for granted. You pay closer attention to details that otherwise might be ignored. My mother couldn't always *say* what she wanted but she always managed to communicate in another way— sometimes even through something as simple and eloquent as silence.

"I like understanding something . . . so well . . . I can turn it into whatever I want. I like the . . . the . . ."—her eyes started to roll in frustration; she was prepared to quit but then it came to her— ". . . the precision. A kind of . . . therapy. Chopping and cutting . . . hypnotic. No tension in cooking. Just . . ."

She tailed off and I thought she was finished until I prompted her one more time and she said, "It just works. I like doing something that works." There was another silence and then she said, "It makes *me* . . . happy. Gives me . . ."

"What does it give you, Mom?"

She shook her head. She'd lost the word. Then she found it: "Definition."

DEFINITION. DESPITE HER aphasia, my mother had nailed it. If there was anything that provides genuine comfort to people, it is finding and defining their own identity.

We use various labels to define ourselves. *I am a Catholic. I am a Texan. I am a scientist. I am a feminist. I am a conservative. I am a rebel.*

We find what makes us comfortable and we put ourselves in that box.

I am married. I am independent. I am rich. I am an artist. I am funny.

I am whatever links me to the world to which I want to be attached.

But food? As a way of providing a sense of self?

On my way home from my mother's, I had a sudden flashback. Years ago, I spent quite a few weeks in Sicily, writing a novel and staying at a small caretaker's cottage on the property of a thirteenth-century abbey. I had edited and published a cookbook by Wanda and Giovanna Tornabene, the mother and daughter who owned the abbey—and within that magnificent walled structure they ran the best restaurant on the whole island. Letting me stay in the cottage while I was on my writing jag was their way of thanking me for publishing their book and getting involved in their lives. And while I was there, they cooked for me—oh, man, did they cook. Their pasta was the best I'd ever eaten, and I ate an immense amount of it every time I sat down at their table.

On the final day of that retreat, I bought the caretaker's cottage in which I'd stayed. It is one of the most beautiful places on the face of the planet, but that's not why I bought it. I bought it because the idea of eating Giovanna and Wanda's food on a semi-regular basis was irresistible. Remembering that momentous decision—and acknowledging the reality that a 175-year-old cottage in what is basically the middle of nowhere in the Sicilian countryside was in my possession because I loved the pasta I could get there—made me realize something rather shocking:

Food doesn't just make me happy. Since my mom went to work at Ma Maison when I was twenty-two years old, every major decision I've made and most key events in my life have revolved around food and drink as surely as the earth revolves around the sun. Whatever definition of myself I've managed to stumble into, it is unquestionably connected to what I have eaten or drunk.

At various times in my life, I've fallen in love, or thought I had, while eating sushi, homemade prune ice cream, and Tex-Mex. Thinking back on the women I fell for, I can't always explain *what it is* I fell in love with, but I do know what I was eating when the lightning struck.

The same goes for the gory finales to most of those relationships. I've had my heart broken over tapas. I've been dumped while chewing on a roasted chicken (and to make it worse, I did the roasting).

In my thirties, I made the decision—over oysters, mignonette sauce, and champagne—to blow up my life, quit my reasonably high-powered job in book publishing, and move to the south of France for a year to write a book and, well, to *live*. My thought process was, in essence: *Why am I wasting my life? I want to eat oysters and drink champagne in France as often as possible while I can still appreciate it.* At the time, I would have moved anywhere for a year if I could have had mignonette sauce several times a week.

I meet a few times a year with a group of my closest friends. We call ourselves the Martini Brothers because our main bonding experience is the imbibing of that revered beverage.

I arrange dinners (or beg to be invited if those dinners are already arranged) geared around wine, almost always red; I spend too much money on the stuff, and I love talking about it. It's possible that the happiest I've ever been—the closest I've ever gotten to a spiritual feeling—has been sitting in the cave of a great Burgundy winemaker, Laurent Ponsot, eating cold chicken and sipping (okay, swigging) Monsieur Ponsot's superb juice. The friends who were with me periodically remark that they have never seen anyone quite as content as I was for those few hours.

It is not an accident, I am sure, that my girlfriend of two-plus decades is a literary agent whose specialty is food books. One of the top agents in the country for food writers and chefs, her first food client was my mom, who in turn led her to such clients as

Maida Heatter, Nancy Silverton, and Suzanne Goin, legends all in the food world.

I still work in publishing and one of the many things I do is edit cookbooks.

I also produce television shows and movies, and the first unscripted TV series I had on the air was a cooking show on the Food Network.

Many of the best times I can recall involve cooking and feeding people, or having other people cooking for and feeding me. I have learned—and am still learning—about the true nature of my relationships with people, including my family, because of our relationships to food.

Food and drink are central to my life and they have been for a long, long time. But until these conversations with my mother, I have never really understood why.

The conversations began a process of understanding.

I'm not exactly sure when I realized what I was going to do with my knowledge, or with the perfect menu I'd managed to drag out of my mom. But when I did come to the realization, it seemed right and natural.

I decided that I was going to cook all of my mother's favorite foods and meals. I'd cook with and learn from her but would also cook with and learn from others, so I could attempt to master the techniques she valued and understood so well and attempt to master the things I valued but of which I had zero understanding.

And once I did, I would make her perfect dinner, not just for her but also for the people she valued and who valued her, the people who'd taught her and shaped her taste and molded her and, by extension, helped mold me.

I was going to learn exactly what made it all work. And what it all meant. Not just the food and drink, but other things as well. I was certain there was a connection between food and relationships and family and personal history. I just needed to find out what it was.

I was going to try to make a whole bunch of people—including myself—happy.

I was determined to find some kind of purpose while deciphering a few of the eternal mysteries that lie within the seemingly simple act of following a recipe and preparing a meal.

In the process, I was hoping to find some definition.

And, if I was lucky, some comfort.

PART TWO

BREAKFAST

Hope is a good breakfast but it is a bad supper.

—Francis Bacon

My Mom's Breakfast Menu

Ratner's Matzo Brei

The Beverly Hilton Coffee Shop's and the
Cock'n Bull's Eggs Benedict

CHAPTER TWO

———————————

My mother was born on August 30, 1922.

Here's what hadn't happened yet at the time of my mother's birth: Lindbergh hadn't crossed the Atlantic; no one had spoken aloud in a movie; there was no such thing as *Time* magazine; there had never been a Winter Olympics; *The Great Gatsby* had not yet been published; and Mickey Mouse had yet to spring from Walt Disney's imagination.

My mom's maiden name was Judith Harmatz, no middle name, and she was raised in Brooklyn by Jacob Harmatz and his wife, Fanny. Fanny's maiden name was Cohen. Jacob's original family name can be traced back to his father, my great-great-grandfather, Yudi Charmatz, spelled with a C in front of it back then. With a name like Yudi Charmatz, your choices are fairly limited: you can be the bearded patriarch of an extended Jewish clan or you can be a George Lucas character and hang at an intergalactic bar with Kylo Ren, Maz Kanata, and Unkar Plutt, who I'm sure will turn out to be a distant cousin.

I knew my grandfather Jake and loved him; to me he was

always Gramps. He was a remarkable man who came to America from what was then the Austro-Hungarian Empire, which, until recently, I thought was just the name of a restaurant on the Upper West Side of Manhattan. I never met my maternal grandmother; she was sick for quite a few years and died when my mom was twenty-three. All I really know about Granny Fanny, as I desperately wish I'd been able to call her, is that she was a good cook and a strict disciplinarian, capable of terrifying anyone who came in contact with her.

Jacob and Fanny had five other children, in addition to my mom. In descending order, they were Natalie (born in 1908); Lillian (1910); Hymen (1912), sometimes called Harold (a far better choice) and more often called Hy; Belle (1914); and Theodore Jerome (1924), whom most people called Ted and the sisters all called Sonny. I came to know all of my maternal aunts and uncles, and responded to them with varying degrees of affection, respect, or disdain.

The most crucial element of the Harmatz family lore is that, according to my mom, Granny Fanny was a wonderful cook. After

Gramps and Granny Fanny as young marrieds. She doesn't look too terrifying. But looks can be deceiving. Maybe she has a rolling pin hidden behind her back.

that, the lore gets a bit murky. The most accurate account seems to be that in 1905, my grandfather Jacob and his one brother, Herman, put up 150 of their hard-earned dollars to open a restaurant on the Lower East Side of Manhattan called Harmatz's. There were three tables in the restaurant. A cup of coffee was three cents and a plate of mushrooms, which seems to have been their signature dish, cost eight cents. When business improved, Jacob, who was more interested in food than Herman, introduced salads and other fresh vegetables to the limited menu.

While the pennies were piling up at Harmatz's, one of Gramps's sisters, Annie, and her husband, Alex Ratner, had been living in Texas. While there, Alex was in an automobile accident and was awarded some money. He used his newfound windfall to yank Annie back to New York, and in 1907, Grandpa Jake, Herman, and Alex decided to open a new and larger restaurant on Second Avenue between 6th and 7th Streets called Ratner's. One family legend has it that a coin flip determined the eatery's name. Another is that Alex's last name was the easier one to pronounce. Either way, however, I feel duty-bound to say that neither Ratner's nor Harmatz's were what one might call welcoming choices for what I assume they all hoped would one day become an A-list restaurant.

Soon after Ratner's opened, Alex developed tuberculosis, so he and Annie moved to California. Annie persuaded her brother Jake to move west with them, and he did, but he soon made the surprising discovery that, just like everywhere else, it required money to live in Los Angeles and they had all run out of the stuff. Jake, being the one with the business sense, returned to New York to build up a nest egg. The Ratner's on Second Avenue was now being run by a cousin, Abe, so Jake became partners with two brothers, Alex and Luis Zankel, and in 1917 they opened up a second Ratner's, this one at 138 Delancey Street on the Lower East Side. For a good many decades, having two Ratner's was a constant source of confusion to anyone looking for a good onion roll and a nice piece fish. Although the food at the Second Avenue Ratner's was never as good as Jake's version, Abe's restaurant became a much hipper restaurant for a while when its location turned into the East Village in the 1950s. Actors in the burgeoning television business and who worked in off-Broadway theaters began flocking there. And in the early and mid-'60s, Bill Graham and Jerry Garcia and Frank Zappa and Jimi Hendrix and other rock-and-rolling denizens of the nearby Fillmore East were hanging out eating rugelach and pickled herring at Ratner's Second Avenue. I still can't quite wrap my mind around any member of Iron Butterfly scarfing down some latkes after a hard night of "In-a-Gadda-Da-Vida"ing.

My grandfather's original tiny restaurant was on Pitt Street on the Lower East Side, which, in those days, was crammed with Jewish and Italian immigrants. It was as close to the Old World Polish, Russian, and Austrian shtetls as could be re-created in the New World. Because the Old Worlders were streaming into the country at a wildly rapid rate, a lot of restaurants sprang up in that neighborhood, all promising quality food at reasonable prices. Harmatz's and later the Delancey Street Ratner's began as—and remained until its final day—a vegetarian-dairy restaurant. No meat whatsoever, although eventually Ratner's did serve fish. That choice, much like the ancient Hebrew dietary laws, came about out of a commitment to safety, cleanliness, and expediency. With no refrigeration and lacking fairly basic sanitary conditions, many of the restaurants that relied on meat products were soon forced to close shop. Dairy restaurants proved easier to keep clean, an essential trait fueling their growth in popularity. The food at the Delancey Street Ratner's began with traditional (and very simple) meals such as soups, kasha varnishkes, and various delicious potato concoctions that, in addition to being superb side dishes, were heavy enough to use as an anchor for any boat that docked nearby. But Gramps knew that tastes would change and evolve. He also knew the kind of delicious food that Granny Fanny could make and, although she never cooked at the restaurant, he made sure her recipes were mimicked. Vegetarian-dairy gradually changed from a description to an acknowledged genre of cuisine. Granted, even by the time I came on the scene and was old enough to gorge myself on Ratner's potato pancakes and potato pierogis and blueberry blintzes, you could feel your arteries actually begin to harden right at the table before your meal was even finished. But a cuisine it was.

The Ratner's at 138 Delancey Street, where it remained for eighty-five years, was a huge success. When it closed in 2002, it

Ratner's in its prime on Delancey Street

was the longest continuously run family-owned restaurant in New York City.

In the 1920s and '30s Ratner's became the haunt of celebrities like Al Jolson, the Ritz Brothers, and Fanny Brice, as well as some pretty well-known gangsters. Word is that these tough guys were quite rowdy but that Grandpa Jake kept them in line. My gramps must have been a fairly tough guy himself because Ratner's thrived and he was never tossed in the East River with a pair of cement gefilte fishes tied to his feet. Some of those kreplach-eating hoods made big names for themselves. There was Louis "Lepke" Buchalter; Benjamin "Dopey Benny" Fein (one of my aunts told me his nickname when I was a kid and he instantly became my favorite gangster of all time); Meyer Lansky (if you Google "Ratner's restaurant photos," a picture of Meyer Lansky pops up with the caption "Ratner's Cheese Blintzes—Meyer Lansky's Favorite Food); William Lipshitz (I liked him, too, because as a nine-year-old it was very hard to imagine a tough guy whose last name was Lipshitz); Abe "Kid Twist" Reles (I loved him because he was fictionalized and played by Peter Falk in the movie *Murder, Inc.*); Arnold Rothstein (who supposedly fixed the 1919 World Series); Arthur "Dutch Schultz" Flegenheimer; and Benjamin "Bugsy" Siegel.

I romanticized Siegel, not just because he founded Las Vegas but because one of his best friends was my uncle Spatzi, who was married to my aunt Natalie. His last name was Spatz. I don't actually have any idea what his real first name was because until he died, when I was around ten, I only called him Uncle Spatzi and never heard anyone ever call him anything but Spatzi. He was an ex-cop turned private detective and he reminded me of William Demarest, the actor who used to play a lot of thugs and wisecracking reporters in 1930s movies. It broke my heart when I heard that Bugsy Siegel had asked Spatzi to come to Vegas with him but my uncle turned him down because he didn't want to get involved with the mob. I'm still a tad bitter about this decision because I love Las Vegas and I think I would have made an excellent mobster. Petey "Muscle Boy" Gethers. Or, more likely, Petey "Grammar Boy" Gethers. On reflection, it's probably a good thing I didn't grow up explaining to guys with names like "Killer" Klein and Chaim "The Hitter" Shmulowitz about the proper usage of "me" and "I" or trying to get them to stop putting apostrophes in the wrong places.

Ratner's on Delancey continued to be a celebrity haunt way beyond those early days. It eventually stayed open twenty-four hours a day and became the lunch and dinner destination for a lot of show business luminaries, the must-stop place for politicians seeking the Jewish vote and a late-night delight for stoners who craved some strawberry cheesecake at three a.m. At any given time, from the 1950s on, you'd see Dennis Hopper, Groucho Marx, Dick Gregory, Walter Matthau, Elia Kazan, or Zero Mostel dining at an adjoining table to Nelson Rockefeller, Bobby Kennedy, John Lindsay, Robert Wagner (the mayor of New York City, not the star of *Hart to Hart*), Ed Koch, or David Dinkins. The restaurant's most famous movie moment came when it was used as an establishing

Meyer Lansky. Ratner's Cheese Blintzes were his favorite food.

shot in the beginning of *The French Connection*—for those in the know, it immediately set the film's locale as the somewhat seedy and run-down Lower East Side of the late '60s/early '70s. More recently, in season five, episode four, of *Mad Men*, a lunch scene was set in Ratner's, solidifying the restaurant's claim as one of Manhattan's great historical sites of that era.

As a boy, it never ceased to amaze me that my family could go to a restaurant, eat to our collective hearts' content, and then stroll out without paying a dime. Not only were our meals free in the dining room, as we left my gramps would make sure that, from the take-out counter, we were loaded up with delicacies, all of them crammed into flimsy white cardboard boxes with the red Ratner's logo on top, barely held closed by thin white string straining to

*Ratner's Onion Rolls. In a much more attractive setting
than their natural habit.*

burst. I've never had food quite like what was served at Ratner's.
For one thing, there were the incredible onion rolls, miraculously
warm and always sitting in a red plastic basket as one sat down to
dine. Those rolls were free not just to descendants and relatives of
Jacob Harmatz but to everyone who sat at one of the tables, which
were set with no-frills white tablecloths and white cloth napkins
that were large enough and heavy enough to double as hospital
bandages.

For breakfast, you could get matzo brei (my favorite as well as
my mother's, and you could get it scrambled or pancake style), lox,
eggs, and onions (also scrambled or pancake style; I got everything

pancake style), or a baked spinach soufflé topped with a fried egg and a side of potato pancakes cut into strips like French fries. Other standouts on the menu were potato and onion pierogis, gefilte fish (a scary, gelatinous blob of cold fish that was somehow delicious when served with take-your-head-off-spicy-hot red horseradish), and blueberry, cherry, and plain cheese blintzes. Or you could just settle for a bagel or bialy loaded with cream cheese and what seemed like an Everest-size mound of thick lox and sliced raw onion, tomato, and cucumber.

For lunch and dinner, you could start with sweet, cold borscht topped with sour cream, or vegetarian chopped liver (it sounds horrible but was incredibly delicious, especially when slathered on an onion roll or a slice of homemade challah), and follow it with grilled fish served on sizzling platters in the shape of a fish along with a side of stewed mushrooms or barley and onions. There was thick, heavy, Jewish cheesecake (way different from the creamy Italian cheesecake) and Dr. Brown's cream and black cherry sodas, which I was only allowed to have in the restaurant, never at home (my mom was one of the earliest anti-sugar people on the planet).

When I wasn't stuffing my face, I was allowed to sit behind the cash register with one of my aunts and push buttons and ring up payments and give change (well, technically, I gave dollars; coins were dispersed through a magical little gizmo that was like a curved slide coming out of the cash register). I could also go into the kitchen; I loved pushing my way through the western-saloon-like swinging doors with diamond-shaped windows carved into the middle. There I could watch sweaty cooks working amid the stainless steel shelves and equipment, churning out all of the restaurant's specialties on stoves that seemed as hot and dangerous as the sun. I could even go behind the cake counter at the front of the store and help out the harried employees who were trying to box up macaroons, cheese or cherry Danish, an amazing strawberry short-cake, bagels and bialys and other doughy treats fast enough to sat-

The Ratner's Menu

isfy the hordes of frantic customers tearing off numbered tickets from a metal dispenser and waving them in the air so they could be waited on next. The action was not unlike what goes on at the commodities market except that we were basically dealing in cholesterol rather than corn futures. It occurs to me now that one of the reasons the staff behind the counter may have been so harried is that they had to let a seven-year-old boy "help" them make their sales.

My grandfather was an extraordinarily generous man. No relative of his ever paid a penny once they passed through the heavy glass doors of Ratner's. My mother tells stories of how he would make up excuses, some pretty far-fetched—he found money on the street or someone paid him a loan he didn't remember loaning—as a reason to pass much-needed cash along to my parents in the early days of their marriage. She once showed me a note he wrote to her, into which he had tucked some money—according to the note it was extra cash that had accidentally found its way into his pocket. Gramps's English was excellent but, probably because he was a native Yiddish and German speaker, he couldn't spell. He never learned to spell his daughter's name properly; the letter she showed me began: "Dear Judit."

Some of his efforts to disguise his generosity bordered on the extraordinary. When my parents were still struggling newlyweds and living in Manhattan, my mother's sister Belle told her about an incredible butcher she'd discovered in Brooklyn. His prices were unbelievably cheap—a third of the price of any other butcher. So every couple of weeks, my parents would give Belle money and Belle would go to this magical store near her house and then pass along steaks, chops, ground beef, you name it—top quality at an insanely low cost. This went on for a year. Then, one day, my parents' friend and neighbor, Teri, said she wanted to get in on this amazing deal. My mom went to Belle, advocating for Teri, and the truth emerged about the too-good-to-be-true cleaver wielder. There was no low-priced butcher. There was only a normal-priced butcher—but my mother's father had been paying the difference in cost. Rather than making my mom and dad feel as if they were charity cases, he'd created this elaborate ruse to make sure they ate well. My gramps, Jake, was all about dignity and generosity.

Jacob Harmatz attended my bar mitzvah and tried to bribe me with money beyond my wildest dreams ($1,000!) to continue with my Hebrew studies. I stayed true to my young-but-already-nonspiritual self, politely rejecting his financial overture. Then I kissed him on his wonderfully stubbly cheek and cried profusely when he died three months after my thirteenth birthday.

As often happens when a strong patriarch takes his leave, the family dynamic changed quite a bit—and it changed quickly. Of the many unfair things in life, one of the most unfair is that while physical traits are often passed along to descendants—baldness, gum disease, high blood pressure, and the occasional high cheekbone and strong jaw line—moral and ethical traits do not seem to be genetically linked to one's heritage. Honesty, courage, altruism, and decency all too rarely make it from one generation to the next.

My mother never worked in the restaurant—or "the store," as my relatives all referred to Ratner's—but three of her four older siblings did. Her brother Hy ran the place and, after my grandfather died, Hy owned it. Or, rather, controlled it—and everything else from Jake's estate. My grandfather was not only an unselfish and decent man, he was a trusting one, with a nineteenth-century view of how families worked.

Although his other four children (the baby of the family, Ted, had been killed in a plane crash a couple of years before) shared equally in the estate, Hy was given the overriding power to dispose of that estate as he saw fit—including giving loans to himself and deciding what money to hold on to and what to pay out to everyone else—and when to pay it out. Jake was certain that his only remaining son would provide generously for his siblings and their own families. The flaw in my grandfather's thinking centered around everyone's dependence on Hy's generosity, a concept that was completely foreign to my uncle. His idea of sharing and playing well with others was to give everything, including the restaurant, to his two sons, put my aunts (his sisters) on a relatively small salary for their work at the store, almost completely ignore (i.e., screw) Ted's surviving family members, and pretend that my parents really weren't part of the family from a financial perspective because they didn't join him walking the hard floor from table to table or punching the buttons of the adding machine in the backroom office at the restaurant.

Over the next three decades, Hy and his two sons ran the restaurant into the ground, due to a combination of sheer greed (they cared far more about the value of the real estate that came with the restaurant than the essence and reputation of the place itself) and a total lack of interest in and knowledge about the quality of the food that Ratner's served—neither of those being great traits when overseeing a revered restaurant. They damaged the brand by going into the frozen food business and pushing a high-profit/ extremely low quality product. They had tunnel vision and refused to expand—a Ratner's in Miami or Los Angeles, for instance, would have been a gold mine, never mind a Ratner's a mere four miles away on Manhattan's Upper West Side. Belle's two children, who were actually interested in food and had good taste, wanted to open an uptown take-out-only Ratner's, but my uncle refused to cut them into the business in any kind of meaningful way. If you weren't *immediate* family—*his* immediate family—my uncle's view was that you weren't really family.

At a party celebrating his 50th wedding anniversary, Hy stood up and made an unforgettable speech. He rambled on at length about how he knew Robert Moses and how important Ratner's was to the community and totally forgot to even mention his wife, Mildred, who was a fairly obvious and equal co-reason for the celebration. By this time, he was starting to lose it somewhat and I think he believed he was being honored by the United Jewish Appeal instead of celebrating half a century of marital bliss. At some point, as he finally veered back to talking about the family, one of his two daughters-in-law stood up and, good-naturedly, called out, "You forgot to mention your wonderful daughters-in-law." My uncle Hy glared at her and, rather viciously, spat out the words, "You're not blood!" It was a touching and lovely moment, treasured by all concerned.

Most relevant for me, the uncle-cousin takeover of the restaurant eventually spelled the end of my free eats. After I'd returned to New York in my minuscule-earning early twenties, I made weekly sojourns to the family restaurant and ate enough to fill me up for pretty much a whole day. Then, one Saturday morning, I went to Ratner's with a close friend for breakfast. By this time, Hy's son Bobby was essentially running the joint. Bobby was five or six years older than I was and didn't have a lot to talk about other than his family, the weather, and golf. And even golf and family conversations were pushing it.

When my friend and I finished our lox, eggs, and onions— perfectly crisp onions, sliced large enough to provide real texture, and small but thick, salty chunks of lox—the waiter came over. I've done an injustice by neglecting to mention the Ratner's waiters, who were as legendary as the food. Most of them had been there forty years, almost all of them shook so much that if you ordered soup you'd wind up with about half a bowlful by the time it got to your table, and most of them didn't actually pay attention to what you ordered—if they didn't like your choice, they would simply bring you whatever they thought you should have. The waiter who was serving us this day, whom I'd known since I was a baby, handed me a bill. At first I didn't reach for it, never having seen a bill before in the restaurant, and figured he'd finally gotten so old he didn't remember who I was. So I said, "I'm family. Judy's son." He had the good grace to look a bit embarrassed when he said, "Bobby told me to give you a check."

I nodded, told my friend I'd be right back, walked to the rear of the restaurant where my cousin was lurking, trying to avoid my seeing him, and showed him the check. "What's this about?" I asked.

He said, with much less embarrassment than the elderly waiter, "We decided it's too expensive when you come in and bring friends. So this is the new policy." And then, I guess feeling awkward since I was just staring at him in disbelief, he said, "I'll give you a fifty percent discount. Starting now."

Quietly, I said, "Gramps would be turning over in his grave if he knew his grandchildren had to pay at his restaurant." Bobby didn't respond—I don't think he cared too much about Gramps or his grave—so I delivered my only possible threat: "Just so you know, I'll never come in here again." He didn't say anything in response to that comment, either, but his eyes did light up slightly and I realized that was not a threat in his book, it was the desired result.

I took the check to the cashier—my aunt Natalie!—and paid it in full, refusing to take the 50 percent "discount." All she said was, "Bobby's running the place now."

Later that day, my parents, three thousand miles away in L.A., heard about this penurious turn of events, so they called Bobby's father, good old Uncle Hy. This wasn't the first time they had had a financial run-in with Hy. A couple of years earlier my dad had found out that the other family members had been getting a weekly check, as per my grandfather's will. The funds came from a somewhat mysterious piece of real estate that my gramps had bought and bequeathed to all his children. It wasn't a lot of money— something in the range of 150 bucks—but it was nothing to sneer at, especially when considering the lump sum that had accumulated over the lengthy period of misappropriation. In the ten years or so since her father had died, my mother had never received one single check, so my dad called Hy and asked him about it. Hy coolly replied that he'd been banking my mother's checks and investing them, since he figured he knew more about finance than my father (who was a very successful TV writer and producer and director, did quite well financially, and actually had a business manager who knew a thing or two about investing money). My dad was furious: he told Hy to send him all the money that was due to them and, from that point on, to send the weekly check as well, he'd do his own investing, thank you very much.

So now, after Bobby's reversal of sixty years of family tradition, all my dad did was ask why I'd been given a bill for my meal. Hy's response was, "It's not about the money." My dad followed that one up with the very logical question: "What's it about then?"

There is an old adage that, in a courtroom, a prosecutor should never ask a question to which he doesn't know the answer. This conversation was proof of something similar: no relative should say anything completely moronic to another relative unless he can defend his statement/bald-faced lie/just plain stupidity to at least some degree. My uncle Hy was completely stumped by my dad's simple question since there was not one single answer to the question that made any sense at all other than, "Money." After a lengthy, painful silence, while my uncle strained to come up with something, my dad decided that enough was enough and told Hy that he should just bill him directly any time I came into the restaurant to eat. My uncle said that would be fine—offering further proof that it *was* about the money.

When my dad called to tell me about the conversation with Hy, I thanked him for his defense—in fact, I was thrilled by his outrage—but told him I doubted I'd ever go back to the family restaurant again. My mother, who was also on the call, spoke up then, telling me not to overreact and anxiously assuring me that this would all blow over in a few weeks and that everything would return to normal. It was very hard, at that time in her life, for my mother to accept anything—or even discuss anything—truly negative about any member of her family; it was only later that she became an unsentimental realist about most things family-related. The more independent she became, the stronger she became and the less she needed to fall back on rose-colored glasses.

From that point on, when friends from out of town insisted on going to the legendary Ratner's, I took them. I always paid in full. Other than that, I never stepped into my family's restaurant again.

That, however, was not the end of my mother's complicated relationship with the Ratner's side of the family.

Although my mother had no work connection to Ratner's, she knew the food well. And her serious interest in food had developed partly as a result of her personal connection to the restaurant. In 1974, she and her niece, Belle's daughter Beth Lefft, cowrote *The World Famous Ratner's Meatless Cookbook*. The publisher decided, in 1981, to try to give the book a new push and to breathe new life into what had been a solid backlist title. The two relevant stories about the book come a little less than a decade apart.

The first is before the book's republication. The publisher was hoping to come up with an appealing cover, something that is especially important for food-related books. They wanted something as irresistible as possible. The editor, doubling as the food stylist on the cover shoot, called me up from the restaurant in a bit of a panic. "We're using a whole bunch of food on a table for the cover photo," she said, "all the dishes they're best known for, and I want one of them to be a beautiful-looking plate of lox."

I didn't really need to ask. My lox radar immediately went on red alert. "So what's the problem?"

"Your family won't give it to me. Your uncle told me it's too expensive for them to hand it over for free."

"Did you explain to him how much the book is going to benefit the restaurant? And how they're going to make money selling the book there?"

"Trust me," she said. "I tried every single thing I could think of. He's not handing over the lox."

"How much is it?"

"I think about fifteen dollars."

"Seriously? He won't give you fifteen dollars' worth of smoked salmon?"

"I swear."

"That's the retail price, right?"

"I think so," she said.

"So he's actually making a profit on this. If he's asking for fifteen bucks, he probably paid five or six. Or two or three."

"It's insane."

"You have no idea," I told her.

I thanked her and told her to sit tight, then called my mom who, when she heard what was going on, was stunned into silence. "How about if I just say that you'll pay for the lox," I said. "I don't want the publisher going into this thinking they're dealing with total crazy people. Even though they clearly are."

"Oh my god, yes."

"They're your family," I said. Her only answer was to sigh. Deeply.

I called the restaurant, got my aunt Nat at the cashier's booth, and asked her to put my uncle on the phone. When Hy picked up the receiver, I didn't ask any questions, I just said, "My mom will pay for the lox. Will you trust her to send you a check and let them use it for the photo shoot or do I have to come down there and hand you cash?"

He made some odd noises, none of which seemed to be any real language, and finally I said, "She'll send you a check. Just tell me how much it is."

We settled on twenty bucks—five dollars more than the price he'd given to my mom's editor, just in case there was any need for a few extra slices. In the end, my mom never had to send the check because the editor gave Hy the money in cash. No way was she going to let the author of the book pay for a plate of smoked salmon.

The book was republished and it did quite well, selling steadily for years.

The coda to the story came about a decade later. I found out that Ratner's—where they'd been selling a lot of copies of the book on

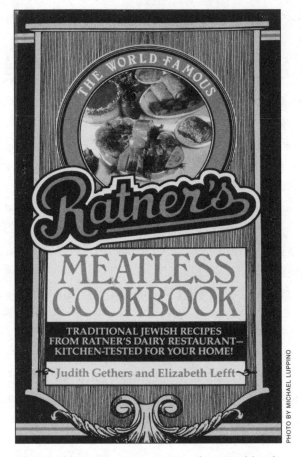

The World Famous Ratner's Meatless Cookbook.
Note the lovely plate of $20 lox.

a weekly basis—had run out of books. They'd been out of stock
for a few months but hadn't said a word to my mom. The publisher had finally let it go out of print; even the couple of hundred
books sold every month at the restaurant wasn't enough to justify
the publisher's printing and warehousing costs. I could not believe
my relatives hadn't bothered to tell anyone they'd stopped selling
the book, although why I was surprised is beyond me. But it
seemed wrong to eliminate such a steady and perpetual market, so
I arranged for my mother to buy the original printing plates from

the publisher and have the plates shipped to her house in Los Angeles.

Right around then, my mom was staying with me in New York so, in person, I explained how the self-publishing process would work: she and her niece/coauthor would pay to print the books and ship them to Ratner's. They'd sell the book at the restaurant, my mom's and Beth's costs would be deducted from the sales, and I told her that if she wanted to be nice, they could split the profit with her brother and nephews fifty-fifty. She thought that all sounded fine and fair. So she called Hy and told him what she wanted to do. My uncle immediately said that he thought it would be better if he oversaw the printing and shipping and paid my mother and her niece a dollar per book (to be clear, that's total, not each, and that is significantly less than the authors would have made if they'd split the profit fifty-fifty, as proposed). I'd been listening to my mother's end of the conversation and at this point I made her hang up. We went through the steps one more time, and I instructed her to tell her brother that she owned the publishing rights to the book, and she also owned the printing plates, which were being stored in her garage, and that it was a take-it-or-leave-it offer. No one was ever going to get rich off the book—it was really just a question of keeping the book in print and providing Ratner's customers with a valuable keepsake. The whole concept of the deal was to be fair to both sides—once again, a way of thinking as alien to Hy as string theory. She called her brother back, followed my instructions quite well—she was steamed and it was impressive to see how much her anger stiffened her spine—and Hy said he would think about it and would call her back. About fifteen minutes later, my brother Eric called from Los Angeles. He informed us that Hy had just called him to say that our mother had given Hy permission to print the books. He told my brother to go to our mom's house, find the printing plates in the garage, and mail them to him. Eric was calling because he said Hy's description of the arrangement just hadn't sounded legit.

My mother was shocked to the point of near paralysis. When we got off the phone with Eric, she just sat in my living room and said, very, very quietly, "I can't believe how dishonest he is."

It was a watershed moment. Up until that point, my mother had always tended to block out the things she didn't want to know or hear, especially about her own family. But now we had a long talk about family and trust. She proceeded to tell me a lot of things I'd never known; her brother's petty treachery seemed to have opened her up emotionally. She talked about how the best thing that had ever happened to her was moving to California and away from her family when she was forty; being away from her domineering brothers and sisters had let her grow up and become confident and finally develop a real sense of self. That's when she told me that Hy had behaved terribly after their brother Ted had been killed. Once he had control of the family finances, Hy basically cut Ted's widow and three children off from the family. We also spoke about the fact that Hy had held on to the weekly check that belonged to her—and she acknowledged that if my dad hadn't confronted him, she never would have gotten the money. As we talked, she kept saying, "I never realized my brother was such a bad guy." But then, at some point, she said, "I should have known."

"What do you mean?" I asked.

"After Pop died"—she called her father "Pop"; all her siblings did—"Hy didn't bother to pretend he cared about the food. The food hasn't been good at the store since he took over. It used to be such high quality. It used to be so respected. He didn't care about any of that." She looked up at me, a real sense of wonder on her face, and even at this age—she was pushing seventy—there was a sense that a rite of passage was taking place. "I should have known not to trust anyone who's so disdainful about the quality of food."

Because she was so rattled, I asked if she wanted me to call my uncle back to give him the bad news that he'd been caught lying his thieving little head off, but she said no, she'd do it. And she did. Calmly, with no anger, she told Hy that she'd spoken to Eric, who'd told her what he had done. She said that she would still agree to give him 50 percent of the profits but that Hy would now have to pay his half of the costs up front. She wanted a check for $11,500—50 percent of the cost of printing two thousand books plus 50 percent of the cover price for the sale of those books. When she got his money, she'd print and ship the books. When the books were sold, Hy could keep all the money and make his nice little profit. She stressed that would be the exact same process going forward, too—he'd send her money and she'd get him the books. He objected, of course, and denied her allegations, saying he had just misunderstood their previous conversation, and tried to cajole his little sister out of such a dastardly scheme.

"I'm sorry," Hy's little sister, my nearly seventy-year-old mother, told him over the phone, "but I can't trust you to do the right thing."

I was a bit awed by the courage it took for my mom to stand up to her brother—and for herself—the way she did. Her anger and firm sense of right and wrong overrode almost seven decades of familial deference. It was a turning point in her life. I don't think she was ever bullied or cowed by anyone ever again.

Hy caved, of course. Making a profit after cheating someone was best but just making a profit was good enough. The book stayed in print, snatched up by Ratner's customers at a brisk rate, until the restaurant closed for good a little over a decade later. It closed because Freddy and Bobby, the sole owners by that point, knew they could make a lot more money renting the building— over half a century earlier, my grandfather had bought the property on which the restaurant sat—than they could by running a kosher meatless dairy restaurant. None of the money from this or future transactions made its way to any other family member, of course.

But their real estate obsession did lead to one last attempt at a sibling swindle. Everything was strictly kosher at the family restaurant except the family's ethics.

In the late nineties, a couple of years before Hy died, my mother called me to say that she had just gotten off the phone with her brother. Sure enough, he'd done it again. On the phone, he told her that their father, my gramps, had many years ago bought another piece of property across the street from Ratner's— this was the same mysterious source of the weekly checks that my father discovered years earlier hadn't been coming my mother's way. On the call, Hy explained to my mom that the property wasn't worth very much but that if they ever wanted to sell it, it would be complicated to do so because each of the siblings, including my mother, owned 10 percent. Well, except for Hy, who somehow owned 50 percent. He said that he had already passed his 50 percent on to his two lovely sons, Fred and Bob. It would be a lot easier, Hy stressed, if the two sons owned the whole thing. Just in case, mind you, they ever wanted to sell.

Because Hy and his brood were so generous, he said that he wanted to give my mom more than the building was really worth— five thousand dollars for her 10 percent share of the property. My mom called to ask me what I thought. I said, "Well . . . I don't really know much about commercial real estate on the Lower East Side, but I would guess two things. One: Any property of that size anywhere in Manhattan can't be worth less than a million dollars and it's probably worth a lot more than that. Two: If Hy says it's not valuable and he's offering you five grand, it must be worth a ton more than what he's offering. Oh, and guess what—he's probably already got an offer for it!"

My mother—having long discarded those rose-colored glasses— called her brother back to say she wasn't interested in selling to her nephews; she would take a chance and see what price they could get if and when they sold it as a group to an outsider. Hy instantly raised his offer to ten thousand dollars. My mother, with no need now to ask my advice, said no.

I can skip the many details. But, of course, there was indeed an offer already on the table. And after nearly three years, Hy's death, a lot of sneaky backroom maneuverings, some breathtaking lies and duplicity by various cousins, and a lot of my screaming incredibly rude insults and profanities at those cousins and their various lawyers, my mother's 10 percent share turned out to be worth six hundred thousand dollars.

She put some of that money into a good investment, courtesy of her protective and wise accountant and financial manager. But she also put a good chunk of it into a fund that her sister Belle had gotten her into nearly twenty years before—Bernie Madoff's fund. That money—and the money she'd had in there for years—disappeared, along with tens of billions of other people's dollars, a few years later when Madoff turned out to be the biggest crook since Ponzi.

Madoff had come into Ratner's to eat a couple of times, so I'd been told, pre-scandal. A nice guy, everyone said. Down to earth. Friendly. No airs. But ate like a bird.

My mother was right. You can't trust anyone who is so disdainful of the quality of food.

MATZO BREI

This is not a food that most people are even aware exists. And just to be clear for any food snobs, don't pronounce this "bree" as in brie cheese; it's not nearly that sophisticated. It's pronounced "bry" as in "bribe" or, more relevantly, "fry." Think of it as a kind of Hebraic French toast. Now remove the toast and the maple syrup. My mom ate this as a child; it was a specialty at Ratner's, but she also made it for me when I was a little boy and I loved it. We used to eat it together on weekends. She liked it with apple sauce on the side. And sometimes a dollop of sour cream. She also sometimes ate it with a small helping of jam, which she often made herself, from scratch. I usually preferred my fried matzo salty rather than sweet.

Matzo brei is the first thing I tried making for my mother once I began my search for the meaning of food, family, and life. It did not require a lot of training or preparation. To be honest, a reasonably intelligent monkey could make a decent matzo brei. But during my cooking process, I proudly went where no simian had gone before.

Before cooking, I did learn a tiny bit about the dish. And that's all there really is to learn about this particular repast. Matzo brei, in Hebrew and in Yiddish, literally means "fried matzo," which gives you some indication of its subtlety and complexity. It is of Ashkenazi Jewish origin and although various sources say that it can either be formed into a cake, like a frittata, or broken up and cooked like scrambled eggs, my mother's version in her Ratner's cookbook disagrees. There, she has one recipe for "fried matzo," which is stirred in the pan and thus scrambled, and one recipe for "matzo brei," which is served pancake-style. I made brei.

Wikipedia points out that, in accordance with Jewish dietary laws, if matzo brei is prepared with any dairy product (e.g., butter), it should not be eaten with meat, nor should it be eaten with dairy if cooked in schmaltz (chicken fat). It is, of course, on the weird side that people follow dietary laws that were dictated by sanitary conditions from thousands of years ago. To make it even weirder, matzo brei is commonly eaten as a breakfast food during Passover, when, according to Jewish law, only unleavened bread is permitted. However, Wikipedia also points out that some Jews refuse to eat matzo brei during Passover because they do not eat *gebrochts*, matzo that has come into contact with water. In case you don't think that religious instruction is insane, please read that last line again. It is against Jewish law to eat a piece of dry, unleavened bread *if it touches water*. If need be, read the line aloud. At some point it'll sink in.

The Matzo Brei recipe from
The World Famous Ratner's Meatless Cookbook

INGREDIENTS:

3 matzohs (NOTE FROM AUTHOR: NO PERSON OR BOOK EVER SPELLS MATZO THE SAME WAY; IT IS OFTEN SPELLED "MATZOH," "MATZO," OR "MATZAH." I DON'T KNOW WHY THIS IS SO; PERHAPS NO ONE BOTHERED TO TRANSCRIBE RECIPES WHILE WANDERING IN THE DESERT FOR FORTY YEARS; PERSONALLY, I WOULD HAVE PREFERRED A TABLET WITH THIS RECIPE CARVED INTO IT TO ONE WITH THE TEN COMMANDMENTS, BUT TO EACH HIS OWN.)

½ teaspoon salt

¼ teaspoon pepper

2 eggs, well beaten

2 tablespoons butter

Jam, applesauce, or sour cream (optional)

DIRECTIONS:

1. Soak the matzohs in lukewarm water until soft (AUTHOR'S NOTE: UNLESS YOU'RE ONE OF THE AFOREMENTIONED ANTI-WATER/MATZOH COMBO LUNATICS). Drain thoroughly. The matzohs will be crumbly.

2. Season with salt and pepper. Stir in the eggs.

3. Heat the butter in an 8-inch skillet. Add the matzoh mixture and cook without stirring. Brown on one side, turn carefully with two pancake turners, and brown on the other side.

4. Serve hot with jam, applesauce, or sour cream.

Serves 2

I felt no need to master this simple dish before attempting to make it. I just decided to take the plunge, so I called my mom on a Saturday and told her I wanted to come over the next day to prepare her a surprise breakfast. The first and only real stumbling block in my plan was, on Sunday morning, finding a market that carried matzo. Apparently, a lot of stores only carry this product during Jewish holidays (and I guess only in places where they can shelve it so it doesn't touch water; I can't bear to think about the matzo that must have been discarded after Hurricane Katrina). But, happily, I live in New York City, so it was easier finding a box of matzo than it might have been if I were searching in, say, Huntsville, Alabama. It was a no go at the high-end Citarella store, and I struck out at my local Korean bodega, but the Gristedes supermarket a few blocks from my apartment had a whole shelf of the stuff, and two kinds at that: plain and onion. Not one to mess with tradition, I went with the plain.

My mother was quite pleased when I outlined my plan. She hadn't tasted matzo brei in years. I asked her if she'd help, or at least oversee my attempt to re-create such an iconic dish from both of our youths, so her home companion pushed her wheelchair into the doorway of the kitchen as I began.

I started by putting everything I needed on the kitchen counter and realized my mom was watching me like a hawk. Suddenly my nerves kicked in. No matter how simple the recipe, I really wanted this to work.

The first step was easy enough—I took a few matzos out of the box and put them in a bowl of water. Done and done.

When the matzos looked appropriately soggy to me, I was about to drain them but my mother commanded me to stop. Her voice contained a note of surprise as well as disapproval. I'd go so far as to say she was aghast. She said, "Give it to me." I held the bowl out in front of me and she reached out, stuck her left hand in the bowl, picked up a chunk of the matzo, and rubbed it between her fingers.

My mother loves manicures—she gets one once a week. It is one of her rare vanities in her nineties and she preens for several days each time she goes to the manicurist, holding up her nails for all to admire. This particular morning, I wasn't paying attention to her perfect nails, though. I was noticing how old her fingers looked. How thin. Her skin seemed to be wrapped tightly around each digit, formfitting and deeply wrinkled. Nonetheless, they plunged strongly into the bowl and rubbed the mushy texture expertly. Those fingers suddenly became sixty years younger. My mother knew how drowning matzos were supposed to feel and it only took her a second or two to nod her head in satisfaction. The nod said: *Now* you can proceed.

No monkey I ever heard of absorbed this kind of knowledge in a kitchen: Sometimes your food needs to *feel* right before you can go ahead and cook it. Texture counts. Don't be afraid to plunge your hands right in.

Now I drained the bowl, getting out the excess water, and added some salt and pepper; less salt than I normally would use because my mom's on a low-salt diet. I love sweets—almost anything that tastes sugary—but I love salt even more. If forced to choose, I'd go with a heavily salted fried egg over even the most delectable chocolate brownie. If it were up to me, I would have sprinkled that salt for another ten seconds or so, but out of consideration, I just flicked in a drop of sea salt and mixed it around. Possibly the first selfless food act of my life.

Next: time for the eggs. I cracked the first of four eggs into the blue plastic bowl containing the soggy matzos. Immediately, a bit of shell fell in the bowl and I stabbed at it with my finger to try to remove it. Before I even managed to touch anything, I heard the words: "You don't crack them over the same bowl."

In all the years I'd been cooking, this is something that had never occurred to me. My modus operandi was always to crack my eggs on the inside rim of the bowl I was working with, then, annoyed, pick out any pieces of shell that had fallen into whatever mixture was already there.

I went, "Really?" and my mother said, "Of course not." She said it rather sternly, too. I told her that I'd always done it this way and she gave me a look that said she was seriously considering the possibility that her younger son was a borderline idiot.

I got a second bowl out, cracked the remaining three eggs into it, picked out the one or two pieces of shell that did indeed drop in, and, when all was clean, dumped the shell-less eggs into the larger bowl with the matzo. My mother looked at me proudly, as if I'd just performed my first successful brain surgery.

I heated the skillet, then added the butter. Even though I'd normally use olive oil, I decided to go with the recipe as printed. Why screw around?

When the pan—on medium heat—was sizzling with the melted butter, I poured the matzo mix in and spread it evenly so it was pancake-like. I turned the heat up just a bit and waited.

One of my many flaws in the kitchen and out is that I'm impatient. At the stove, I always turn things over too quickly, trying to will my food to cook faster. I also want the people I work with to talk faster and the guys I play poker with to deal faster. I'm impatient to get to the point as well as to things I want to enjoy. But I forced myself to wait until I was fairly certain the matzos were properly brown on one side. It wasn't easy but I held firm. I poked at the stuff with a spatula, trying to get a sense of where things stood and when the timing seemed right, I flipped the pancake, exactly as instructed.

Perfection.

The cooked side was a lovely, evenly spread brown. I'd say it looked professional, if there was such a thing as professional-looking matzo brei, which I doubt. I took the pan off the heat for a moment to show my mom. She looked impressed. Avoiding too much hubris, I made sure it went quickly back on the fire.

A couple of minutes later, the B side was also done and we were ready to eat.

I asked my mom if she preferred applesauce, sour cream, or jam. She chose jam, saying that this was always her favorite combination. She had a fancy raspberry jam in her fridge, as well as an equally fancy cherry, so I put both out. We both used the cherry and it was the right call.

As we ate this perfect combination of savory and sweet, I could tell that my mother was delighted. Since her stroke, she has had to learn to eat mostly with her left hand—she is naturally right-handed—so she eats slowly and deliberately, as it's difficult to maneuver a knife and fork. She will rarely ask for help, though, even when cutting a tough steak, and she does way better than I ever could as a lefty. This breakfast required no cutting, however, so she ate heartily and, for her, quickly. Her delight ultimately overcame her decorum and she pretty much wound up skipping the fork completely to just go with the thumb and forefinger of her left hand.

"As good as I remember," she said when we'd both finished. "It felt authentic."

Watching her lick the last remaining bit of cherry preserve off a knuckle on her left hand, I must admit I felt authentic, too.

EGGS BENEDICT

Real chefs have lots of help. Take a peek into the kitchen of a first-class restaurant—not a family-style eatery like Ratner's or your local Italian joint but a place owned by Daniel Boulud or Thomas Keller—and you'll see a line of people preparing nothing but salads. And another line tucking, folding, and spooning out appetizers. There will be a line of people working on meat and one fussing over nothing but fish. And another for sauces. It's not just that they are preparing meals for hundreds of people, it's that all these cooks are preparing meals for hundreds of people where every part of the meal has to come out at the exact right time. You can't serve a steak to someone and then, ten minutes later, come out with the potatoes and, five minutes after that, shove the spinach onto the table. You don't want someone finishing a main course and ordering dessert while someone else at the same table is still halfway through the meal. It's not all that hard preparing good meals for a group of people—I'll bet a top-notch chef could make dinner for a hundred people all by himself. It's getting the timing of those meals right that can make a strong man or woman weak-kneed.

I didn't want help on this particular Sunday morning. I wanted to do this on my own. But even cooking for just two people—me and my mom—getting absolutely perfect eggs Benedict on the plate at the exact same time almost did me in.

I think my mom put eggs Benedict on her list—and wanted me to try cooking it—not because *she* loved it but because *I'd* loved it as a boy and she could never get over the fact that I craved such an exotic food at such a young age. I discovered the dish when I was eight years old and my whole family was staying in a hotel in Los Angeles for an entire summer. We were still based in New York but my dad's work was in L.A.—he was writing and producing a TV sitcom and had to spend six months a year there. He had the tough job of being separated from the family for half a year, but my mom had the tougher job of raising two sons and holding her marriage together during those periods. This arrangement went on for almost three years. We'd get to spend the summers together out in L.A. and the second summer we stayed in the Beverly Hilton Hotel. This was the early '60s and it was Beverly Hills, so it was perfectly safe to leave me alone to roam the grounds, which my parents did on quite a few occasions. I was like the boy version of Eloise in the Plaza—I got to know all the hotel staff, so basically had about twenty-five friendly babysitters at all times. I learned many things over that summer—how to swim and how to play tennis, among others—but the most amazing step forward in my education was when I found out that in a hotel, with one phone call, it was possible to get food sent directly to your room. So, in the mornings when my dad would go to his office at the studio and my mom would go do whatever she was doing—it was a well-deserved vacation for her—I would dial the number for the miracle known as room service.

There were two things on the menu that astonished me. One was something called eggs Benedict. I'd never tasted anything like it. Never *seen* anything like it. The second thing I discovered was that you could eat *steak* for breakfast in a dish simply called steak and eggs. Steak for breakfast! It was like being able to order up an oil well! So I alternated: one day eggs Benedict, one day steak and eggs. Sometimes—remember, I was a kid—I ordered both. It never occurred to me that all of this cost money; I thought it was just part of the whole living-at-a-hotel fantasy. I remember very distinctly when my dad's bill was delivered after the first two weeks of our stay. My guess is that there were many people on our floor, possibly even on other floors, and possibly even in other cities, who also remember it quite distinctly. I was in my room but I could hear him through the wall wondering, rather loudly, "Who the fuck's been ordering steak and eggs Benedict every day?" It wasn't pretty when the culprit was tracked down.

When I was eleven, we moved to L.A. full-time and in the fall my father would often take me to Rams football games at the Memorial Coliseum on Sundays. The games started at one p.m., so we'd go to a family brunch first, dining, almost always, at a restaurant called Cock'n Bull. I had gotten over my steak-for-breakfast addiction and my dad had recovered from his shock at the bill I'd run up, so whenever we'd go there, I would order eggs Benedict. I loved the hollandaise sauce, I loved the shape of the arrangement on the plate, and I loved Canadian bacon, the name of which seemed as exotic and foreign as the taste and the thickness of the cut. Forever after, whenever my mother asked me what

I wanted for a special-occasion breakfast, I always said eggs Benedict. And she always made it for me. I never knew anyone else's mother who would or could make eggs Benedict.

To prepare it for the first time, I went with a recipe from an excellent food website, SeriousEats.com. They titled it "Foolproof Eggs Benedict." I liked the sound of that. I also liked that they said the prep time for the hollandaise sauce, which is the key to a great eggs Benedict, was all of two minutes. I figured how hard could the timing be if the hardest part took two minutes?

Hmmm . . . let's see . . .

There's one thing I probably should mention at this point in the food trajectory: I hate following recipes. Even worse, I'm almost incapable of doing so. It's not that I don't have the attention span to do it; my problem is that I hate being told exactly what to do: it goes against my creative—or just plain stubborn—grain. I like to get a vague sense of how to get someplace and then I like to get there on my own. I never liked school for this exact reason. I appreciated it when a teacher would open an intellectual door, but I always insisted on going through that door by myself. I fought vigorously against music lessons and language lessons when I was young (for which I'm still kicking myself repeatedly), and I never successfully built a model plane in my life because I couldn't read a set of instructions all the way through, much less obey them. I don't read reviews of movies, books, or plays because I don't want to know what a critic thinks of anything. Get the picture? I am not the ideal person to follow a complicated recipe that demands, above all, precision.

But I've spent enough time in the kitchen to know that it is impossible to make certain dishes without following instructions. With sauces, for instance, one *must* be precise. Cooking is definitely part science, but unfortunately I am far less Louis Pasteur in the lab than I am Jerry Lewis in *The Nutty Professor*.

Still, it had to be possible to focus on a simple recipe. I could do precise for two minutes. Couldn't I?

Foolproof Eggs Benedict,
adapted from the Serious Eats recipe
by J. Kenji López-Alt

ABOUT THIS RECIPE:

Yield: Serves 4

Active Time: 30 minutes

Total Time: 30 minutes

Special Equipment: Immersion blender

INGREDIENTS:

1 tablespoon butter

8 slices Canadian bacon or ham steak, cut into English muffin–size pieces

4 buttered and toasted English muffins

8 Foolproof Poached Eggs (see separate recipe)

Kosher salt and freshly ground black pepper

1 recipe Foolproof 2-Minute Hollandaise, kept warm (see separate recipe)

Minced fresh parsley or chives (optional)

DIRECTIONS FOR EGGS BENEDICT:

1. Melt the butter in a large skillet over medium heat until foaming. Add the Canadian bacon and cook, turning occasionally, until heated through, golden brown, and crisp on both sides. Transfer to a paper towel–lined plate to drain.

2. Divide the English muffin halves among four plates. Place one ham slice on each English muffin half. Drain the eggs on a paper towel–lined plate and place one egg on each ham slice. Season the eggs with salt and pepper.

3. Spoon warm hollandaise over each egg. Sprinkle with parsley or chives (if using) and serve immediately.

FOOLPROOF POACHED EGGS

ABOUT THIS RECIPE:

Yield: Makes 4 poached eggs

Active Time: 10 minutes

Total Time: 10 minutes

Special Equipment: Fine mesh strainer

INGREDIENTS:

4 eggs

DIRECTIONS:

1. Bring a medium pot of water to a simmer, then reduce the heat until it is barely quivering. It should register 180 to 190 degrees F on an instant-read thermometer. Carefully break 1 egg into a small bowl, then tip it into a fine mesh strainer. Carefully swirl the egg around the strainer, using your finger to rub off any excess loose egg whites that drop through. Gently tip the egg into water. Swirl gently with a wooden spoon for 10 seconds, just until the egg begins to set. Repeat straining and tipping with the remaining eggs. Cook, swirling occasionally, until the egg whites are fully set but the yolks are still soft, about 4 minutes.

2. Carefully lift the eggs from the pot with a slotted spoon. Serve immediately, or transfer to a bowl of cold water and refrigerate for up to 2 days. To serve, transfer to a bowl of hot water and let reheat for 2 minutes. Serve immediately.

FOOLPROOF 2-MINUTE HOLLANDAISE

Yield: Makes about 1½ cups

Active Time: 1 minute

Total Time: 2 minutes

Special equipment: Immersion blender with a cup that barely fits its head

INGREDIENTS:

1 egg yolk (about 1 gram)

1 teaspoon water (about 5 grams)

1 teaspoon lemon juice from 1 lemon (about 5 grams)

Kosher salt

½ cup (1 stick, about 112 grams) butter

Pinch cayenne pepper or hot sauce (if desired)

DIRECTIONS:

1. Combine the egg yolk, water, lemon juice, and a pinch of salt in the bottom of a cup that barely fits the head of an immersion blender. Melt the butter in a small saucepan over high heat, swirling constantly, until the foaming subsides. Transfer to a 1-cup liquid measuring cup.

2. Place the head of the immersion blender into the bottom of the cup and turn it on. With the blender constantly running, slowly pour the hot butter into the cup. It should emulsify with the egg yolk and lemon juice. Continue pouring until all of the butter is added. The sauce should be thick and creamy. Season to taste with salt and a pinch of cayenne pepper or hot sauce (if desired). Serve immediately, or transfer to a small lidded pot and keep in a warm place for up to 1 hour before serving. Hollandaise cannot be cooled and reheated.

Now might be a good moment to make a second confession: the first time I actually read this recipe 100 percent all the way through was when I just typed it out for this book. I tried, I really did. But as soon as I saw things like "swirling" and "fine mesh" when it came to making simple poached eggs, I got woozy. There was no way I was going to attempt to make eggs by trying to cook them in a "barely quivering" pot of water and straining them through some apparatus I couldn't imagine owning.

But I did check what was required for the rest of the recipe and, before going to my mom's apartment, as I was rummaging for tools, I was struck by this vague memory that somewhere in my distant past I had bought an actual egg-poaching pan. So I went poking and probing through one cabinet in my kitchen in which I keep things that haven't been used for decades but which I can't bring myself to throw out and, sure enough, there it was: an egg poacher. On the dirty side, with a cobweb or two clinging to the handle, but it was there, safe and sound.

It was a small, white pan with three round indentations—nice little spots for the raw eggs to slide into. The idea is Dutch oven–like: the pan fits on top of a pot filled with boiling water and the heat from the water cooks the eggs. This seemed a lot more efficient than going free form with swirling and a wire mesh. So my egg poacher made its way uptown to my mom's.

The hollandaise sauce recipe called for an immersion blender. This was a stumbling block, since I had absolutely no idea what that was. But I couldn't help but notice that all other eggs Benedict recipes that didn't use an immersion blender took twenty to thirty minutes of prep time as compared to two minutes. Solution: a call to Janis— who knows everything about food, utensils, and science (and thus the theories behind almost all recipes) and who provided a crucial bit of information.

"You *have* an immersion blender," she said.

"I do?"

"Yes. Your mother gave it to you a few years ago. It's that white thing that, periodically, you ask me what it is and I tell you it's an immersion blender."

"Well, there's the problem—you're not specific enough."

She didn't say anything but I was pretty sure she was shaking her head.

"Um . . ." I said, hoping my boyish lack of eloquence would charm her into allowing me back in her good graces, "Do you happen to know where it is?"

"In your pantry. Upper shelf, right-hand corner."

"I have a pantry, too?"

I was pretty sure there was more head shaking on the other end of the phone but I didn't care because, as far as I could tell, I was now all set. I had my weird white immersion blender—which was still in the unopened box—and my egg-poaching pan, cobweb-free after a good washing. All I needed now were the ingredients.

The eggs and English muffins were easy. So was Canadian bacon, although when I was ordering from the guy behind the Citarella take-out counter, several very simple questions occurred to me. I'd loved Canadian bacon since I was a wee lad but I had absolutely no idea what it was. Did it really come from Canada? Was it actually bacon? Was it always round? Was there a required thickness that allowed it to be called Canadian bacon as compared to, say, North Dakota bacon or just plain regular bacon? So I asked.

"It's smoked pork loin," the counter guy said. "And as far as I know, it doesn't have anything to do with Canada. And all you gotta do is tell me how thick you want it and that's how thick it'll be."

That took a little bit of the glamour out of the process, but it was still valuable information. Knowledge could be deflating but it was never a bad thing.

And now, with everything in tow, it was time to cook.

My mom's Upper East Side apartment has a small but serviceable kitchen, like many New York City apartments. When I got there, I went straight to work.

Since the recipe promised that the sauce took two minutes, I decided to leave that for last. Confident in my ability to pull off the non-sauce parts on my own, I ignored all the recipe's other instructions. Deciding that the thick-cut Canadian bacon would take the longest to cook, I placed it in a skillet. Then I cracked the eggs—in a separate bowl, as previously learned—and transferred them to the poaching pan. I arranged the pan on top of a form-fitting pot filled with water and turned the heat on medium, figuring it would only take a few minutes, tops, for the eggs to poach. I then put the English muffins in the toaster oven and turned that setting to low.

Cool, calm, and collected, I spent a few minutes chatting with my mom (we discussed, to the best of her ability, immersion blenders—it turned out, of course, that she had not one but two— and other fascinating topics), and then I decided it must be time to make the sauce.

After all these years believing that hollandaise sauce was some miracle concoction that only a three-star Michelin chef could master, it turns out it wasn't much harder to make than matzo brei. The hardest part was finding a cup into which, as per the recipe, "the immersion blender barely fits." I sorted through a few different cups and glasses and then found a fairly narrow coffee mug that was the perfect width. Into that went all the ingredients and then I turned the blender on. For those of you who have never used this remarkable appliance, it looks and operates much like a dildo. And watching it turn the various ingredients into actual rich, creamy sauce gives—or so I imagine—a similar level of satisfaction.

My glee at the wizardry of the immersion blender sent my mom into a laughing fit.

"Come on," I said. "This is a major discovery for me."

"Very major," she agreed. "Like discovering the wheel."

"How come you can suddenly speak perfectly?" I demanded. And that set her off laughing again.

The recipe specified that the hollandaise sauce had to be served immediately when ready—it could not cool down or it would turn into some other alien form. That's when I realized that things were not going as wonderfully well as I had thought. For one thing, I'd forgotten to turn the flame on underneath the Canadian bacon, a serious hindrance to the cooking process. I instantly turned the heat under the skillet to high.

I also became aware that the eggs were not exactly cooking. The water was boiling fine underneath them but they were still runny and, as near as I could tell, still downright raw. I timidly said to my mom, "So these eggs don't seem to be cooking." She took a peek into the kitchen from her wheelchair and said, "They should be covered." That's when I saw that there was a top to the little poached egg pan. So I covered the eggs as my mom instructed and, lo and behold, they started firming up. But not before I got the "what have I spawned?" eye roll again. And more laughter.

"I'm glad you're enjoying this," I said. "I slave for hours and all I get is scorn."

"You've been in there ten minutes," my mom said.

"It's the principle of the thing," I insisted.

Meanwhile, I did not want rock-hard English muffin slices so I turned the toaster oven down to about 150 degrees F, keeping them warm but not cement-like (I hoped).

Panicking that these delays would cool my hollandaise sauce down and reduce it to the texture and taste of Silly Putty, I kept low heat under it and stirred constantly.

A few miraculous minutes later, the eggs seemed ready, the Canadian bacon was the right degree of crispness on both sides, and, amazingly enough, when I popped open the front of the toaster oven, the English muffin slices were hot but still pliable. Who needed line cooks?

I put the lightly buttered muffins on two plates, carefully placed a perfectly fitted Canadian bacon slice on top of each muffin, slid three nicely poached eggs out of the egg pocket with a spoon, and then ladled my warm hollandaise sauce on top of everything. I hate parsley and never intended to use it. And I completely forgot about the chives. No matter—I had two beautiful egg/muffin arrangements; my mom had one.

We sat down to eat. My mother's home companion—who only wanted scrambled eggs; she wanted no part of the sauce—cut my mom's food for her. It cut without too much trouble. Rather than dig in right away, I watched as my mom put a forkful of the breakfast in her mouth and chewed. After she swallowed, she said, "Delicious!"

"Seriously?" I asked.

"Taste."

I did, and I must admit that she was correct. Delicious.

Food conjures up sense memory unlike anything else except, possibly, music. You can hear a few strains or lines of a song—the same way you can bite into a specific food—and suddenly be transported back into the past. The people you were with—those your memory connects with the music or with the food—are real again, not just ghostly apparitions from the past. The smells, the emotion, the visual images all reappear as if everything were happening at that moment. Biting into my eggs Benedict didn't take me to the Grateful Dead concert at Winterland in 1971 where I found myself trapped in a beam of light coming from the ceiling, but it did take me back to the Cock'n Bull when I was fourteen years old. It made me feel as if my dad were sitting at the table with my mom and me. I could hear his voice. See his graying beard. I felt as if I were sitting on the wine-colored leather seats in our favorite booth, already anxious to head to the Coliseum to see the Rams play.

I don't know exactly what sensations my mother was experiencing. Her aphasia had kicked back in—or at least I suspected she was pretending it had kicked back in because she did not want to share her eggs Benedict–induced flashback. That was all right with me.

A recipe is a blueprint for a finished product. It is a guide that connects otherwise unconnected individual elements, showing how to blend them together to create something whole and new. It is both science and art with a touch of magic. As with anything in life, when creating something new you run the risk of burning it or under-seasoning it or over-seasoning it or making it too sweet or not sweet enough. It is possible to follow a recipe too closely, removing any sense of creativity or personal involvement. It is also possible to stray too far from the structure and the elements that make it jell, creating the risk that the thing one is striving to create becomes unrecognizable, transformed into something different and undesired or just plain bad.

But everyone has to start, at some point, with a recipe.

This time I'd followed one to the best of my ability. And it had worked. The disparate elements had not just come together to create a whole new dish.

They had come together to provide a link to the past.

PART THREE

LUNCH

Ask not what you can do for your country.
Ask what's for lunch.

—Orson Welles

My Mom's Lunch Menu

Barbara Apisson's Celeriac Remoulade

Louise Trotty's Chocolate Pudding

Joël Robuchon's Mashed Potatoes

Yotam Ottolenghi's Quail

CHAPTER THREE

It's relatively easy to see what brings people together to form a family. And it's very easy to see what makes a family fall apart. It is usually harder to understand what holds them together.

My mom adored my father; when they were young, it was almost to the point of hero worship. The older she got, the more she realized she was his equal and she was able to see him for what he really was: not a hero but a flawed and wonderful man. The flaws did not alter the feelings she had for him; to the contrary, they made her love him even more. Looking back, I am struck by how much their relationship changed over the years—and it didn't just survive, it got stronger, and they became even more intertwined. In some ways, my mother's weaknesses when she was young—her insecurities, her lack of a definition unconnected from being a wife and mother, her inability to create an identity for herself other than the one her brothers and sisters insisted on foisting on her— drove my parents' relationship for the first part of their marriage. My dad knew he had to toughen her up, to help her define herself as a separate human being. Later on, *his* weaknesses—his career frustrations, his compromises in certain areas, his inability to compromise in other areas, ultimately his illness—came to the forefront and added a new dimension to their already strong bond. My dad understood the specifics of the world. My mom has, in her quiet way, always understood the world as a whole. The older I get, the more like her I strive to become.

As with my mother, I have two distinct images of my dad that glow like neon reminders of the past. And as with my mom, they, too, are food- and drink-connected.

One mental snapshot captures any fall or winter Sunday morning in the 1960s through the mid-'70s. My dad is in bed watching football, a six-hour endeavor that basically involves not moving his body except for his arms to eat, drink, or clap, and his mouth to chew and to roar in appreciation or groan in dismay at the changes in score and the final point spreads. He is wearing a dark brown terry-cloth kaftan, a bit of leisurewear that made him look vaguely Roman emperor–like, and is propped up against a thick wad of pillows that rest against my parents' king-size, freestanding, elaborately carved wooden headboard. Across his knees is a sturdy breakfast tray, on which sits a large plate of scrambled eggs, along with smaller plates that hold a bagel, sliced raw onion and tomato, slabs of cream cheese, and several slices of smoked salmon. My dad is as relaxed as he gets, laughing, reveling in the athletic performances on his enormous TV screen (a console; this was pre–flat screen) and enjoying the presence of his younger son, sprawled on one side of the bed, also absorbed in being a football fanatic, also munching on a bagel with lox and cream cheese and onions. When I am older and living in New York City, we bet on the games every Sunday over the phone and keep a careful, running track of our wins and losses. We bet real money, either ten or twenty-five dollars a game, and any debts have to be paid promptly. Sometimes my dad even lets me put twenty-five dollars down in a separate bet that he places for me with his bookie, whom he calls

Big Al, even though I find out later he is much closer to an accountant than to some sort of thug. When we place these bets, I know my dad's in his giant bed in L.A. watching his enormous TV. I'm in a similar position on my smaller, less imposing bed, watching my much smaller, less imposing TV, wearing jeans and a T-shirt, wishing someone was plying me with Ratner's-like delicacies. To this day, conjuring up this picture of my dad makes me smile and yearn for something I rarely yearn for: my childhood.

The second image is much later, late fall of 1989. My dad is propped up in a different bed, a hospital bed. He is thirsty, making short, gasping noises that emanate from his cancer-ravaged lungs. The large black male nurse, a would-be actor who had given me his 8×10 headshots, just in case my dad makes a miraculous recovery and goes on to direct another TV movie, hands my father a cold root beer. My mom keeps him supplied with a constant stream because that has always been his go-to soft drink. My dad sips it through his straw urgently, deliciously. Unlike many years later when my mother bites into Dominick's croquembouche, the root beer is not a reason for my dad to stay alive. At this point, he does not have a real reason to stay alive. To him, I am certain, it is simply proof that he *is* alive.

My parents met at summer camp in 1936 when they were both fourteen years old. Camp Mohican was the boys' camp, Reena was for girls, and both camps straddled a lake on the New York–Massachusetts border. My mom won awards for Best Archer and Best All-Around Camper, which used to make her blush because she didn't like being remembered as such a good girl, but now she'll boast about it, saying, "Well, I was very good at everything." My dad won Best Performer in the Camp Play. Other than that, his biggest claim to fame was that he almost got kicked out one summer because he and his younger brother, George, snuck into a rival kid's cabin around five o'clock one morning, kidnapped him, tied him, naked, to a flag pole, and then waited for reveille to be blown so the whole camp would come out to stand at attention and see the kid's penis, which was probably *not* standing at attention by that time.

When they met, my father's name was Seymour (usually called Sye) Gushen. It changed to Steven Gethers a few years later when he resisted the opportunity to go into the family business—a leather tannery—and decided to become an actor, perceptively realizing that the Cary Grant roles he sought were not going to come to guys whose names sounded like a Hebraic sneeze. He took the name Steven because he wanted to keep the same first letter of his given name. To keep the same surname initial, he borrowed his new last name from his family's housekeeper's boyfriend, Johnny Gethers, a black man from South Carolina.

The housekeeper's name was Louise Trotty and my father met her when he was thirteen. His mother was quite ill—she died a year or so later—and his father sent him out on the Brooklyn streets to the employment agency to have them recommend a few house-keeping candidates who could clean, cook, and deal with a dying woman. Louise had just arrived from South Carolina and was wait-ing at the bus station when my dad passed by. She was young her-self, only twenty-five, probably not truly equipped to run a Gushen household comprised of a domineering father, a bedridden mother, and three young children. But she and teenage Sye started talking, she needed a job, he convinced her to head home with him, and she not only helped raise him, his brother, and his sister, she later helped raise my brother and me. Years after we were grown, she went on to also help raise several of my young second cousins.

In the early days of my parents' marriage my dad was a broke and often out-of-work actor. Ten years after the fortuitous bus stop meeting, Louise would come to the newlyweds' apartment in Stuyvesant Town, a postwar middle-income apartment complex in Manhattan, to clean the place. She adored my dad; thought of him as her own son in many ways. So she'd work for half a day and, instead of taking money for her labor, she'd leave my dad twenty bucks because she knew he needed it. Later on, she lived with us for years, first in a move to the New York suburbs and then in Los Angeles. She provided solace when needed (as a baby I can remember her letting me play with her fake pearl necklace, which would snap apart and then back together, a never-ending source of great delight), discipline when called for (as an older child, I remember her swatting at me and my brother with her shoe to keep us in line), and she made certain foods I still dream about: crispy, perfect fried chicken; ice box pie with slices of frozen bananas and peaches; meat loaf with hard-boiled eggs placed strategically throughout the middle of the loaf, which I always thought was something magical; and chocolate pudding, the remains of which I was allowed to scarf up while the chocolate skin was just beginning to harden.

As a result of her arrival in our lives, and the ensuing name change, I have a strong suspicion that I am one of very few Caucasian Gethers living in the United States. This is because in the early eighties, as a present for my dad, I bought one of those let-a-retired-school-teacher-research-your-family-history-and-put-it-in-a-cheesy-leatherette-binder mail-order books. It listed every Gethers in America and a number of them had names like Alfonia and Vernell. Fine names all but a far cry from Chaim and Schlomo. I recently met an African American Gethers but didn't explain our name theft. He said, "Distant cousins," and we both shrugged and smiled.

Judy and Sye/Steve got married in 1943 when they were twenty-one and my dad was home on a brief leave from the army. A portent of the way he'd go through life, my dad insisted they honeymoon at the ritzy Essex House, on Central Park South, in Manhattan. They checked in on August 23, 1943, the day after their wedding. There was a note waiting for them in their room, number 1608, from the managing director of the hotel. It was addressed to Corporal and Mrs. S. Gushen and in it the M.D. promised to do everything in his power to guarantee "a delightful stay."

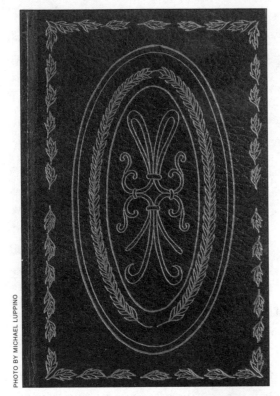

Lovely fake leather book with all living Getherses in the United States, circa 1983

Names from my fake Family Tree. I feel particularly close to Vernell and Alfonia Gethers.

JAMES GETHERS
R1 BX. 172
ST STEPHEN, S.C. 29479

JAMES GETHERS JR
R1 BX. 237
SUMMERVILLE, S.C. 29483

JAMES GETHERS JR
R3 BX. 237
SUMMERVILLE, S.C. 29483

ALFONIA GETHERS
R1 BX. 57
WALTERBORO, S.C. 29488

FLORENCE GETHERS
100 MYRTLE ST
WALTERBORO, S.C. 29488

FRANK R. GETHERS
R1 BX. 547
WALTERBORO, S.C. 29488

RICHARD L. GETHERS
BX 163
WALTERBORO, S.C. 29488

SHERMAN GETHERS
R1 BX. 515
WALTERBORO, S.C. 29488

SAMUEL GETHERS
R 1 BX 34
WANDO, S.C. 29492

VERNELL GETHERS
34 WANDO R1
WANDO, S.C. 29492

Corporal and Mrs. Sye Gushen a few months before their wedding

At the bottom of the stationery, in a banner, is the hotel's slogan: *Home of the Casino on the Park, where smart New Yorkers dine and dance.*

I suspect that my father's lifelong path of living as well as possible and somewhat beyond his means was because he was a fugitive from his own family.

My dad did not go into his father Irving's leather tannery business outside of Boston. Instead, he set out to be the next Clark Gable—and as a result of that rejection, my grandpa Irving refused to have anything to do with him. They didn't speak for years. When my older brother, Eric, was born in 1946, my mother—who revered her father-in-law—decided to take matters into her own hands. She sent Irving a letter, saying he had a grandson and she didn't want him to grow up without one of his grandfathers. She told him it was time for a reconciliation and invited Irving to come see the baby. My grandfather sent a brief response, the essence of which was: *No thanks. Not interested.*

COURTESY OF PETER GETHERS

Irving Gushen at the racetrack

My father's family was, on the surface, less bizarre than my mother's. But only on the surface. All one had to do to see the weirder and darker side was to dig a wee bit deeper into the worlds of my aunts and uncles, my great-aunts and great-uncles and my second cousins. My father fled from them—and there were plenty of things to flee from: hidden alcoholism, pathological cheapness, extraordinary negativity, and self-absorption.

And, just like with my mom's siblings, there were a few financial transgressions. Or, as they might be called if they weren't contained within the family circle, fraud.

My father never discussed any of this with me. Ever. But my mom did. She told me that although my father had rejected the idea of going into the family business, when Irving died my dad inherited a third of it. His sister, Helen, and her husband, Jack, along with my dad's brother, George, and his wife, Hope, inherited the other two-thirds. Soon after my grandpa Irving's death, my mom said that the Massachusetts foursome came to my dad with a proposal: He had no interest in running or even knowing about the leather business, so why didn't they buy him out? He'd get some needed money and avoid any unnecessary aggravation that might come with being part owner. My dad quickly agreed and everyone was happy. It didn't take long to negotiate a fair buyout price. Well, except for one minor detail that was left out of the negotiation. According to my mother, my dad's siblings and in-laws knew something that he didn't know: there was an interested buyer for the business and that buyer was going to pay a lot more than the price my dad had agreed to.

And voilà: a near-lifelong family feud.

WHEN MY PARENTS got married, their families lived a few blocks from each other in Brooklyn. My mom's family lived at 251 Montgomery Street, directly across from Ebbets Field, where the Dodgers played. My mom was something of a tomboy—I wish that word hadn't faded from use—and she had baseball cards autographed by almost every National League player from the 1930s. Naturally, her mother, Granny Fanny, threw them all out when my mom got older. Or, as I like to think of it, my grandmother burned up my million-dollar inheritance!

In his early twenties, my dad didn't want to just change his name, he wanted to separate himself physically from his family—and separate my mom from hers. He wanted to move forward into the future with his wife while both his parents and his in-laws much preferred clinging to the past. The future, for my dad, was all of three or four miles away, across the Brooklyn Bridge, in Manhattan. So after the war—my dad served in the Pacific, where his most harrowing moment came when he tripped over a tent and broke a finger—he yanked my mom along with him to Stuyvesant Town, which had started construction in 1942 and was finished in 1947.

The Stuy Town complex had—and still has—8,757 apartments spread out over eighty-nine buildings, from 14th Street to 20th Street and ranging from First Avenue to Avenue C and the East River. All the buildings looked the same and in front of most of them were small gardens protected by chain-link fences and wonderful cement playgrounds, all designed for happy, safe, inexpensive family living. For their parents' families, though, it was as if they'd moved to Berlin at the height of Hitler's reign. Manhattan equaled danger. And far worse, separation.

Not surprisingly, my most powerful Stuy Town memories all involve food.

As a very young boy, while my dad was off trying to get acting gigs—he eventually became one of the leads on a soap opera, *Love of Life*—my mother used to coax me into the kitchen to help her cook. Well, "help" is a bit of a misnomer. What she would do is let

Stuyvesant Town 1949. Paradise for my parents. Siberia for their parents.

me put all sorts of things in a bowl—eggs; eggshells; flour; sugar; toys; mud; you name it. Then I'd gleefully mix it all up and she'd put it in the oven at a robust 350 degrees. An hour or so later she'd call me in, take what she swore was my concoction out of the oven and, lo and behold, it had transmogrified into a delicious home-made cake. I'm a little embarrassed to say that it was quite a few years before I figured out that my mom was making the ol' switcheroo while I was off napping or playing with my blocks. At age two, I was pretty certain I was already a master baker, but at age seven I learned to handle the disappointment of finding out otherwise.

I heard my very first swear word when I was around three or four. This incident was also food-related. My mother was still far from being a gourmet foodie, but she was very interested in healthy cooking. I vividly recall a Sunday family breakfast—my mom, my dad, my brother, and me—for which my mom decided to make buckwheat pancakes, which were supposedly better for us than the normal flapjacks. She served it to the three of us—three sensitive guys. We each took a bite and chewed. And chewed. And chewed some more. That's when my dad said, "This tastes like shit." I didn't quite understand what it meant, but I knew it was something naughty. Then he said, "I don't mean it tastes bad. I mean it tastes like actual shit." My mom did not take this too well. I remember some crying—but then she tasted her portion. And then, without another word, she cleared the plates. We never had buckwheat pan-cakes again.

My parents had two couples they considered their closest friends. One was a married couple named Teri and Irv who lived in the building next to ours in Stuy Town. They had three children and I was always over at their place for dinner. If I ate there early in the month, we'd have a normal dinner—meat and potatoes and a good dessert. Toward the end of the month, we'd sit at the din-ing table and out would come peanut butter and jelly sand-wiches for all. I never minded but years later I found out why the food followed such an odd but consistent serving pattern: Irv, a gruff high school principal—he always reminded me of Ralph Kramden—was a compulsive gambler. By the end of each month, he'd run out of money and thus Teri couldn't afford to buy the same level of groceries.

Teri fantasized about going to Japan. Her apartment was decorated in a kind of pseudo-Japanese style and she often wore kimono-type clothes and put her hair in a bun, held together with sticks that looked like Japanese chopsticks, and she sometimes made what then passed for Japanese food: teriyaki. She often talked about one day fulfilling her dream and going there. When I was in college and living in California, fifteen or so years after I'd eaten my last teriyaki beef or peanut butter sandwich at their dinner table, she and Irv finally did save up enough money to live the dream and go to Japan. Before they landed, however, their plane crashed into a mountain and they never made it.

My mother was also in L.A. when word reached us about the crash. My dad was in New York. She and I were both wrecks, sad beyond belief, and didn't know what to do. So we went to a movie, *The Sting*. Neither of us thought we could possibly enjoy it but it turned out to be an extraordinary release from the gloom of real life (or death). We walked out practically giddy, went to a Hamburger Hamlet, once a great restaurant chain in L.A., to get some excellent burgers and fries and a few glasses of beer—until that night, I never knew my mom drank beer—and we talked about what had happened, able to reminisce about her close friends without either sobbing or crumbling into silence. *The Sting*, the sheer pleasure of the movie, provided some perspective and we both saw a glimmer of hope in the future. It was also the first time I'd ever sat alone with my mother and drunk alcohol, and I believe there was an extra added comfort for her that I was now grown up enough to deal with the tragedy as an adult. For the first time, I didn't have to lean on her for support; I could be the crutch. At least for a few hours. And a few beers.

My parents' other best friends were Esther and Albert, who also had three kids with whom I was friendly. Esther and Albert both worked in the garment center. Esther was lovely, smart, and soft-spoken but with a will of steel. A fairly high-powered executive in the garment business, she was a slightly scarier version of my mother and with less of a sense of humor. Albert, also a garmento exec, was always puffing on a large cigar and running off a string of jokes—he reminded me of a Catskill or Vegas comedian, a cross between Alan King and Jackie Mason—and he had a secret life that I thought was the coolest thing ever: every Monday night he played the drums in a Dixieland band on Grove Street in the West Village, at a place called Arthur's Tavern. I learned two valuable lessons from knowing Albert: 1) Being funny all the time does not mean you're not angry—in fact, it usually means you *are* angry and doing your best to hide it; and 2) Doing the one thing you really love only one night a week does not equate with happiness; it leads to frustration—repressed anger and frustration: not a recipe for a glorious life.

Esther and Albert were responsible for the next big step my mother took in the food world, though.

Albert convinced my dad that the two families should find a place to summer together—someplace out of Manhattan where the grown-ups and children could all experience nature and breathe some non-city air. So the two men drove up to Central Valley, a forty-minute or so drive out of Manhattan, right near the West Point military academy. While driving around, they accidentally stumbled upon a place called West Point Farms, a restaurant that also had a few guest rooms. The main building was modern but the whole place had a remarkably old-fashioned feel. The owners were an elderly couple—at least they seemed elderly to me at age three; they were probably in their late forties or early fifties—Henri and Barbara Apisson. Henri was an architect in France—he designed their restaurant—and he was Maurice Chevalier–level French: a thick and charming accent; an ever-present twinkle in his eye.

Whenever someone complimented him on the food or service, his answer was always, "Zat's because everysing we do and make, we do and make weez love." Barbara was Armenian and she was almost a caricature of a perfect grandmother. In my mind's eye, I picture her always wearing an apron and bustling around and tsk-tsking anyone who wasn't being productive; she was small and spindly and brittle-looking but overwhelmingly kind.

Half an hour after meeting Henri and Barbara, Albert and my dad agreed that both of our families would spend a month or so at the farm. On their drive back to the city, my father mentioned how amazingly inexpensive the place was. Albert kind of shrugged and said it didn't seem *that* inexpensive. It turned out that Henri, generous gent that he was, determined that my dad was not in Albert's financial league and, even though they'd never met before, decided my father was a nice guy and deserved a break—so he charged my father half of what he charged Albert.

My family wound up spending the next few summers at West Point Farms. It was a magical place. But the most magical thing of all was that Mrs. Apisson was a brilliant cook. She made amazing phyllo dough and stuffed it with various savories and sweets. My favorite was something called *beureks*—phyllo triangles filled with different cheeses. She served them piping hot and they practically melted in your mouth. She also cooked the most delicious vegetables imaginable—so good that even a four-year-old would eat them.

Barbara (I never called her anything but Mrs. Apisson) was the first person who really taught my mother about food and how to prepare it. She was not just a superb cook, she was a superb *healthy* cook, back in the late '50s and early '60s when healthy cooking was hardly the rage. In the mid-'70s, she even coauthored a cookbook called *A Diet for 100 Healthy Happy Years: Health Secrets from the Caucasus*. In the book, Barbara describes herself as a woman "of Caucasus-Armenian extraction" and says that healthy eating is the reason people from the Caucasus often live to be a hundred years old. My mom paid close attention to Barbara's preaching about organic farming and healthy eating, and the place was so informal that within days of our arrival, Barbara just took my mom into the kitchen and began showing her how things were done. Soon, my mother was going into the kitchen on her own to cook. And it wasn't long before she was coming out of the kitchen having made her own jams and mustards and mayonnaise and yogurt and pastries with made-from-scratch phyllo dough.

My mom particularly loved a dish that Barbara made called celeriac remoulade. It was not particularly healthy, nor was it an Armenian dish; it was about as French as it could be. Barbara made it because it allowed Henri to feel as if he were back in Paris.

Barbara was not just a great cook but also a great teacher, and her belief in healthy and natural foods profoundly changed my mom's approach to shopping and cooking. We stopped having sweets—especially packaged sweets—and suddenly our dinners were as locally focused as they could have been in those days. I never again tasted a frozen or packaged food until I went off to college and lived on frozen chicken potpies and Cocoa Puffs for most of my freshman year.

A couple of years after our summers at West Point Farms had ended, we were up in Massachusetts, visiting my dad's family. A tenuous peace between Grandpa Irving and Steve/Sye had been made sometime after I was born; the détente went in and out over the years. Late one afternoon, I headed over to a friend's house to play. As it started to get dark, my friend's mom asked if I wanted to stay for dinner and I immediately said sure. She called my mom to make certain it was okay. Then she asked me if I had anything I'd really like to eat. I said: "Cold cereal." She explained to me that she could make pasta or hamburgers or anything that was really good and I said that was fine but if I got to choose, I wanted cold cereal. She called my mom again to tell her about my offbeat request and my mother explained that she didn't keep anything like Sugar Frosted Flakes or Sugar Pops or any kind of sugared cereal at home so she wasn't surprised that I craved such forbidden fruit. She graciously gave her blessing—so that night, the parents and kids ate a real meal and I ecstatically gobbled down several bowls of Trix.

The next night, back at the house in which my parents, my brother, and I were staying, my mom made dinner. As an appetizer, she made Barbara Apisson's cheese beureks (sometimes spelled boreks or bouregs; they are delicious under any spelling), which she had perfected by then. I liked them just as much as the bowls of Trix.

That was the first time I ever realized that something delicious you ate in a restaurant could also be made and eaten at home. Good food wasn't something that magically appeared from behind closed doors (unless you had a mother who turned mud-and-eggshell pies into perfect cakes). Cheese beureks were something that normal people could cook if they only knew how.

It was a major revelation at an early stage of my development: like almost everything good in life, good food was the result of hard work.

Celeriac Remoulade

INGREDIENTS:

1¼ celery root

½ lemon for rubbing and for juice

½ teaspoon salt

3 tablespoons sour cream

2 tablespoons mayonnaise, preferably homemade

1 tablespoon Dijon mustard

¼ teaspoon freshly ground black pepper

DIRECTIONS:

With a sharp knife, slice off the ends of the celery root and then most of the brown peel. Trim the bits of brown remaining and slice the root in half. Remove the spongy area in the middle by cutting it out. Rub the pieces with the half lemon to prevent them from browning. Cut the pieces in half again for easier grating. Shred/grate the celery root now (you can use a food processor with a grater attachment). Transfer to a bowl and toss with 1 teaspoon salt and juice squeezed from half the lemon. Let marinate for 30 minutes but no longer than 1 hour.

For the dressing, mix together the sour cream, mayonnaise, mustard, and pepper. You may want to loosen it up with a little more lemon juice. Fold the dressing into the celery root. Cover with plastic wrap and refrigerate for 1 to 2 hours.

OKAY, THIS IS pretty simple to make. It is also the biggest surprise, for me, of all my mother's choices for her fantasy menu. I never got attached to this dish. It's too sour for my taste and too refined. Over the years, I've gotten to appreciate sour, although it's not my favorite taste, but I'm not quite grown up enough yet for refined. But my mom loves it and it's an important recipe to her, so here it is.

I did make my own mayonnaise because that's what my mom used to do, and once again I was surprised by how easy it was. Even though the celeriac recipe only uses two tablespoons of the stuff, it was pretty cool to dip those measuring spoons into a jar of freshly made mayonnaise. I recommend taking the extra ten minutes or so it takes to create a jar of mayo because you can use the leftover concoction on a BLT or a tomato sandwich, which are pretty much the only other things I can imagine using that mayonnaise for, except for the once-every-three-or-four-year craving I get for a tuna fish salad sandwich.

Recipe for Homemade Mayo, adapted from my mom's
recipe found in her recipe card box and that seems to be
adapted from a Julia Child recipe

———————

INGREDIENTS:

3 egg yolks

3 tablespoons lemon juice

½ teaspoon salt

¼ teaspoon dry mustard

2 pinches sugar

1½ cups olive oil

DIRECTIONS:

Warm the mixing bowl by running it under warm water. Dry the bowl and add the egg yolks, beating for 1 to 2 minutes, until they are thick and sticky.

Add 1 tablespoon of the lemon juice, the salt, sugar, and the dry mustard. Beat for 30 seconds.

The egg yolks are now ready to receive the olive oil. Add it a teaspoon at a time while beating the mixture constantly. Watch the oil and not the sauce. When the egg yolks have absorbed the oil, add another teaspoon and not before! **(NOTE FROM AUTHOR: I BASICALLY HAD NO IDEA WHAT I WAS WATCHING OR LOOKING FOR OR ACTUALLY DOING DURING THIS STAGE, BUT IT WORKED OUT WELL, SO DON'T BE TOO NERVOUS DESPITE THE STERN INSTRUCTIONS.)**

Keep doing this until you have added ⅓ to ½ cup of the oil. At that point, you'll see the sauce thicken and you can take a deep breath because the "crisis" point is over. If you are beating the sauce by hand, you can rest for a second. **(ANOTHER NOTE FROM THE AUTHOR: I CONFESS, I RESTED FOR ABOUT A FULL MINUTE. THIS CONSTANT BEATING IS EXHAUSTING; ALL THIS PRESSURE AND TALK OF CRISIS POINTS DOESN'T HELP.)** Then keep adding the oil, 1 to 2 tablespoons at a time, blending thoroughly after each addition.

When you have added all the oil, beat 2 tablespoons boiling water into the sauce to keep it from curdling.

Season to taste with wine vinegar, lemon juice, salt, pepper, mustard, curry, or any other spice you like. (FINAL AUTHOR'S NOTE FOR THIS RECIPE, I SWEAR: I WENT FOR SALT, PEPPER, AND A DAB OF WHITE WINE VINEGAR, MOSTLY BECAUSE I LOOKED AT VARIOUS MAYONNAISE RECIPES AND A LOT OF THEM USED WHITE WINE VINEGAR AS AN ESSENTIAL INGREDIENT; PLUS I LIKE VINE- GAR AND IT SEEMED LIKE A GOOD IDEA.)

If the sauce is not used immediately, scrape it into a small bowl and cover it closely so a skin will not form on its surface.

THE CELERIAC REMOULADE recipe is Julia Child's, from *Mastering the Art of French Cooking*, because my guess is that Mrs. Apisson used a similarly authentic French recipe for her version. The same era, the same sensibility, and all that. I also used it because my mom wound up becoming friends with Julia Child. They worked and taught together when my mom eventually ran the cooking school at Ma Maison and they hit it off. Julia even once cooked lunch for my mother in Julia's home in Santa Barbara. I had moved back to New York by then and my parents were living in L.A.—this was circa 1979–1980. My mom called me, as excited as I've ever heard her (except for the time she once sat next to Paul Newman at a dinner party and all she could do for several days afterward was sigh and repeat sentences with the words "hunk" and "those eyes are so blue!" in them). She told me that Julia had invited her and my mom's close friend Joan to her house for lunch and they were about to start their drive up the coast. It all seemed pretty thrilling to me and I told her to call me afterward and let me know all the details.

She didn't call me that night or the next day. I finally called home and when my mom answered the phone, I just went, "So how was it? What did she make?"

There was a lengthy silence. Finally my mom said, in a very quiet voice, "I'm going to tell you something but you can never tell anyone."

Well . . . of course I promised. And for many years I never did tell anyone what I heard. But eventually I spilled the beans, so to speak, because this story was too good not to share. After quite a few years passed, my circumspect mother gave me her official permission to spread the word.

The word was that Julia Child made a horrible lunch.

My mother said she had never been more disappointed in her entire life. The salad was overdressed, rendering the greens way too wet and soggy, and she served some kind of chicken that was too dry. My mom no longer remembers what else was served, but she does recall that it was all tasteless. Describing the lunch to me on the phone that day, she was deeply apologetic.

She kept saying, "She's a wonderful, wonderful teacher."

I kept saying, "But she can't cook?"

"No, no, of course she can cook," my mother insisted, over and over again, "but she's a better teacher than a cook."

We went round and round until I said, once again, "I just want to get this straight: Julia Child is not a great cook."

My mom sighed deeply and said, "She is not a great cook. The lunch was inedible."

I don't think my mother ever told anyone else, other than my dad and my brother, about that particular dining experience. She felt as if she would somehow be betraying the entire food community and striking a blow against the American way of life. In later years, when I'd bring up the touchy subject, she'd wave her hand and say, "Oh, it wasn't that bad. It wasn't *inedible*." I'd just look at her until she'd shrug and nod in acknowledgment that I was remembering things correctly and then she'd say, "It was pretty bad."

I KNEW I would not be swooning over the taste of Julia's celeriac remoulade, but I also was aware that the recipe called for some fairly demanding knife work, so I decided to use the opportunity to take a cutlery class. I periodically thought about—and envied—my mother's serenity when I discovered her chopping those carrots or onions lo those many years ago, but I'd never done anything about it. This was my chance to see what this serenity thing was all about.

The few days leading up to the class were anything but serene as most of my swing-thoughts—or chop-thoughts—tended toward picturing what my hands would look like with several fewer fingers than I currently had. Manual dexterity was not my strong suit. Quite a few people in my inner circle felt quite firmly that I should not be allowed to handle anything with a sharp edge. Several would add the phrase "or with a point." One or two would probably include pencils in that equation.

But I was determined.

My mother has told me several times over the years that food preparation worked in lieu of psychiatry for her. She used her chopping and cutting time both to clear her head and to fill it with the thoughts that mattered. Dicing onions calmed her. Quartering mushrooms relaxed her. Slicing carrots into perfectly uniform quarter-inch circular pieces allowed her to focus on solving problems for her husband or her kids.

My first knife class was at Manhattan's Institute of Culinary Education or, as it's known to all who work and attend classes there, ICE.

I've mentioned my aversion to formalized instruction. And to precision. Add to that my growing fear of slicing off several digits on my left hand. So, heading to ICE headquarters—I kept picturing it as akin to Dr. No's secret underwater den of evil—I was a bit trepidatious. But the space turned out to be fairly non-imposing, even kind of cool, with all sorts of different kitchens and workrooms and, given that it was on a very high floor at 25 Liberty Plaza, way, way downtown, it was the opposite of underwater.

My class had nine students in it, including me: five women, four

My mom with a drinking buddy . . .

. . . and a cooking buddy.

men. They seemed like a reasonable and pleasant group, anxious to learn basic cutlery skills.

Everyone called the teacher "Chef," which rubbed me the wrong way. Normally, I'm totally intimidated by uniforms and experts. I have no problem calling my doctor "Doctor" rather than Phil or Bob or Frieda. In fact, I prefer it. Calling doctors by their first names makes me think they're too much like me and I prefer to get poked, probed, and cut by someone higher up on the food chain. And if I ever talk to the pilot of an airplane, I am happy to refer to him or her as "Captain." I give them my blind faith that they will be able to get me from New York to L.A. by somehow making a couple of tons of metal sail thirty thousand feet in the air, so I'm happy to call them whatever they want. But I absolutely cannot bring myself to call some person in white pants, a white Three Musketeersy–looking coat, and a toque by a title. I know that kitchens are run somewhat militaristically, but it still seems off to me calling a chef "Chef" just because he is better at making béchamel sauce than I am.

Our chef/teacher turned out to be a nice guy and a good teacher. Everyone else in our class immediately started calling him "Chef" when addressing him, but I maintained my self-respect by calling him nothing or coughing into my hand and mumbling his name incoherently so he had no idea what the hell I was calling him.

His first bit of business was to tell us what he wanted to accomplish in this three-hour session and to give us a bit of his cooking and cutlery philosophy. It wasn't quite Sartre or Kierkegaard but it was interesting—he was all about good, fresh ingredients; he thought knowledge about how best to use one's tools was essential in any profession; and he made a passionate case for kitchen safety (yes!). Best of all, it was realistic. He broke it to us that we wouldn't become Daniel Boulud–level chefs after three hours of learning how to handle different knives, but he did think we'd have a base of knowledge that would either suffice for our needs or be a good stepping-stone from which to go upward and onward if we so desired.

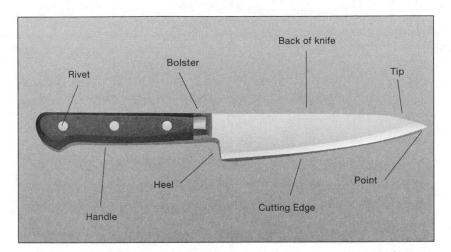

Diagram of a Chef's Knife. I paid particular attention to the Tip and the Point, to avoid severing several knuckles. I was most comfortable with the Handle and I feel very confident in my Bolster ability.

We were each sent to separate workstations that all had folders with a few printouts tucked inside, various vegetables, different sized bowls, a cutting board, and several sharp-looking knives.

Chef—or ahemHmmnamlman, as I referred to him—asked us to look at one of the printouts, which had line drawings of different kinds of knives and labels for each of the various parts.

We were then shown what each of the knives at our station actually were, got a definition of each and a demonstration of how best to use them. I ate all this stuff up with a spoon, so to speak:

Paring Knife: This baby has a thin three-to-four-inch blade that usually tapers to a point and is used when intricate work is called for—it allows for a greater amount of control than a larger knife (so better for peeling fruit, for instance).

Chef's Knife: The ultimate utilitarian cutting tool. It can be used for everything that has to do with chopping or slicing. It's a medium-size knife and is the least intimidating because it doesn't look like it does anything special. It just looks like a knife.

Cleaver: This is the blade that looks like it can do some serious damage and belongs in the hands of Luca Brasi in *The Godfather*. It chops through meat and can be used for vegetables or to remove meat from bones. We were told it was also good for scooping ingredients into cookware. I decided I'd have to work my way up to that one.

That was it for us. There are other types of knives, of course—a boning knife, a bread knife, a carving knife, for example—and all of them can have different types of blades (curved, serrated, wavy) and handles. But the three we were given seemed sufficient to get us going.

As I stood studying my printout, our teacher pulled out a long, thin, rounded tool. I knew I had one in my knife set at home, but I had no idea what it was. Turns out it was a knife sharpener. He then showed us how to sharpen our blades on it—rubbing the cutting edge first in one direction (down), then the next (up). It had to be done at the correct angle, about a forty-five-degree slant, and carefully. Having been given one of these sharpening sticks along with our three knives, we all went to work sharpening our blades. After a minute or two, I was sure I was getting the hang of it.

Chef—Coughahemmenfffgh—then showed us how to actually cut things up.

He began by showing us how to hold the knife—by the handle, naturally, but also keeping one's index finger on the bolster. Not only does this grip provide more leverage and stability when chopping hard and fast, it also prevents carpal tunnel syndrome. It is indeed a dangerous life being a chef.

Using a paring knife, he showed us how to core a tomato (in my naive appreciation of learning these skills, this was kind of thrilling) and how to peel an orange so that the peel came off in one, long, curling piece (this was showing off because he made it look really easy; it isn't). Using a cleaver, he slashed down on a thick potato, demonstrating the tool's power. He also told us a story about how a student in one class almost cut him—Chef Phlemmermannn—in half by waving the cleaver around carelessly. He explained how to properly dismantle an onion (you're supposed to cut off the end so the onion can lie flat while you chop—a genuine revelation to me). After that, he showed us how to place our fingers on the chopping block, our knuckles square to the knife, so even if we slipped up we wouldn't do any serious severing. He explained the differences among mincing, chopping, dicing, and cubing; then he had us practice on garlic. He also showed us how to smoosh the garlic pieces with the flat edge of the blade. "Smoosh" is not the technical term, I'm sure, but I didn't take note of the word he actually used and "smoosh" does justice to the process.

After that, we paired off (except for me: I was the odd person out, which was fine with me; I'm not much of a team player in or out of the kitchen) to make salsa—using our onion, tomato, garlic, and hot pepper (also provided for us). We quietly chopped, minced, smooshed, and spiced—he urged us to taste as often as necessary and bring it to the level of heat that we most liked (I like things as hot as possible, so I used my entire pepper). The same urging applied to the use of salt and pepper, with which we were also provided.

As we worked, our teacher for the day went around and appraised our work for each segment and vegetable. He seemed impressed with my garlic mincing/smooshing but not so much when it came to dicing the onion—I was left with several long onion strands, no matter how I tried to imitate his turning and angling demonstrations. From his raised eyebrow and slight nod, I suspected he gave my tomato coring and dicing a solid C.

The last part of the lesson was the tasting. We each received a spoon and there was one large tray of toast points that had been prepared by an invisible person in a nearby test kitchen. The team to my right won the group vote. I preferred my level of heat but theirs was definitely the best overall from a texture and taste perspective.

The end result?

I didn't cut myself. Not even a nick. And I am determined to get myself a set of really perfect and beautiful knives. That will probably be my gift to myself when I type the words "the end" on these manuscript pages. And yes, the class did help me when making the celeriac remoulade. I used the cleaver—with surprising confidence—to cut off the ends of the celery root. The paring knife was used—not exactly expertly but competently—to remove the peel and the spongy inside. I used the chef's knife for the rest of the cutting.

When I took the concoction up to my mom's apartment, I brought a cutting block into her bedroom—she wasn't up for a trip to the kitchen that day—to proudly show off my newfound skills, dexterity, and knowledge.

I explained to her that I'd learned something in class I'd never realized before: the reason you are supposed to cut an onion or a carrot, or, literally, anything else, into the same size pieces is that those pieces will all cook at the exact same rate. My chest swelled up with this revelation as if I were telling her about my Nobel Prize–winning physics theory. Her response to this was, after several attempts at getting the right words out: "You couldn't have figured that out on your own?"

I told her that of course I could have, but it wasn't anything I'd really thought about. "Sometimes," I told her, "the best educational process is to just understand something simple that you might not have focused on before." Even as I said it, I knew it sounded fairly lame. But she nodded politely in response.

Undeterred, I then gave her a demonstration of my new mastery of the cutlery world. The whole flat-finger-knuckle thing. The anti–carpal tunnel grip. The smooshing and the paring and the skin peeling (which, I must admit, I had not mastered to the degree I should have before trying to show off).

I performed for my mom as if I were an eight-year-old Penn and Teller, amazing my audience with this view into a world of magic where few dared to tread. When I was done, my mom smiled.

I'm not sure she was impressed.

But I am sure she was pleased.

CHAPTER FOUR

When I was around three or four, various members of my
mother's family, including my gramps, Jake, gave in and followed
their wayward daughter and son-in-law into the wilds of Manhattan. Not to Stuyvesant Town but to the near-identical but slightly
more upscale development called Peter Cooper Village (adding the
word "Village" rather than "Town" to the official nomenclature
was a clever attempt to make the look-alike redbrick complex sound
superior).

Jake and Ceil, his second wife, my mom's sister Belle (with her
two children but minus her husband, who had died), and eldest
sister Natalie with Spatzi and their two sons, all moved into Peter
Cooper. It was hard to split up families in those days. Or maybe it
was just the Harmatz clan that liked to cluster around each other
forever.

Peter Cooper, directly across 20th Street from Stuy Town, ranged
up to 23rd Street and, like Stuy Town, sprawled from First Avenue
to the East River. The apartments in both places were very similar,
but Peter Cooper had security guards (I'm not sure what they were

guarding other than the tenants' egos) and the grounds were slightly nicer and less family friendly. The most important difference was that the Peter Cooper residents were allowed to have air conditioners in the apartments whereas Stuy Town inhabitants were not.

Not long after my mother's family moved next door to us—and not exactly by coincidence—my parents moved out of the city altogether. The Gethers family became ensconced about forty-five minutes north of Manhattan in West Nyack, New York. We lived in a very cool and eccentric house that was owned by the local water and electric company. It was pre–Civil War and was actually used as a stop on the underground railway to hide slaves traveling north to Canada. As a result, and to my delight, there were all sorts of strange, secret hiding places scattered throughout the place. The house was situated on three and a half acres of land, bordered on the back by a lake and, according to what I could understand from my parents, quite cheap. I have no idea how my dad was able to find it and rent it, but he always had good taste, was quite confident in his taste, and had a knack for deciding that he wanted something and then finding a way to make it happen.

West Nyack was more farmland than suburbia back then. It was like a benign version of the Billy Mumy *Twilight Zone* episode town: kids rode their bikes everywhere, schoolteachers came over to their students' houses for dinner, parents didn't need to supervise trick-or-treaters on Halloween, and the town doctor made house calls and knew everybody's medical history without checking his charts. It was the kind of place Ronald Reagan crazily thought all of America was like before the rebellious 1960s. Even West Nyack wasn't really like that. But it sure seemed that way to me from the ages of five through ten.

The town had Boy Scout troops galore and bowling teams and Little League battles and killer dodgeball games on the school playgrounds. I instinctively shied away from any activity or group that involved uniforms and uniformity. That five-year period is when my basic perception of mankind seems to have been formed: stay away from any gathering of more than two people if they think they know more about life than you do—*especially* if they're all wearing the same clothes.

The one thing West Nyack didn't have was my father. At least on a regular basis. Out of necessity he became a part-timer.

The television industry had rather abruptly relocated from New York to Los Angeles. Since this is what put bread on our table—he had abandoned acting to become a screenwriter—my dad had to move with it. He resisted as long as he could, for several years spending six months on the West Coast working on various television series and movie projects, and then coming back to Nyack for the next six months to write or just be a dad. I thought it was all pretty exotic having a half-time father who, when he was home, was home twenty-four hours a day. I thought that six-month, twenty-four-hour-a-day period more than made up for the long absences. I was happy in my youth-spun cocoon. My brother, six and a half years older than I, and going through all the normal traumas of teenage-hood—hormonal, psychological, and emotional—wasn't nearly as sanguine without a dad. And my mom . . . well . . . at the time I had no idea how hard it was on her and how strong she had to be to deal with my dad's disappearances for such long stretches, especially to the land of starlets and glamour. But I never saw a trace of any difficulty. Instead, I saw a mom who would throw the football around with me in the backyard (she was a way better athlete than my dad) and drive me everywhere and help me with my homework.

My mom began to really get serious about cooking around this time. It was the era of horrible frozen TV dinners—whole families used to sit down in front of the television at dinnertime with prepackaged aluminum foil trays that had come out of the freezer and gone into the oven, and they would eat small portions, subdivided by aluminum foil walls, of turkey with gravy, mushy potatoes, mushier carrots, and some form of pudding. They basically were

COURTESY OF PETER GETHERS

A semi-single mom with her two angels. Somewhere around this time she was explaining sex to Eric and showing me how to hit a baseball.

the precursor to airplane food. Eric and I got none of that, though. My mom used to make her own TV dinners. She'd prepare steak or pot roast and roasted potatoes and vegetables (horribly enough, I remember portions of Brussels sprouts) and rhubarb cobbler and she would freeze them, so we'd always have healthy and nutritious dinners ready to heat up. Then, when my dad popped in for his extended visits, she would prepare new and elaborate dinners.

I remember my mom making something that I thought was totally exotic: quail. It's not the perfect food for small boys because it's delicate and that's not something we boys do very well. It was delicious, though, and no one else in West Nyack that I knew of ever ate quail. Years later, I learned there was a very specific reason she came to love cooking this small, tasty bird. All the men in the Gethers family liked the dark meat sections of their fowls. So did my mom. But when she made chicken or even turkey, because she was who she was, she let us take the parts *we* liked best and she took what was left, which meant no dark meat for her. I grew up assuming she preferred white meat. Uh uh. She just ate it because it's what remained after her husband and two boys had ravaged the legs and thighs of the large birds. But quail was too small to share. Everyone got his or her own tiny bird to pick up and rip apart and try to figure out how to eat. Which meant my mom got her share of dark meat, even if quail legs were not the meatiest.

My mother wasn't the only person doing kitchen duty in our West Nyack house. Louise Trotty, the woman who had helped raise my dad and who was responsible for the Gethers family name-change, lived with us. She had a bedroom in the converted base-ment—I went down there at all hours of the day and night to watch a black-and-white TV with her—and she came out of loyalty to my dad, who knew she would make my mom's life easier. As an extra bonus, he could now afford to pay her. Louise often cooked for us, even when my mom was home—her food was delicious but limited in scope—and when my mom was visiting my dad in Cal-ifornia, it was Louise who disciplined us, often with her potent shoe swat.

There were advantages to being the baby in the family. I didn't get into nearly as much trouble as Eric did. As a result, I was often rewarded for being "the good one." My favorite reward, by far, was Louise's chocolate pudding. She made it from scratch. I remem-ber her pouring lots of milk into a pot, melting dark chocolate, and stirring with a wooden spoon for a long time while a skin would form on top of the pudding and around the sides of the pot. While it was still warm, she would spoon it into small bowls, put a strip of cellophane over each individual bowl, and put the whole col-lection into the fridge. But there was still that pot. And that spoon. If I timed it right—and especially if this wonderful delicacy was being made anywhere close to something bad Eric had done, which was not very difficult because he was usually doing something bad—I'd get to lick the spoon. And then use that spoon to scrape the sides of the pot and lick that sucker until the cows came home.

When I was seven years old, my mom disappeared for a couple of months. I was aware that she was in the hospital in the city—I visited her a few times—but I didn't fully comprehend what was going on. What was going on was that she had cancer. A melanoma, to be specific. On her calf. She was given a 5 percent chance of being able to stay alive for twelve more months.

Melanoma was and still is the most severe and scariest type of skin cancer, but all I really understood was that when my mom eventually returned from the hospital, she had a huge chunk of her calf missing. The gouge in her leg was probably six to eight inches long and several inches deep and I thought it looked monstrous. I'm sure she was self-conscious about it but she never hid it, at least not that I recall. And I think one of the reasons my dad was such an excellent husband is that he never treated her enormous and rather grotesque wound and subsequent scar as anything but a part of her that he loved like all the other parts.

My dad's heart was quite large. And his pockets were equally deep. My dad loved spending money (a trait I unfortunately inherited in a big way), especially on my mom. He had never been happy with the wedding ring he'd bought for her because when they'd gotten married, all he could afford was the equivalent of one of those rings found in a Cracker Jack box. So when he found out that my mom had a terrible, life-threatening cancer, he immediately took out a bank loan and bought her the most beautiful diamond ring he could find as a replacement. To this day, if anyone asks my mom to tell the story of him giving her the ring when she was in her hospital bed, she will start to cry at the sentiment and sense of loss and laugh at the same time, thinking of the absurd romantic instinct of going into hock to buy a diamond ring for a supposedly dying woman.

Once my mother was home, she was still very weak and had to spend a few more months in bed. My dad was present, of course, for the operation and immediate aftermath, but he had to return to his work in L.A. for a chunk of the lengthy recuperation period.

I was given a very specific role to aid in her recovery. My mom had lost a lot of weight—she never weighed much to begin with—so my job was to make her a milk shake every day when I got home from school and to make sure that she drank it. Her favorite flavor was coffee, although she also liked chocolate and mocha, a combo of the two. She and I had the same taste in shakes; we liked them thick and kind of icy—chunky if possible, so they were more flavored sludge than smooth milk.

My dad gave me another marching order, as well: I was to monitor my mom's eating habits and make sure she ate dessert every night after dinner—an excellent assignment for a seven-year-old since it meant I got to eat the same dessert. She and I ate a *lot* of Louise's chocolate pudding.

My mother never accepted the fact that she was supposed to die within a year of her diagnosis. Quite the opposite. My father had written a play and it was opening on Broadway in October 1961, some nine months after my mom's cancer was revealed. She insisted that she would walk into the theater for Opening Night and be completely healthy and she never wavered in her belief.

The play, *A Cook for Mr. General*, is notable for three reasons, at least to me. One is that it was Dustin Hoffman's first Broadway role. He didn't even have a speaking role. He played a character called Ridzinski. My dad told me—after I saw *The Graduate* years later and Dustin Hoffman became my acting idol—that he'd been so talented in rehearsals that even though he wasn't supposed to speak, they let him do some birdcalls onstage, just so he'd have something to do. Reason number two is that an actor named George Furth played one of the lead parts; his character had the tasteful moniker of Jockstrap Jordan. Furth later went on to write *Company* with Stephen Sondheim, a play that I found life-changing in its cynicism and dark, complex view of relationships when I saw it on Broadway years later. And the third reason the play was so memorable is that I very distinctly recall my mom, dressed to the nines, leaving our house in West Nyack to go to Opening Night.

Reflecting back, my hope is that her dress was a little bit tight due to all the milk shakes I made her drink in my role of Master Sergeant of Desserts. But I don't really know if that was true.

I do know that she looked beautiful. And unbowed.

And very much alive.

LOUISE TROTTY'S CHOCOLATE PUDDING

Louise Trotty was an amazing person. It feels a bit funny to say that she raised me because my mother was very present in my life as a kid, as was my dad. My parents were my parents and filled that role to the hilt. But Louise was also my parent. I could go to her when I was upset but didn't want my parents to know how upset I was. She could comfort me and bring a sense of peace to my life that no one could do in quite the same way. I know that she loved me like I was her own son, the same way she loved my dad. And I loved her deeply in return.

Louise did not suffer fools and she believed that hard work was essential to a good life. I have no idea what religion she was or even if she was religious at all. I do know that she consistently demonstrated a bottomless capacity for love, a deeply embedded kindness, and a somewhat scary impatience when Eric or I did something we weren't supposed to do.

I called her Trotty much of the time rather than Louise. I don't know why but I liked it and she liked it, too. I would holler from upstairs, "Trotty, when are we gonna eat?" and she would admonish me for yelling, not for calling her by her last name.

She was the first black person I ever met, and it's probably the main reason I'm fairly color-blind when it comes to humans. She did not seem angry about her lot in life, and I suspect she would have shared that anger with me, or at least I would have sensed it.

Trotty had a medium dark-brown complexion and several large moles on her face. I never knew her to have a date with a man. I know that, when she wasn't living with us, she shared an apartment in Harlem with her aunt Martha, who was two years older than Louise. When I was young, I was absolutely incapable of understanding how her aunt could be only two years older than she was, and I was fascinated by the math.

I was also fascinated by the fact that Louise never learned to read. She could write out very simple names or phrases, sometimes with baffling misspellings, but couldn't string together a complex sentence on paper. I offered several times to try to teach her, but she would never engage in that discussion. I remember that she once got angry at my persistence, so I dropped the subject, never to bring it up again. I don't know whether her resistance was out of embarrassment or fear or some sense that there'd been a miscarriage of justice, or perhaps it was just resignation that she was too old. I never thought it was anything she should be embarrassed about. It was just something she couldn't do.

She and my mother had an uneasy truce over the years. They never had the relationship that Louise had with my dad or with me (my brother was older and far less interested in having an extra mother—he was mostly concerned with avoiding any extra punishment). There was a minor rivalry between my mom and Trotty, I suppose, for the affection of the men/boys in the household, but there was also a friction that resulted over control of the kitchen. My mother was trying to make healthy food that tasted good. Louise made fried chicken and icebox pie and meat loaf with mashed potatoes that tasted all the better for their unhealthiness. There was never any open hostility, not at all. They liked and appreciated each other. They just didn't love each other the same way my dad and I loved Louise and she loved us.

The truce became a lot easier when my mom was sick and laid

up in bed. She then became like a daughter rather than the wife of one of Louise's surrogate sons. Each day after I made my daily milk shake and delivered it, Louise would check the glass to make sure that my mother drank every last bit. If she didn't, Louise would talk to her the way a parent talks to a recalcitrant seven-year-old, explaining that it was for her own good. Then she'd tell me, quite sternly, that the next day I had to add more coffee ice cream or more chocolate syrup because that's the way my mom liked it.

The truce turned shaky again when we moved to California. Louise never liked it there; she had no friends and felt isolated living up above Coldwater Canyon in my parents' new and large house. She couldn't take the bus into Harlem to see her aunt Martha on weekends. She was unhappy, and that probably made her not so much fun to be around for my mom. She spent a lot of time alone in her bedroom, downstairs, next to the kitchen. On Saturdays, she and I would often go to the movies together, one of my parents dropping us off in Beverly Hills or Westwood or Hollywood and picking us up when the film was over. On weeknights, I would still go into Louise's room and watch one of her corny TV shows with her. I liked keeping her company and watching her enjoyment.

We moved to Los Angeles in 1964 because my dad got a job writing and producing a sitcom, *The Bing Crosby Show*. It was no longer viable for him to make his six-month commute. My mom had been ready to make the move for several years, but they waited for Eric to graduate from high school and head off to college— they didn't want him uprooted twice. I was ambivalent about the move. As much as I liked West Nyack, I didn't really mind putting it behind me. On the other hand, I didn't take to Los Angeles right away. I hated the Dodgers and the Rams and was never taken in by the supposed glamour of the place. On my first day of school in my new sixth-grade class, I wore my San Francisco Giants team jacket, alienating just about every boy in the school.

Life was quite different there, no question about it. For our very first L.A. Christmas, Bing Crosby came to our house for a big party. His musical director, John Scott Trotter, had, without telling my parents, arranged for a group of carolers to show up. They sang holiday songs in the seventy-five-degree winter wonderland and then—honest to god!—Bing Crosby sat down at the piano in my parents' living room and sang "White Christmas." After dinner, he went into the kitchen, kissed Louise's hand in a courtly fashion, and told her the meal was delicious. Louise didn't just swoon—she fainted dead away.

Trotty moved back to New York when I was fifteen. She went back to living with her aunt Martha and worked for my cousin Nikki, looking after her two young sons.

I moved back to New York when I was twenty-one and, of course, saw her whenever possible. It wasn't often enough. By this point, her eyesight was starting to fail and she didn't love going too far from her apartment. We did speak on the phone at least once a week. The discussions tended to be about baseball (she'd become a Mets fan). And I saw her around her birthday every year—it was on September 23—as well as every Christmas. For both occasions, I'd take her out to a Chinese restaurant in the Times Square area. She would order a large portion of shrimp fried rice and that's all she would ever eat. I'd give her a bottle of bubble bath or perfume, and, in return, she'd bring a big shopping bag of her fried chicken. I definitely got the better end of the deal.

I went up to the Harlem apartment where she and Martha lived two or three times; I took the subway up. The apartment was clean and comfortable, with few frills. There was a warmth to it that didn't come from the furniture but from its inhabitants.

When she was ninety-one, Louise took ill and went into the hospital. I went to visit her with my mom and Janis, who had met Louise once before at my apartment, and my friend Paul, who knew her when we were kids together in L.A. but who had by that time moved east with his wife and kids. Louise had always been plump but she was now skin and bones—she must have lost fifty pounds. Nonetheless, when she saw us, she lit up. Her smile was huge.

She was in a room with two other elderly black women and she said, by way of introducing us, "This is my family." Taking my hand, she said, "This is my son, this is one of my sons. His brother's my son. Their father was my son, too." Pointing to Paul, she said, "And this is another son." Then she turned to her roommates and said, "Ask them if I met Bing Crosby." The women told us that Louise talked constantly about the time she spent in Los Angeles, especially about all the famous people she met and how Bing Crosby had liked her cooking and kissed her.

We stayed about an hour and reminisced with Louise—she seemed to remember every stupid thing Paul and I had ever done when we were kids, and the stupider we'd been, the more she enjoyed the remembering. She talked about how much she loved my dad and how she still couldn't believe he had died before she had. She cried a few tears thinking about him. We talked about her fried chicken and her chocolate pudding and how she used to let me lick the spoon. She remembered trying to fatten my mother up when she was sick and she told everyone in the room that my mom had become a famous chef and Louise said how proud she was of my mom. We all kissed her and said we'd see her soon.

One of the women stopped me on our way out and said, "Did she really meet Bing Crosby?" and I said, "I swear. Everything she told you was true." The other women were very impressed and Louise lorded it over them, I am positive, until the day she died, which was just a week or two after our visit.

At her funeral on West 145th Street in Harlem, the minister delivered a touching eulogy and there was some lovely singing from a small choir. My mom, Paul, and I went to have lunch at Miss Maude's Spoonbread Too, a venerated Harlem soul food joint. There, my mom told me that my dad had been paying Louise's salary until the day he died and that, ever since then, my mom had been sending her a weekly check for the same amount. She felt that

Trotty

she not only owed it to Louise, she owed it to my dad, who said that for many years Louise had been his lifeline.

Then we had fried chicken, meat loaf, icebox pie, and chocolate pudding. It was delicious. But not as good as Trotty's.

Chocolate Pudding Recipe, adapted from the Taste of Home Website

Louise did not, of course, cook from recipes or write any of her recipes down, since she did not know how to read or write. So I searched the Internet and tried various pudding recipes, attempting to replicate hers. Some of them were too good, if that makes any sense—they didn't taste plain and simple enough. Some used chocolate that was too dark or too fancy. Everything Louise made was simple. They were recipes for people who didn't have much money and I think their simplicity (and sincerity) is why everything she made was so delicious.

This is the recipe I stumbled upon that comes closest to the chocolate pudding Louise Trotty used to make. It comes from the Taste of Home website. I have changed only one thing: the author of the recipe puts M&M's on top, which is totally antithetical to the simple hominess of chocolate pudding (not to mention repellent). I left the M&M's line out of the recipe. Trust me: don't even think about it. Trotty would sometimes whip up a bowl of cream and use that as a topping, but I'd recommend just eating it the way chocolate pudding was meant to be eaten—either right out of the pot, still hot, with a big wooden spoon, and getting it over way too many parts of your face, or chill it in small, individual bowls and be civilized.

One final observation on this whole chocolate pudding thing. The recipe calls for ½ cup of baking cocoa. When re-creating this, I remembered that, when we lived in West Nyack, Louise used Hershey's cocoa and that was fine. In L.A., my mom had gotten a bit fancier (as did her pantry) and she started using Droste Dutch-style cocoa. I did a little research and found out that there is an actual difference between Dutch-style and regular cocoa powder.

Cocoa powder is—who knew?—the solid remains of fermented, dried, and roasted cacao beans. The beans are cracked, then ground into a paste made of cocoa solids suspended in almost flavorless cocoa butter. When the butter is extracted, what's left are crumbly solids, which are then ground into a fine powder. So cocoa powder is basically the essence of a cocoa bean's chocolate flavor, without any extra fat, sugar, or liquid to get in the way. This is what's called natural cocoa powder and it's what most of the brands of cocoa are that you find in U.S. supermarkets—Hershey's, Ghirardelli, etc.

Dutch process cocoa powder does not actually have anything at all to do with Holland, dikes, Hans Christian Andersen, or those doors that open from the top and bottom. The Dutch process simply makes cocoa less acidic and gives the powder a notice-ably darker hue than the natural powder. It also—you can try it yourself—tastes earthier and woodsier. There are various scientific differences, too—Dutch process cocoa isn't acidic so it doesn't react with alkaline leaveners like baking soda—but 1) none of that is rel-evant to chocolate pudding and 2) I don't have a clue what any of it means. What I can tell you is that I prefer the Dutch-style when making this pudding. They both taste like Trotty's recipes, only for me one tastes like age seven and one tastes like age thirteen.

ABOUT THIS RECIPE:

Yield: 6 to 8 servings (NOTE FROM AUTHOR: OR 1 SERVING, MAYBE 2, IF YOU'RE A TWELVE-YEAR-OLD BOY)

Total Time: 10 minutes prep time plus chilling

INGREDIENTS:

1 cup sugar

½ cup baking cocoa

¼ cup cornstarch

½ teaspoon salt

4 cups milk

2 tablespoons butter

2 teaspoons vanilla extract

(NOTE FROM THE INDIGNANT AUTHOR: THIS IS WHERE I HAVE REFUSED TO TYPE IN THE WORDS "M&M'S OPTIONAL.")

DIRECTIONS:

In a heavy saucepan, combine the sugar, cocoa, cornstarch, and salt. Grad-ually add milk. Bring to a boil over medium heat; boil and stir for 2 minutes. Remove from the heat and stir in the butter and vanilla. Spoon into individ-ual serving dishes. Chill until serving.

When I told my mom I was trying to re-create Louise's chocolate pudding, her face lit up instantly and all she said was, "Oh my."

The dessert turned out perfectly, and it is extraordinarily easy. All you have to do is measure, pour, have the dexterity to turn on one of the burners on the stove, and stir. It takes ten minutes, tops.

Note, however, the final line of the recipe: "Chill until serving." That had no relevance for me. I wanted to re-create my fondest memory of this dish: licking the warm pudding off a wooden spoon that had just circled the inside circumference of the still-warm pot. So after I dished out most of the dark brown pudding into individual serving bowls and stuck them in the fridge, I carried the pot over to my mother who was visiting me in Sag Harbor. She sat at the dining room table, expectantly. I scraped a medium-size wooden spoon around the edge of the pot, capturing a nice portion of the pudding and a tiny bit of the skin, which was already beginning to form. I held the spoon up to my mom's lips and the pudding was suddenly gone in one fell swoop.

There is something that inevitably happens between parents and children if the parents live long enough: a reversal of roles. The child often becomes the parent to the parent. It is not always a pleasant process, nor is it something to which either side looks forward.

This tasting of the chocolate pudding—yes, it felt almost like some kind of royal ritual: the Tasting of the Chocolate Pudding—was a role reversal. There I was doing for my mom what both she and Trotty used to do for me. I was carefully circling the spoon around a large, deep pot, then holding the spoon out toward her mouth so she could sample the warm, chocolaty concoction. But this interaction was not painful or awkward. It was a moment in which my mother and I both happily and of our own free will returned to our respective pasts through my ability, as an adult, to re-create that past. Magically, there was my mom, forty years old and unmarried by time, delighted as she experienced what her ten-year-old son had so delightedly experienced. And there I was, licking my own spoon after scraping the warm pot, once again an untroubled boy, blissfully unaware that real troubles could even exist.

We both knew exactly what we were tasting as we partook of my re-creation of Louise Trotty's chocolate pudding.

It was the delicious taste of youth.

JOËL ROBUCHON'S MASHED POTATOES

(PUREE DE POMMES DE TERRE)

My parents went to Europe together for the first time when I was around nine years old. While they were gone, Louise took care of my brother and me in West Nyack and what I remember most vividly from that three-week period is Eric coming home after going drinking with some of his sixteen-year-old suburban rabble-rousing friends and doing his best to enter the Guinness Book of World Records for most vomiting by a drunk teenager. Louise let him pass out and sleep on the linoleum floor in the entryway (after first smacking him with her shoe, of course). I also remember getting postcards from London, Paris, and Rome. These brief missives from my mom and dad definitely fueled my romantic imagination.

When my parents returned, I heard talk of theater seen and museums visited and friendly people speaking in languages other than English (or speaking English with a much nicer accent than ours). Mostly, or so it seems to me, I heard about the food. It was bad in England (no longer true at all), it was great in Rome, and it was best of all in Paris. My mother couldn't stop asking the question, "How can a ham sandwich taste that good?" I was fascinated by their tales of amazing cheeses, and croissants that exploded with flavor when you bit into them, and something called chocolate mousse. My mom waxed poetically about the texture and deep chocolaty taste and how you could turn over a spoonful of the stuff and it would just stay there on the spoon. That all sounded pretty amazing, but what I really liked about the dessert was its name, which I assumed was "chocolate moose." *That* I wanted to see. I was more than a little disappointed when my mom finally broke it to me that this particular delicacy was nothing more than French chocolate pudding.

My parents went back to Europe a few more times after that first trip. In 1985, they spent a good amount of time in Paris because my father was directing a TV movie that he also wrote called *Murder or Mercy?* It starred Robert Young and was based on the true story of Roswell Gilbert who, after fifty-one years of marriage, murdered his wife, Emily, who had been suffering from Alzheimer's for the previous eight years and had often begged to die. Gilbert said it was an act of mercy but he was tried for murder and convicted. The case became a big part of the national debate about euthanasia and my dad was thrilled to cast Robert Young, conceivably the most liked and likable TV star between the 1950s and the 1980s, as Gilbert. My parents came back to Los Angeles from Paris with my dad raving about Bob Young and my mother unable to do anything but rhapsodize about the meals they had, in particular the mashed potatoes, at Jamin, Joël Robuchon's first and arguably greatest restaurant. From her rapturous descriptions, it was as if she'd had an affair with the young Alain Delon instead of having eaten a bunch of smooshed-up potatoes on a plate.

Robuchon, like so many of the great European chefs, started cooking professionally when he was fifteen years old. It proved to be a good career choice since not only has he accumulated twenty-eight Michelin Guide stars for his many restaurants around the world, the most of any chef in history, but he was also named Chef of the Century by the French restaurant guide Gault et Millau in 1989. My mom clearly thought he deserved every accolade he earned. She could not stop extolling the virtues of his mashed potatoes.

By this time, my mom was already working with Wolfgang Puck, who had, three years earlier, opened the legendary Spago, overlooking Sunset Boulevard in West Hollywood. The day she got back from Paris she went running to see Wolf at the restaurant and said, "Why can't you make potatoes that taste like Robuchon's?" Now, asking Wolf, "Why can't you make something" as delicious as another chef's version of the same dish is a bit like asking Stephen Sondheim why he can't write a song as good as "Feelings." Wolf's slightly peevish response was, "I can. But nobody would eat them here." My mom couldn't believe her ears, so she asked why not. Wolf said, "Those potatoes taste that way because they are all butter. Nobody in America, certainly nobody in L.A., would ever touch them knowing how fattening they are."

He may have been wrong about whether anyone in the United States would eat Robuchon's potatoes, but he was definitely right about how fattening they are. Here's Robuchon's original recipe:

1 kg (NOTE FROM ME: LET'S JUST SAY 2 POUNDS) la ratte potatoes

454 grams (ANOTHER NOTE FROM ME: LET'S CALL IT 1 POUND [2 STICKS]) unsalted butter, cold, cut into small cubes

¼ cup milk

Salt to taste

THREE THINGS TO NOTE:

1. There are only four ingredients. I am a firm believer in the cooking credo that the fewer ingredients there are in a dish, the better that dish tastes. Potatoes, milk, butter, and salt. What could be bad?

2. Good luck finding *la ratte* potatoes. *Félicitations à vous* if you do. If you don't, it's fine to use Yukon Golds or yellow fingerlings. I used yellow fingerlings. I thought it would be a nightmare to peel the little suckers but not at all—once they were

boiled, the skins came off as easily as anything Lena Dunham ever wore on *Girls*.

3. Yes, that proportion above is correct: two pounds of potatoes to one pound of butter. It seems like a lot just reading it. Wait until you actually cook it. Mixing that much butter in with so few potatoes makes the ratio feel as if it's ten pounds of butter to one pound of taters. It made my head spin even before I tasted it.

THE INSTRUCTIONS FOR COOKING ARE EQUALLY SIMPLE:

—Put the unpeeled potatoes in a pot and cover with water. Bring the water to a boil, then reduce the heat to medium and simmer and cook for 35 to 40 minutes or until tender. Drain and peel the potatoes. Transfer the potatoes to a bowl and let them cool slightly.

—Turn the potatoes through a food mill on the finest setting, squishing them back into the cooking pot (**AUTHOR'S NOTE: "SQUISHING" IS MY WORD. IT IS AN ACCURATE DESCRIPTION OF THE PROCESS**). It turns out that a food mill is another piece of cooking equipment I didn't have. So I found something else on my shelves that looked like it would work. I had no idea what it was or why I had it, although eventually it came to me: I worked with a wonderful cook, Amy Thielen, on a cooking show called *Heartland Table*. She used this thing called a ricer and, while filming, I watched her squish something through it and immediately decided I had to have one. So, lurking behind the cameraman and the sound guy, I surreptitiously used my phone to go online and ordered one on the spot. Proof that there is a purpose to everything that happens in life.

—Heat the potatoes over medium heat, stirring until heated through. Add the butter in five additions, allowing each addition to be almost melted before adding the next until it all has been incorporated.

—Stir in the warm milk until combined (**AUTHOR'S NOTE: THIS IS THE FIRST TIME THE RECIPE SAYS THE MILK SHOULD BE WARM. BY THE TIME I GOT TO THIS STAGE, BECAUSE, OF COURSE, I HADN'T CAREFULLY READ THE RECIPE ALL THE**

The mysterious thing called a ricer. It worked perfectly to
squish up the mashed potatoes.

WAY THROUGH BEFORE I PLUNGED INTO THE COOKING, I JUST POURED IT IN
COLD. I PAID FOR THIS MISTAKE AT THE LUNCH TABLE!). Using a whisk, vigorously stir potatoes until fluffy. Season with salt.

—Smooth the top of the potatoes with the back of a spoon or a spatula.

Makes 5½ cups.

WHEN I MADE these irresistible potatoes for my mom, she didn't
care one iota how fattening they were, since at the time she weighed

a hundred pounds tops. She did, however, care about a few other things when I presented her with my interpretation of the food she'd thought about rapturously for thirty years.

My mother forgets nothing when it comes to food: not taste, not texture, not appearance. So I was more anxious than usual when I scooped a large portion of Robuchon's potatoes onto her plate. I had smoothed the top of the potatoes in the serving bowl, as instructed, so I was pretty sure I had the appearance down pat. And, before bringing the finished dish out of my kitchen, I'd slipped a spoonful into my mouth and was positive I'd nailed it. No question in my mind: I was ready to start work on the mashed potato line at the best restaurant in Paris.

I waited confidently for my mom's reaction as she carefully took a forkful with her left hand and ate slowly and deliberately. My confidence faded while she sat in silence. And kept sitting in silence. And then *kept* sitting in silence. I assumed that either full aphasia had kicked in or she hated my version of her beloved potatoes. It was one of the few times I was rooting for aphasia. Fantasies about that Paris potato line job faded in the silence.

Finally, I timidly asked, "So . . . ?"

With no hint of aphasia, she answered, "I'm thinking."

She thought for another minute or two until I couldn't take it anymore and blurted out, in a way that no professional chef would ever consider, "Come on already! Do you hate it? Is it any good at all? I thought it was fantastic! What do you think?"

Here's what she thought: the potatoes were too lumpy. She was right, unfortunately. Robuchon's version, according to my mother and every other person who is lucky enough to have ever tasted the original, had no lumps. Not one single lump. Mine were smooth enough for me but not for my mother. Remember those instructions in the recipe that said, "Vigorously stir until fluffy"? Well, I stirred vigorously until I thought my shoulder was going to fall off, at which point I decided, "Screw it, this looks good enough." And that cold versus warm milk error? Turns out the warm milk would have dissipated some of the annoying lumps. Those damn potatoes did look good. But they weren't really fluffy, just reasonably smooth. There weren't *many* lumps. And they were small, tiny to be precise. But they were lumps.

Next up on my mom's assessment: the potatoes didn't taste the same as the potatoes that Robuchon had used. She was polite when she made that comment but she could taste the slight difference from the French potatoes. I didn't tell her that I'd subbed in fingerlings for *la ratte*, but she knew.

Her final comment: the butter hadn't been incorporated thoroughly enough. She was right on this count, too. As soon as she said it, yes indeed, I was suddenly and painfully aware of all the tiny lines of butter flowing through the bowl. I hadn't even noticed them in the kitchen, but now each stream of butter looked to be the size of the Mississippi.

Deflated, I pouted a bit and then said, "So not good at all?"

My mom looked at me like I was crazy and said, "Delicious!"

I said, "Really?"

She smiled an angelic smile, and I was certain she was reveling in a flood of lovely memories of Paris, my dad, and the perfect meal. After a few moments, she said, "Delicious!" again, before the aphasia kicked back in. She really struggled with the next sentence, which took a while to come out. But come out it did:

"But . . . they're . . . not . . . Robuchon."

The truth is not always kind. But in the food world, as in the real world, it is always better to know than not to know.

YOTAM OTTOLENGHI'S QUAIL WITH RHUBARB SAUCE

My mother's career in food didn't just change my palate and my personal life. It had a huge effect on my career.

A few years after starting out in the publishing business, I became an editor at Random House (now part of the enormous Penguin Random House complex). One of the first books I bought in my role there was Wolfgang Puck's first cookbook. I didn't edit it because I didn't know nearly enough to critique and fix his recipes; once I acquired it, the book was taken over by legendary editor Jason Epstein, who was not just a better editor than I was, he was a better cook. As my career and skills with a pencil (and later e-editing on my computer) progressed, I started to get more comfortable delving into the minds and intents of various chefs and more comfortable trying to tell them how to make their books better. I have now edited and published such chefs and cooks as Nancy Silverton, Suzanne Goin, Kenny Shopsin, and Lidia Bastianich. None of this would have ever happened without my mother's immersion in the food world.

Eventually, I was doing more in the food world than just editing cookbooks; I began producing food shows under the banner of Random House Studio, a company I started in order to take full TV and film advantage of the corporation's extraordinary access to talent. Of all the shows and films I've been involved with, by far the most fun experience was producing the show *Heartland Table* for the Food Network. The show sprang from a cookbook by Amy Thielen called *The New Midwestern Table*. I didn't have anything to do with editing or publishing the book, but I did coproduce the show with Lidia and her daughter Tanya's production company. The premise was closely based on Amy's real life: she and her artist husband, Aaron Spangler, spent years living in Northern Minnesota in a cabin that Aaron built by hand (mostly with no power tools! So, he was not at all impressed with the fact that I learned how to cut a clove of garlic without slicing off my index finger at the knuckle). For several years, they lived there with no electricity or running water, something to which I never aspired, although I kind of admire their ability to do it, along with their sheer stubbornness not to give in to the modern world. At some point in their lives, they shifted to New York, where Amy worked

in various chef-like capacities for some of the city's top restaurants, and then they shifted back to Minnesota, where Amy gathered authentic midwestern recipes (as well as characters and stories)
and wrote a wonderful cookbook. Tanya, our coproducer Shelly,
an intrepid crew, and I spent several weeks filming twelve episodes
of *Heartland Table* in and around Amy and Aaron's cabin. While we
were there, the average temperature was minus twenty-six degrees.
One day it hit minus thirty-two. It was so cold that if your hair was
a tiny bit wet when you went outside, it turned white because the
water in the follicles froze. One day, one of the crew members took
a cup of hot coffee outside, threw it in the air, and the entire cup of
joe turned into a powdery white dust before it came close to hitting
the ground. On one insanely cold day, I whined to an eighty-year-
old Minnesotan that, with the windchill factor, it was minus forty-
two degrees. Her response to me was: "Windchill factor's for
pussies."

Despite having my manhood maligned by an octogenarian,
shooting *Heartland Table* in outer space–level frigid temperatures
was incredibly fun. And it made me even more determined to keep
doing food-related shows. That determination happily led me to
one of the smartest and loveliest food-related people I've ever met:
Yotam Ottolenghi.

Ottolenghi is one of the great stars of the contemporary food
world. His books are not just huge international bestsellers, they are
brilliant, creative recipes within the context of a philosophy of food
and cooking that has resonated with his readers in a way that few
chefs have ever been able to achieve. Yotam Ottolenghi is also as
charming as a person can be, wildly intelligent (he began life as a
journalist and is a remarkably astute observer of politics and human
nature), handsome, personable, and . . . wait for it . . . incredibly
nice. He also has a fascinating background: he is Israeli and his
business partner is Palestinian. He's too good to be true. Except he
is true.

Partnering this time with a company called Jupiter Entertainment, I went to London and had breakfast with Yotam at Nopi, his Soho restaurant. Well, to be honest, the night before I met the master chef for breakfast, I had dinner at Nopi. My logic was twofold: I thought I should have some firsthand knowledge about his food before our meeting. And I thought I might never have another opportunity to get a table at a restaurant that was so difficult to get into. It was an excellent call. The meal was spectacular, particularly the quail with rhubarb sauce.

Despite my mother's insistence, for her own secretive reasons, on cooking quail, I have never been a quail fanatic. I usually prefer things I can rip apart in a vaguely caveman-ish fashion rather than something with small bones that would work well while listening to a piano recital. But I had never tasted anything like Nopi's quail. It was satisfyingly meaty but also delicate and elegant. The rhubarb sauce was neither sweet nor sour, it was a sauce that somehow seemed as if it was destined to be drizzled on top of this fowl and had been there since birth. I couldn't imagine eating quail again without this red rhubarb sauce drizzled over and under it.

It was a unique experience: eating something I had eaten many times before yet having it taste as if I were eating it for the first time. It was a thrilling dinner that gave me the same charge I've had eating Wolfgang Puck's food at Chinois (where he reinvented Chinese food) and the original Spago (where he reinvented Italian food) or dining at Robuchon's restaurants in Paris or eating Alice Waters's food at Chez Panisse. To me, it was like going to the Museum of Modern Art and seeing van Gogh's works for the first time. Nobody has ever painted like that. No one *could* ever paint like that because his art came from someplace inimitable.

I was equally exhilarated during our breakfast the next morning, where I had the best French toast I ever tasted. The glow continued after the breakfast came because Yotam and I were 100 percent on the same page. We wanted to do something similar: a show that was smart and different, pushed a few limits, and aimed high.

The process has been slow—it's not a snap to sell something smart, clever, and fun—a combination of great food and social journalism—to a TV network. The Food Network, for instance, clearly adhering to the Donald Trump School of Creativity and Artistic Vision, said they wouldn't do a show with someone who had a foreign accent.

It will happen eventually, though. Yotam will continue to open wonderful restaurants and write books and will eventually have a hit TV series. But this process of trying to create something fresh and intelligent and, most important, different reinforced something I've been trying to deal with for a long time: inside the kitchen, things might be complicated, but there's a high percentage of success. Knowledge and preparedness actually pay off, providing an end result that is satisfying and pleasurable. It might take time and lots of repetition, but a certain degree of success is almost guaranteed.

Outside the kitchen, however, all bets are off. You can have the knowledge and skill as well as the tools and the right plan, but you're as likely to run full speed into a closed door as you are to succeed.

Outside the kitchen you must deal with the human factor.

Outside the kitchen, in other words, you must deal with real life.

Which is why cooking is usually way more satisfying.

As MUCH AS she loves quail and as often as she made it, by the time my mother and I began discussing this dish, she could not give me a favorite recipe. Nor could she remember or describe the best quail she'd ever tasted, so I had no starting point to figure out how to make the perfect quail for her. I did, however, have Yotam Otto-lenghi's e-mail address. I wrote him a note, describing my orgas-mic reaction to Nopi's quail with rhubarb sauce and asking for his recipe. Here's what he e-mailed back:

So . . . I went looking for the dish you had and found something which is highly confusing, written in kitchen shorthand and I doubt very much you'll be able to decipher it (I know I can't). Have a look, see what you think and try at your peril.

Warmest,

Yotam.

At the end of the e-mail was exactly this:

QUAIL WITH RHUBARB

Stuff 2 butterflied quails with 80 gr of stuffing. And sous vide for 25 minutes in 85 degrees, then pan fry until golden brown.

STUFFING

2.4 kg pork sausage (minced)

400 g shelled pistachio (roughly chopped)

50 g Baharat spice mix

100 g fresh ginger (grated)

2 g black peppercorn

30 g salt

Mix together.

GLAZE FOR RHUBARB

2 tbsp tamarind

100 g caster sugar

50 ml lemon juice

200 ml cold water

100 ml red wine vinegar

1 bay leaf

100 g pomegranate molasses

1 star anise

Reduce to a thick glaze.

QUAILS

16 quails

De-bone/butterflied cut.

RHUBARB

1 bunch rhubarb

Roast in oven 3–6 minutes with some icing sugar, slice and caramelise in a pan with the glaze.

YOGURT (TAKEN FROM THE NOPI COOKBOOK, SO SMALLER QUANTITY THAN THE REST)

320 g Greek yogurt

1½ tbsp. date syrup (30 g)

1½ tbsp. pomegranate molasses

Coarse sea salt

Place the yogurt, date syrup, and pomegranate molasses in a medium bowl with ⅛ teaspoon of salt. Whisk until smooth and then transfer to a sieve lined with muslin (or a clean j-cloth). Draw together the edge of the muslin and tie together so that you have a ball of yogurt. Keep the yogurt in the sieve held over a bowl to collect the liquid which drains out and store in the fridge overnight (or less, see introduction to Nopi cookbook). Remove from the fridge 1 hour before serving: the thickness should be that of ricotta.

LIQUORICE GEL (INSIDE THE SOIL)

150 gr liquorice (sweets) (NOTE FROM SNOBBY AUTHOR: YOTAM USES THE BRITISH SPELLING OF LICORICE, SO I'LL CONTINUE TO DO SO BECAUSE I LIKE IT BETTER.)

120 gr caster sugar

150 gr water

Slowly cook until dissolve and blitz to a gel.

LIQUORICE SOIL

250 g ground almonds

160 g liquorice gel

160 g sugar

110 g cocoa powder

25 g ground star anise

100 g butter

Mix all together, spread on silicon mat, and dry in an 80°C oven for about an hour.

Um . . . Okay, where to start?

Yotam was correct: his recipe is a tad confusing in parts. In other parts, I had no concept of what the hell he was even talking about. But I decided that wouldn't stop me. I also decided I was going to need some help with this one. So I asked Janis to co-cook with me. I had a slightly devious motivation in asking for her assistance: I also wanted her to serve as a co–guinea pig tasting this concoction before I dared to prepare it for my mother.

Janis and I, over the years, have proved to be very different types of cooks. She knows a lot about the science of food. I know absolutely nothing about the science of food. To be fair, I know nothing about the science of just about anything, so at least food isn't my worst category. She doesn't like to experiment; I love to experiment. When throwing a dinner party, I will happily throw myself into cooking something I've never tried to make before, a concept that absolutely horrifies her. My attitude is: *What's the worst that can happen? It's no good, we'll order in Chinese food. Friends will understand.* Her attitude is: *The worst will happen. The food will be terrible. We'll go hungry. Friends will never call again and we'll be humiliated.* What can I say? It's a different perspective on life.

Janis was essential to the making of this meal for several key reasons:

1. Grams vs. ounces? Kilograms vs. pounds? And what the hell is a milliliter? I needed someone who understood such things and wouldn't look at me as if I were a complete moron when I said things like, "Milliliter—doesn't three yards equal a milliliter?" It turns out Janis was not actually that person. But I dealt with it.

2. Don't ask me why but I have always been afraid to cook with rhubarb. I love rhubarb and order it every chance I get. My mom, when I was young, made stewed rhubarb and it was one of my favorite things in her repertoire. But it always mystified me. Do you skin it? Would you really die if you ate the leaves? (Apparently yes, but happily most places sell it sans leaves.) I needed someone with no rhubarb phobia who also wouldn't roll her eyes at the thought of *my* rhubarb phobia. Turns out Janis wasn't actually that person, either. But I dealt with it.

3. Most of all, I needed someone who would let me try to figure this out and trust my judgment but who would have my back just in case. Janis was totally that person.

First thing to figure out from the recipe: at the start of Yotam's jottings, he says that two quail are needed. Later on, the recipe calls for sixteen quail. Actually, the first part says that two "butterflied" quail are needed, but for some reason I read that as "butterfield" quail. Do you have any idea how humiliating it is to say to a butcher, "Do you have any Butterfield quail?" as if you were asking for "Perdue chickens" or a "Smithfield ham"? The answer: pretty humiliating. But I did make an executive decision and decided to make this with two quail and only two quail.

Of course, once I made the decision, I couldn't find any quail. So I substituted poussins. They worked splendidly—no normal person could tell the difference. And best of all, I got to make amends for my Butterfield query. When I asked the butcher if he had any quail he said, "No, I just have quail eggs." I told him, "Okay, then I'll come back in nine months." I got a good thirty-second roar out of him.

The rest of my shopping was much more straightforward. Or it was until I went looking for liquorice. The only liquorice I could find was the black and red candy type. I figured: How different could it be from whatever the "liquorice sweets" thing Yotam says should go into this concoction? I hesitated over the red kind; black seemed more Ottolenghi-appropriate and less Halloweenish, but when I asked one of the aproned helpers on the floor of the store, he said, "It all tastes the same. It's liquorice." So I bought red and black.

The next quandary was "Baharat spice mix." That's not something that's readily available in the good old USA unless you're shopping at a specialty spice store or online. But I didn't have time for that: I wanted to cook this damn thing ASAP. So I turned to Google. Sure enough, within seconds, I had a recipe for Baharat Middle Eastern seasoning on my phone screen:

1½ tablespoons dried mint

1 tablespoon dried oregano

1½ teaspoons ground cinnamon

1½ teaspoons ground coriander

1½ teaspoons ground cumin

1½ teaspoons ground nutmeg

1 tablespoon freshly ground black pepper

DIRECTIONS:

Using a pestle or the blunt end of a wooden spoon, mash all of the ingredients in a mortar or small bowl for 2 to 3 minutes. Can be made 1 week ahead. Cover and chill. Makes ¼ cup.

No problem. Done and done. Although this did bring up another issue, brought to the forefront by the "makes ¼ cup" at the end of the preparation paragraph. Was the ¼ cup of Baharat spice supposed to add tang to two quail or to sixteen quail? Hard to know, since I'd never made this before and basically didn't understand at least 50 percent of the measurements anyway. So I decided to just buy what my eyeballs told me should be right for two small birds.

By now, I was on a roll: when I couldn't find any date syrup, I opted to get a few dates instead and decided I'd just mash them up and see how that worked. When I couldn't find any star anise, I bought an extra few strings of black liquorice and decided that, if need be, I could use some Sambuca I had stashed in my liquor cabinet at home. And when I couldn't get hold of tamarind, I didn't panic since I wasn't 100 percent sure what tamarind actually was. I decided I could add another dollop of pomegranate molasses and that would cover it.

Voilà! Ready to cook up a storm.

Oh, wait. Not quite. First I needed to clear another roadblock: something called sous vide.

Until I read Yotam's recipe, I'd never heard of this cooking technique. But since it seemed fairly crucial—the recipe calls for the quail to be cooked "sous vide" for twenty-five minutes before pan frying—I immediately went out and bought a sous vide machine, determined to do Ottolenghi justice. I also did a little research and learned that sous vide is a kind of slow cooking. You have to put food into an airtight bag, drop the bag into the sous vide machine, which is filled with boiling water, and the hot water cooks any kind of food at all—vegetables, meat, fowl—evenly and perfectly. It seemed simple enough.

Janis rolled her eyes when I pulled out my sous vide cooker. For one thing, she thinks I have too many gadgets. For another, she heartily disapproves of the whole sous vide craze. "It basically poaches things," she explained. "It doesn't brown them. Yes, it cooks everything evenly but it leaves food slimy." For good measure, she added, "I think the whole sous vide thing is idiotic."

Nonetheless, I wanted to do this right. That quail at Nopi was truly spectacular and if sous vide was a contributor to that, I was all in.

The stuffing was easy. True, none of the measurements quite matched up with cooking two birds, but I decided I was a good enough cook to eyeball it. Once I had the sausage chopped, I could see what proportions of the other ingredients felt right. The recipe did leave out little details: Were the peppercorns ground or left whole, for example? I went with ground—but I adapted as I went along. And let's face it: it's hard to screw up stuffing when it involves sausage, ginger, and pistachios.

Next came the rhubarb with the glaze. I did the unthinkable this time and read the recipe carefully, every last step, before trying anything.

Still somewhat shaky about the mysteries of rhubarb, Janis showed me how to skin it, which neither of us really thought was necessary, but since I'd actually read the recipe, I was determined to follow it. The cooking part was straightforward, although I overcompensated for the lack of star anise with too much Sambuca. And not bothering to measure 100 milliliters of red wine vinegar, I took a guess at what that meant and put too much in. But, quick thinker that I am, I added more sugar to compensate for the extra vinegar.

The glaze took longer than I thought to cook down but cook down it did, as all things liquid with heat under it must.

Here's where things got particularly tricky.

The heading for the liquorice gel had this parenthetical state-ment next to it: "(inside the soil)." I had absolutely zero idea what that meant. I wasn't really sure what liquorice gel was supposed to look like, but I had a vague concept of gel in general, so decided I'd just stop dissolving the stuff when it looked something like toothpaste coming out of a tube. I tossed in the red and black liquorice—which made me feel less like a true gourmet chef than a guy at a cheesy candy stand at a circus.

While the gel was dissolving pre-"blitz"—and I had no idea what it meant to blitz something, so I decided I'd just turn the heat on really high and see what happened—I went to work on the liquorice soil. I was as lost as can be on this one. I not only had no notion of what this was supposed to look like, I couldn't figure out how it even related to the rest of the recipe. The gel goes inside the soil? Okay, but where the hell does the soil go? It's called soil, after all, so maybe it goes under the bird? That seemed plausible. But the rhubarb sauce is supposed to go under the bird, as well as driz-zled on top of it, so does that go on top of the soil and gel or beneath them? The only thing that kept me going was that Janis was as clue-less as I was. That didn't just give me courage, it meant that she couldn't make fun of me when I wound up with something that looked right and then also had a mound of soil and gel I didn't know what to do with.

By now, the gel was looking vaguely gel-like, so I pounded the almonds until they seemed ground, adding what I hoped was 160 grams of gel. (Google told me that 1 gram equaled 0.035 ounces. I got too impatient to even use a calculator so did a quick estimate and decided that it was close enough. It was at this point that I realized why the producers of the PBS show *The Mind of a Chef* had not called me as yet to appear on the show.)

I blew off the instructions to use a silicon mat—I didn't know what that was and had no intention of finding out—so I just put the mixed-together soil on a baking sheet and put it in the oven at

200 degrees F. The recipe said 80 degrees centigrade, which comes out to 176 degrees Fahrenheit—so 200 seemed close enough.

While I was roaming in gel and soil purgatory, Janis handled the yogurt sauce.

I checked on the soil after forty-five minutes and it seemed dry. Of course, it seemed pretty dry before I put it *in* the oven. I took it out, not sure if it was supposed to be hot or room temperature. Since I wasn't even sure what it was or where it was supposed to go, I figured that particular difference wasn't going to be crucial to the end result.

But now that it was as ready as I could get it, it was finally time to sous vide.

The sous vide had a thermometer in both Fahrenheit and centigrade, so it was reasonably easy to set it to 85 degrees centigrade. Actually, it wasn't quite that easy. It took me about ten tries to figure out how to work the buttons on the goddamn thing, and the cooking time doesn't begin until the water reaches the proper temperature, which took half an hour. But, sure enough, once the temperature hit 85 and I dropped the bags in, twenty-five minutes later those birds were cooked through and through. They also looked remarkably unappetizing. Slimy-looking, as my co-chef had said they would. But they went into a hot cast-iron pan right away and before long turned golden brown on all sides.

I slipped those birdies onto two plates. The glazed rhubarb went on top (I lifted the little guys up slightly to spoon some of the red-brown sauce underneath them, too). I still had no idea whatsoever what one was supposed to do with the liquorice soil, so I just scooped a few spoonfuls underneath the poussins and another few spoonfuls on one side of the plate. The yogurt sauce went on the other side of the small fowls.

Much to my surprise, the poussins looked remarkably good. I poured two glasses of a superb Burgundy, took a few sips to steady my nerves, then Janis and I dug in.

I don't have my mother's razor-sharp memory for taste, so I

don't know if I came close to re-creating the quail at Nopi. I suspect not. But my version was absolutely delicious.

I looked at Janis and I could tell from the expression on her face that she agreed. I said, "This is really good. I could make this for my mom."

She just nodded.

She was too busy eating to actually say anything.

PART FOUR

DINNER

There is only one difference between a long life and a good dinner: that, in the dinner, the sweets come last.

—Robert Louis Stevenson

My Mom's Dinner Menu

Before-Dinner Drink: Peter Kortner's and The Martini Brothers'
Perfect Martini

Wolfgang Puck's Salmon Coulibiac

The Tornabenes' Buccatini with Cauliflower, Pine Nuts, Currants,
Anchovies, and Saffron

Solferino's Steak with Truffle Cream Sauce

My Almost-Made-Up Fava Bean Puree

Nancy Silverton's and Abby Levine's French Boule and Challah

Romanée-Conti's Greatest Red Wine: La Tâche

Smoothest White Wine There Is: Bâtard-Montrachet

Burgundian Store-Bought Cheese: Époisses

Martha Stewart's Tarte Tatin

CHAPTER FIVE

When I was seven we started going out to L.A. for summers because summers are when TV sitcoms go forward in full throttle—writing and shooting—and my dad was in the TV sitcom business.

The first summer we stayed in the guesthouse of a mansion, an enormous ghost of a house, that belonged to a friend of my dad's. Jerry Wilson was really a friend of my grandfather Irving's but he had taken a liking to my dad and felt, for some reason, an obligation to house his entire family for three months. He had long white hair, his face was very creased and craggy—at least to the eyes of a seven-year-old—and he drank fairly constantly, muttered a lot in a cranky-sounding way, and was intimidating in a non-yelling, flashing-eye way.

Jerry Wilson and his three sons owned and ran a clothing store called, cleverly enough, Wilson's House of Suede, which was a Beverly Hills landmark right on the corner of Wilshire and Santa Monica (naturally, it is now a Starbucks). Jerry obviously liked my dad just fine, and tolerated having kids in his house, but he was absolutely crazy about my mother. My mom had that effect on gruff, tough, unhappy men. As I learned, it was because she neither judged them nor was afraid of them. Most of them were awful with and around women. But they could relax and be themselves around my mom. My mother, in those years, did not have any close women friends who were separate from relationships she and my dad established with other couples. That came later. When she was young, men loved her because she was not threatening. When she got older, women loved her because she was not threatening *and* she was so damn tough.

The second summer was the steak-and-eggs-Beverly-Hilton June through August. But for the two summers after that, my dad rented us a house. Being in our own home for those months allowed for a more normal lifestyle. My parents enjoyed entertaining and my mom, with Louise Trotty's help—she, too, now came out for the summers—began throwing dinner parties. This was the next phase of my mother's maturation process. She had begun as a shy Brooklyn girl, the youngest daughter in the family, whom no one took too seriously. The growth process began when she met my father and developed when they moved to Stuyvesant Town. The independent, non-Brooklyn Judy continued to develop in West Nyack as she dealt with problems and shouldered the burdens of everyday life in my dad's absence. In L.A.—not coincidentally, situated farther and farther away from her family—she gained confidence in leaps and bounds. She was thrown into a far more sophisticated crowd and held her own. And the identity of the new Judy Gethers was becoming more and more clearly defined.

One other thing helped define her—and me—during this period: in 1963, not long before we were flying out to L.A. to spend the summer there, my mother's brother Ted was killed in a plane crash. My father flew back immediately from the West Coast to be with my mother and to attend the funeral in Philadelphia; I was petrified when I made the connection that to be with us he had to get on a plane. At the funeral, my parents put Eric and me up in a motel, not far from Ted's family's house (Eric was old enough to stay on his

own and to watch over me). We stayed up all night and watched TV and had a weirdly good time, separated from the stifling family grief just a mile or so away.

A few weeks after the funeral I had to get on a plane to go to L.A. for the summer and that was something I absolutely refused to do. Getting on a plane meant that I was going to die.

My mom talked to me at length about why I needed to make the trip. I was adamant and refused to budge. And then I got the first of only three letters I ever received from my father. He had gone back to L.A. and he mailed me a one-page thoughtful, typed-out message. I don't have that letter today, sadly, but I remember it in great detail. He wrote that he understood my fear, that he had had many fears he had to deal with throughout his childhood and adulthood, that fears never quite go away, and that everything in life is a risk: crossing the street, riding in a car, going to school. Everything that brought pleasure also carried with it some kind of danger, whether physical or emotional. So he explained that I had two possible paths: Was I going to give up all the pleasurable things in life because I was afraid or was I going to conquer my fear and keep on living life the way it was meant to be lived? He said that, like everything else, it was my choice. I remember crying when I read that letter, and I remember my mom coming into my room to discuss it with me, which could not have been easy since it was her brother who had so recently been killed. I was being let into the inner world of both of my parents, seeing their fears when I had assumed that grown-ups *had* no fears, seeing their sadness when it had never occurred to me that sadness wasn't something that one outgrew. By the end of the conversation with my mom, having done my best to grasp the bigger meaning of my dad's note and implicit challenge, I knew I was going to L.A. A few days after that, I went to the airport with my mom and my brother. Eric didn't seem to have the same fear I had. I guess he was older and his wider range of experience gave him more perspective. Or maybe he was as afraid as I was but, unselfishly, had conspired with my

mom to keep it from me, so as not to exacerbate my own terror. Or maybe he was just old enough and male enough to want to keep his fears all to himself. I know that my mom never mentioned my fear during the time it took us to get on the plane, nor did she say anything at all to me when the plane was taking off or in flight. She watched me carefully to make sure I was all right. But my dad had given me a choice, I had made my decision, and my mother was smart enough to let me be so I could deal with that decision on my own.

I must say that although I was anything but calm when the plane was taxiing down the runway prior to takeoff, once we were in the air I relaxed. The decision to board the plane was far scarier than the trip itself. And I've never been afraid to fly since. I've not been afraid of most things that are out of my control.

In 1964, my family finally left New York behind and officially made the move to Los Angeles.

Over the next few years, all of our lives were reshaped and redefined, as was the family unit.

My dad became an even more successful TV guy, writing and producing and ultimately directing two-hour television movies, writing the occasional feature film, and even writing two more plays, both of which toured the summer stock theaters, never quite making it to Broadway. He wanted to be Arthur Miller, would have accepted being William Goldman when it became clear he wasn't writing *Death of a Salesman*, and wound up being Steven Gethers, which was pretty damn good but also frustrating. His compromises—some necessary, some of his own choosing—tortured him more than a little bit. Providing for his family was important to him; it was a priority. And his lifestyle was important to him. He loved entertaining people and he loved going to restaurants and getting his regular table and having the owners or maître d's or waiters welcome him with open arms. He also started drinking and learning about good wine, so food and drink, in a

pleasantly insidious way, became an even bigger part of our daily lives.

Because my dad loved to entertain, my mom became a better cook and better entertainer. They had people over for dinner on a regular basis, and I spent a lot of time with adults, my parents' friends, during my early teenage years, probably more time than I spent with kids my own age. I liked the grown-ups' stories better, I found them more interesting, and some of them took me to baseball and football games, which was pretty much like taking me to heaven.

The producer of *The Farmer's Daughter*, one of the TV shows my dad worked on, was a wonderful man named Peter Kortner. Kortner, as my dad and I called him, became a close friend of my parents as well as mine. In my preteen years until I was around fifteen, he was my sports buddy. I went to Dodgers games with him and my dad, but sometimes Kortner would take just me. We were both UCLA nuts so I got to accompany him to some great UCLA football games at the Coliseum. Even though he was in his forties and I was twelve, we became true pals. He talked to me as if I was an adult, which made me feel as if I *was* an adult. I also envied him because he always seemed to be on a date with one beautiful actress after another. He was often out and about with Inger Stevens, whom I lusted after in a major way, once I began to understand what lusting was.

My brother left for the University of Denver the year we moved to L.A., so for four years he was a bit separate and, except for summer vacations, didn't really participate in our Los Angeles life. He didn't become close friends with many of the grown-ups I got to know as a child. He didn't come to the dinner parties for which my mom cooked (not that I was too often actually at the dinner table; I was usually upstairs doing my homework and wearing my very attractive night brace, which was basically like having a ham radio set attached to your teeth and surrounding your head. But I would meander through the party and participate in conversations whenever it was appropriate and I felt welcome).

My mom, dad, and I were changing as a threesome while Eric began experiencing life on a separate plane. As a result, he and my father began a constant tug-of-war, a battle that dominated much of our family life. I was usually standing off to the side watching, but my mom was inevitably caught in the middle. I don't know on which side her true sympathies lay, but in those years she was not one to break with wifely tradition. She showed quiet support for her children and absolute love with no strings attached, but there was never any question that her relationship with her children was secondary to her relationship with her husband.

My mom told me many years later that she always felt guilty about her motherly role with Eric. Before he was born, she said that she and my dad made a pact: they would love their children but they would not let their kids come between their own relationship. She, to this day, feels as if a wall was put up that somehow kept Eric separate from their world of two. By the time I popped into the world, I guess they weren't as concerned about preserving their own love match. Or else I didn't care all that much about being in a secondary position.

Families are delicate things. Who's to say why or how we end up the way we do or become who we are? Parents make mistakes. A child's job is to overcome those mistakes. We can blame our parents—and our own past—for only so long before it becomes an excuse and a crutch. That's my position on family dynamics and I'm sticking to it. Sometimes you just have to assume responsibility for your own life and grow up.

My mother's dynamic with the siblings she left behind changed quite a bit during this period. Being in L.A. gave her some perspective on them and she began to see them for what they were, the good, the bad, and, in some cases, the ugly.

My mother's sister, Belle, the sibling who was closest to my mom, came to visit regularly and always stayed with us. When I was eleven or twelve, Belle was scary. She was a no-nonsense and zero-tolerance person when it came to behavior she disapproved of, and she was certain she was right when it came to just about everything. By the time I grew to adulthood, I came to realize what a remarkable person she really was—devastatingly funny, deeply kind, and rather sad. She was born at exactly the wrong time in the family chronology: because she was a Depression Baby, she was the one sister who didn't get to go to summer camp and who couldn't go to college because it wasn't affordable. When Belle was around eighty, she had dinner with me and a bunch of my friends (all of whom adored my aunt). We were telling college stories and someone asked Belle where she went to school. Without missing a beat, she said, "NYU." Later that night, after dinner, she came up to me and told me that she'd lied, that she not only hadn't gone to NYU, she hadn't gone to college at all. I asked her why she would bother to lie to my schmucky friends and she said, "Your friends are accomplished and smart and I've always been ashamed of the fact that I didn't have a good education." I told her that she was smarter than almost everyone I knew and that was what counted. But it didn't count with her. She asked me not to reveal her secret, which I haven't, until now. And I'm only doing so because I find it so telling and touching.

Belle was the one regular family visitor during that period in L.A. She came out two or three times a year and while she was there she taught me how to play poker, honeymoon bridge, and gin rummy (she also took my money on a regular basis; she didn't care that I wasn't even a teenager yet). She was a different person when she was in L.A. She shed the hassled Ratner's persona, stopped feeling like the family martyr, and just enjoyed herself.

When she was young, Belle was tough: tough on her husband, tough on her kids, tough on the world, but she is one of the few people I've ever met who got better as she got older. She softened a bit—or let herself reveal that softer side, which was probably always there under the protective layers of cynicism and sarcasm—and opened herself up more to the world around her. For my fortieth birthday, I went down to New Orleans with about twelve people to eat, drink, and be merry. That began a tradition that lasted for over a decade. It became known as the Spring Trip and it was the same group of pals, more or less, who went to some interesting spot every April. We did Annapolis and the eastern shore of Maryland; Washington, D.C.; the Napa Valley wine country; a farm in eastern Pennsylvania; Charlottesville, Virginia; Providence, Rhode Island; Charleston, South Carolina; Savannah, Georgia; Key West; and Havana. Belle and my mom were invited to that first weekend in New Orleans because it was specifically to celebrate my birthday, but they wound up coming to almost all the others. My friends all knew my mom. As I had befriended my parents' friends when I was young, my mom and dad were pals with my pals when I got older. But Belle was a revelation and the hit of the weekend: she refused to drink an actual Hurricane, the official get-shitfaced drink of NOLA, but she convinced several bartenders to make her scotch hurricanes—scotch was her drink of choice—and she proceeded to guzzle everyone under the table. She also made one of the greatest toasts ever. After three days of serious eating and imbibing—we went to Emeril Lagasse's first restaurant, not long after it had opened (I can still taste the salmon cheesecake—a savory, not a sweet); Brigtsen's (best chocolate pecan pie anywhere, ever!); the Acme Oyster House and its main rival, Felix's (nothing complicated here: raw oysters by the dozens and beer); Café du Monde for beignets and coffee with chicory; and lots of dives for po'boys and fried shrimp and oysters—we were at our final dinner of the weekend. A large white napkin was passed around, on which everyone was supposed to write a toast. Some were funny, some artistic, some sarcastic, some touching. All were good; Belle's was by far the best. She wrote: "Happy to be here. At my age, happy to be anywhere." The phrase immediately went into the group's lexicon. We even had buttons made with Belle's picture on them, to commemorate her wisdom on her eightieth birthday.

HAPPY TO BE HERE

HAPPY TO BE ANYWHERE
HAPPY 80th

PHOTO BY MICHAEL LUPPINO

Belle's eightieth birthday button

Belle had a soul, which none of my mother's other siblings did. She was protective of my mother, always thought of Judy as her baby sister, worried somehow that she was frail and delicate. But Belle was also the only one who was respectful of my mom. She understood that my mother had made a conscious break from the family, something I think Belle would have also liked to have done but never could, and she respected my mother's strength. She also admired my father's strength; she understood that he wanted my mom to attain her full potential, even if that meant he had to buck my mom's family and Belle herself.

Belle didn't have an ounce of bullshit in her. She didn't allow it in others and she didn't partake herself. Her honesty and sense of humor won over a lot of people. But so did her compassion and her unselfishness (she was not a saint, don't get me wrong; she was selfish in many ways, especially when it came to her son and daughter—she held on to them with a firm grasp—but she was selfless when it came to my mom).

In Los Angeles, in the mid-'90s, my mother got breast cancer. It was her third dangerous cancer (I skipped over the thyroid cancer: for my mom, that was just an ordinary procedure, which she got over quickly, seemingly with a wave of her hand). Belle went out to stay with her during the operation and recuperation period. I couldn't get to L.A. for those first few days—I was on a book tour but said I would come as soon as I could. Belle decided that Eric, who was living in Dallas, should come. She called him up, told him she thought he should be there for the operation, and, because he was having some financial difficulty, said that she would pay for his flights.

By the time I got to L.A. to see my mother, a week or so after the breast cancer operation, Eric had returned to Dallas. When I saw my mom she said that he had been an enormous help and she was thrilled that he'd come. I nodded at Belle, a silent "job well done" acknowledgment. My mom then said to us that she'd felt guilty that my brother had to spend money to come to L.A., so she'd given him a check to cover the expense of the flight there and back. I saw Belle turn red; I thought her head was about to burst into flames. I signaled her to keep quiet; then she and I quickly went downstairs. She immediately turned ballistic, enraged that my brother had "double dipped," as she put it. I told her to forget it, that yes, it was kind of horrible, but it was also sad and understandable, and there was no sense upsetting my mother.

"What's the point?" I asked.

"The point is it's the truth," she said.

My mother's journey to becoming the ultimate realist, someone with few illusions and able to confront life exactly as it is, was in its infancy. At this point, she still, to a degree, preferred denial to the truth. I didn't think she would fully absorb this news; it was a difficult thing to absorb. I argued with Belle. My side was: *we* knew what had happened and, going forward, Belle could deal with it accordingly if she wanted to but that nothing was to be gained by sharing this with my mom. Belle's side was: people should always know the truth. I realized that Belle's core belief, her brutal honesty, was why I'd been somewhat frightened of her as a child and why I'd become so close to her and adored her as an adult.

After half an hour or so, I thought she'd calmed down and that I'd convinced her to keep things between us. She went upstairs to check on my mother, came back down a few minutes later to join me at the small round table in my mom's kitchen, and said, "I told her."

I was annoyed, more than annoyed, angry, but also curious. "How did she react?"

"She defended him."

"That's what she does. And in a few weeks, she won't remember what you told her. She'll block it out."

"That's her choice," Belle said. "My choice was to tell her the truth."

From that point on, Belle and I grew even closer. She was great fun, with a sharp, biting sense of humor and an appealingly cynical view of the world, but there was also something that touched me about my mother's sister. Her honesty was directed not only to others but also inward. She was smart enough to have wanted something more from life than what she wound up with. But she understood that she'd made choices and had to live with them. And that choices had been made for her, leaving certain things beyond her control. I think this is one of the things that connected her and my father—they were both very aware of their own compromises and what they considered to be failures. Belle also appreciated the fact that my mother had made very different choices than she had. Belle thought of herself as the strong one, yet she realized that many of my mom's choices had come from an inner, invisible strength while some of Belle's had been made out of fear. There was no jealousy on Belle's part, none at all, only support.

She reveled in my mother's rise and my mother reveled in Belle's ability to share and enjoy her and my dad's new life. Everyone else in the family was suspicious of that new life. I think their suspicion came from the fact that my parents were happy. More than that, they were suspicious of happiness as a concept. Belle wasn't happy—not with the life she'd chosen or the way her life had turned out—but she enjoyed coming upon happiness in others, as well as sharing it when she dipped in and out of my parents' lives in L.A.

Belle understood food. In New York, she had a few restaurants she'd escape to where she was treated royally. Belle was a restaurant person; she knew what a difficult business it was and how hard everyone involved had to work. As a result, she tipped well, encouraged everyone, and didn't make unreasonable demands. In return, she expected everyone to do his or her job as well as possible. Good service was not a bonus; it had to be the norm.

When her brother Hy and his sons ran Ratner's into the ground, she never said a bad word about them. But deep down, she must have been devastated. Not only did they dismantle a legendary restaurant, they shattered a way of life that she cared for deeply.

Belle smoked constantly and loved to drink. When she'd make her twice- or thrice-a-year trip to L.A., every day around five or five thirty, she'd call up from the entryway to my dad, who was usually upstairs in his office, sitting at his snazzy electric typewriter working. Her raspy voice carried throughout the house: "It's cocktail hour." Within moments, Belle would have a glass of scotch in her hand. My dad's drink of choice varied. He was definitely bourbon and rye rather than scotch. But he also liked Manhattans and stingers and old-fashioneds. With dinner he was a serious wine guy, mostly reds. My mother rarely drank hard liquor in those days— two sips and her legs were as rubbery as Reed Richards's—so she usually stuck to white wine.

So, during this period in Los Angeles, my dad flourished professionally, my brother drifted in and out of the city, and my mother began to appreciate being three thousand miles away from her family and slowly was discovering her independent streak, with a tinge of guilt mixed in.

Me? I went through a fairly normal and exceedingly gawky early teenage period that turned into a reasonably gawky and dorky late teenage period. I developed what was to become a lifelong friendship with my aforementioned buddy Paul. My shnozz seemed to me to be the size of a 1955 Buick and unfortunately the only part of my body bigger than that was my Adam's apple, at least the only part that was getting any use. I discovered girls, most of whom rejected me. Got solid grades in school, although was already beginning to resist the idea of anyone forcing me to learn anything I didn't want to learn. Got my driver's license. Discovered drugs (Hallelujah!) and went off to college, to the University of California at Berkeley, where I found more girls who rejected me, friends who would last a lifetime, lots of interesting classes and professors, and way more drugs. After two fun-packed years at Berkeley, I spent a year at University College at the University of London (serious scholars, brilliant tutors, total absorption in learning, plenty of drugs, and non-American girls who thought I was exotic and thus attractive). Leaving for London was a big step in my growing-up process: it was a big geographical separation from my family, a completely new environment where I knew few people and had no real concept of the world I was entering.

As adventurous as I felt—or as least as I was pretending to feel—my mom, under the guise of wanting a vacation, accompanied me to London. I insisted I didn't need any help in adjusting or finding a place to live and then gratefully (if silently) allowed her to help me adjust and find a place to live. We went to good restaurants and, once I was settled, even spent a few days in the English countryside. In London, we went to Rules, where I had my first pheasant and my first Stilton soup and my first trifle, and to Simpson's-in-the-Strand, where I had roast beef and my first-ever Yorkshire pudding. In the countryside, we had game pie and, one

night, at a lovely country inn, I stayed up late into the night, shot
a few games of snookers with an Irish priest, and sipped quite a lot
of my first bottle of single malt scotch. My mom brought along
Belle's daughter Beth on this trip. Although she and Beth were very
close, I think this was my mother's way of showing me that she
wasn't really there to take care of me, she was there to have fun
with her niece—and if she happened to make sure I was well fed
and had a nice flat to stay in for the year, that was just the luck of
the draw.

One of the complications when growing into adulthood is that
you learn about nuance. You realize that people and life in general are often far more complicated than they seemed when you
were ten.

Several years before I left for school in London, my dad's close
friend—and mine—Peter Kortner, had moved there. I was thrilled
to be reunited with him (we'd been exchanging letters the whole
time from one side of the Atlantic to the other) but when I arrived,
he was very distant and hard to pin down. I didn't understand it
and was deeply hurt. He was one of my favorite people in the
whole world, an adult with whom I could communicate honestly
about anything and everything. I finally wrote to my parents and
told them that I'd been in London almost a month and my great
pal Kortner was refusing to see me.

Four days after mailing the letter, the phone rang in my flat. Both
of my parents were on the line. My dad said they had something
they needed to explain to me. I said, "Okay." And my dad said,
"Kortner's very worried about seeing you."

"Why?" I was bewildered.

"He's gay."

It took me a few moments to absorb this news. And the only
reason I needed the absorption time was because he seemed so
not gay.

"But what about all the women he was always with?"

"Do you know what a beard is?" my dad asked.

I didn't yet know all that many openly gay people when I was nineteen years old, but I knew what a beard was.

"But why?" I asked. "Why did he have to do that?"

"Because he thought it was better to pretend," my mom said.

"You both knew? I mean, the whole time?"

They both said that they had.

"But," I said, "what does this have to do with not seeing me?"

"I guess he's not sure how you'll respond," my dad said.

"I don't care what he is," I told them. "He's, like, my favorite person in the world."

"Then you should tell him that," my mom said.

So that's what I did. I called Kortner and insisted that he take me out for a high tea; I wouldn't let him off the hook. When we met at the Dorchester Hotel, he looked wildly uncomfortable, so before our cucumber sandwiches and clotted cream even arrived, I said, "Look, I spoke to my parents. They told me you're living with some guy here and that for some reason you think I give a shit. I just want to say that you really hurt my feelings and all I really care about is that you're the grown-up and I'm the college kid and you're supposed to take me out to dinner every couple of weeks so I actually don't starve to death. Plus, they show American football games every Sunday at a café near Hyde Park Corner and you're the only person I know within five thousand miles who likes football. So can we get past this and just be friends again?"

We could and we did. For the rest of the year, I saw Kortner once every week or two, although he only let me meet his partner once. He'd take me out to neighborhood restaurants and we'd meet to drink bad American beer and watch football at Café Royal near Piccadilly Circus, and every so often he'd take me someplace reasonably fancy. It was at one of those fancier meals that I had my first vodka martini. He ordered one, it seemed like an extremely sophisticated concoction, so I ordered one, too. Kortner explained to me about the various options: onions or olives or a twist, vodka or gin, dry or less dry. I liked it immediately; there was no learning curve—and it instantly became my drink of choice, especially because we once saw Sean Connery at a restaurant and that meant I was having a martini in the same place as James Bond. I ordered mine "shaken not stirred" that night and the waiter, properly, looked at me as if I were a lunatic.

In the mid-'80s, Kortner moved back to the United States and settled in Northern California. I went to see him there once—he was in a very stable relationship with a new guy, whom I was allowed to meet with no to-do—and we spoke every Sunday morning because we bet football over the phone, the same way I did with my dad.

In 1990, I went to Tampa, to the Super Bowl—the Giants won their second one, over the Bills on the famed "wide right" kick by Scott Norwood—and called Kortner at halftime from a pay phone in the stadium. I did my best to torture him over the fact that I was seeing the game live and told him I'd bought him a Super Bowl XXV hat, which I would send to him when I got back to New York. He sounded weak, and I knew he'd been feeling ill for quite some time. I asked him if he was okay and he said he'd tell me all about it when we spoke in a few days, when there wasn't all the Super Bowl hoopla in the background. I said, "Fair enough," hung up, and went back to my seat to watch the thrilling game.

The day I got back to New York, my mom called me to say that Peter Kortner, whom she also loved dearly, had died the night before. He was the first person I ever knew who died of AIDS.

PRE-DINNER DRINK: VODKA MARTINI

When my mother finally acquired a taste for hard liquor—it didn't really happen until she was in her seventies—Absolut Citron over ice became her drink of choice. In her eighties she started drinking non-flavored vodka and even the occasional martini. She knew how much I liked an ice-cold vodka martini, and I considered it a personal victory when we went to dinner at a restaurant near her apartment one night and she admitted that a martini is a superior cocktail.

It needs saying right up front that technically a vodka martini is not a real martini. A martini uses gin as its main ingredient. Now that I've dispensed with that formality, I can also say that my attitude is: Screw it. I don't like gin and I like vodka. So to me, a vodka martini is a real martini.

The recipe to make a perfect vodka martini is not very complicated:

1 martini glass (any glass will actually do, since the glass does not affect the taste one iota, although it does make the drink more enjoyable and feel more sophisticated.)

Vodka (as much as you're comfortable pouring into your glass; I maintain it's better to have 2 or 3 small to medium-size martinis rather than one giant bomb of a martini. If in doubt, just think WWJBD—What Would James Bond Do? Also, I like Ketel One but the truth is, that's pure pretentiousness since I can't really tell the difference between different types of vodka.)

Ice (or no ice—but the colder the drink is, the better, of that there is no doubt; so best to keep your vodka in the freezer if, like me, you prefer it straight up.)

Dry vermouth (just a drop or two—the tinier the drop, the drier the martini.)

Dab of olive juice (optional) (This is what makes it a "dirty martini." I prefer mine slightly dirty.)

That's all there is to it. Except . . . not really.

To those who drink them, a martini is not just a drink, it is a way of life. Much about drinking good alcohol becomes a way of life, celebrated and ritualized, and that's as it should be.

In the 1980s, my dad was a member of a wine group called

WOW—World of Wine. It was a bunch of Hollywood guys with white shoes and white belts—writers, directors, producers, and agents—who had two things in common: they loved sitting around telling stories and they particularly loved doing that if they were drinking sensational wine. The group used to meet once a week in a famous L.A. restaurant, Le Dome, on Sunset Boulevard. I was allowed to go a WOW lunch once when I was visiting L.A. The lunch itself was fun but the highlight was seeing something these middle-aged, mostly Hebraic scions of the TV and movie business had managed to pull off. Le Dome had a wine cellar beneath the main dining room. And the WOW guys had their own private wine cellar within the restaurant's cellar. It was behind a small iron gate and each member had a key. If they went to Le Dome for lunch or dinner on their own, away from the WOW group, they were allowed to take any bottle out of the private stash as long as they quickly replaced it with an equivalent bottle. I have to say, I thought then and think now that that is about as cool as it gets.

I drink plenty of the stuff, although I never joined a wine group. I am, however, a member of a group of fellows who call ourselves the Martini Brothers.

The Martini Brothers' hallowed history began in the suburbs of New York in the mid-1990s. Three friends, Lee, Zig, and Paul (yes, the same best friend from childhood Paul) wound up living within twenty miles of each other outside the city. Periodically, since all there is to do in the suburbs (at least in my biased view) is exercise, wash your car, grill outdoors, coach Little League, wife swap, and drink, they would get together, eschewing the first five choices, and drink martinis in someone's living room or den. At some point, I was invited to drive out and join them.

Twenty years later, there are now thirteen Martini Brothers and our three- or four-times-a-year meetings are glorious celebrations of life, friendship, and male idiocy. We go out to excellent restaurants, we see movies that few women (or responsible male adults) would ever agree to see with us, and we have as many refills as we can of our favorite cocktail. We have, in the process of glorifying the martini, ritualized every element of our get-togethers, down to our individual club names. We have strict initiation rituals, printed business cards with the official Martini Brothers logo and slogan (*You buy us martinis, we buy you martinis*). We have a Martini Brothers Summer Extravaganza every year, as well as a Martini Brothers Winter Holiday Extravaganza, at which we award the extraordinarily prestigious award, the Golden Olive, which goes to the Martini Brother of the Year. We even have a secret handshake (I'd describe it but then I'd have to kill you).

What we also have is a lot of warmth and a caring connection among all the members. We insult everyone, always good-naturedly (although, seriously, Brother Pinky Martini is an idiot), and I'm going to get a lot of shit for writing this, but we do actually love each other because we all understand each other; we share

PHOTO BY MICHAEL LUPPINO

The Martini Brothers logo. Our motto: "You buy us martinis, we buy you martinis."

something that we can't fully share with anyone else (and, let's face it, hardly anyone else wants to share it with us).

To open every sacred Martini Brothers event, after Brother Father Paddy Martini's benediction, we begin by raising our glasses while one of us asks the question "Who lives better than we do?" The answer is a heartfelt chorus: "Nobody!"

That answer is not to be taken lightly. Nobody does live better than a bunch of friends eating well and drinking martinis and enjoying each other's company.

At some point during every Martini Brothers evening, I think of Peter Kortner, sipping a martini in a cozy London restaurant, and I think of my dad, my mom, and my aunt Belle at cocktail hour in my parents' L.A. home. And I conjure up the toast that Belle wrote down for my fortieth birthday in New Orleans: "Happy to be here. Happy to be anywhere."

Another worthwhile slogan to eat, drink, and live by.

CHAPTER SIX

During the last week of December 1975, at the age of fifty-three, my mom took her very first job.

Like almost everything in life, it started as one thing and turned into something else, completely changing her life as well as the lives of her immediate family, her siblings, and her friends.

Happily, even though I was now living three thousand miles away, I managed to be there at the very beginning.

You know how in sitcoms, the screen goes wavy and suddenly your favorite character is wearing a bad wig and unfashionable clothes and is twenty years younger? Picture this page getting wavy. I'm taking you for a bit of a ride via a family flashback.

AFTER MY YEAR in London, I returned to Los Angeles to spend my senior year of college at UCLA. My passion for learning was still great but my passion for the piece of paper saying that I was learned was fading rapidly. So with one day and my last set of finals to go, I dropped out.

My parents were remarkably understanding about my decision
not to graduate and they weren't at all surprised when I announced
I was moving back to New York. But they were more than a little
bewildered when I chose to move to a rat-infested (well, one rat, but
that was more than enough) basement apartment in Manhattan's
West Village. I loved that apartment. It was on Perry Street just off
Seventh Avenue, around the corner from the Village Vanguard jazz
club, my fantasy hangout, and it had a brick wall and an incredibly cool tin ceiling. There were a few things it didn't happen to
have, like a complete floor (I solved that problem by putting a
sheet of plywood over the dirt hole that led to the subway below),
a shower, a bathtub, a stove, or a refrigerator. I never managed to
get the bathtub but I did figure out how to add the other three
luxury items at a reasonable price. It was a railroad flat—fitting,
considering it often felt as if I were living in a moving subway
car—with a fairly large front room that functioned as a bedroom
and living room, a small square room in which I fit a low dining
table (low because I couldn't also fit chairs, so it was Japanese sit-
on-the-floor style minus the elegance or, in fact, any semblance of
style), and another square room that ultimately housed the stove,
fridge, and shower. There was a closet-size room after that with a
toilet. That room didn't have a door but I solved the problem by
putting up what I was certain was a very attractive burlap cur-
tain. Separating the other two rooms were strands of multicol-
ored beads that I thought were totally cool. The view from my
bedroom/living room looked up onto the building's garbage cans,
which were stacked in front of the only two windows in the whole
apartment, and the first time it snowed after I'd moved in, I came
home at night, flopped down on my bed (my *water*bed!) to find
some very cold, very wet sheets. It had snowed through the rick-
ety window into my apartment.

My parents came east soon after I was ensconced. Before seeing my new living situation for the first time, my mom lectured

my father, telling him that no matter what they thought, they had to be supportive and enthusiastic (they'd been prepared for the situation by their friend Edward, who occasionally took me out to dinner so I wouldn't have to subsist solely on my Saturday visits to Ratner's, and told my folks that he was afraid to sit down in my living room). My mom repeated her lecture to my dad several times, the last time during their entire cab ride downtown from the Upper East Side, where they were staying. When they finally arrived, descending beneath the garbage and through the dingy underground hallway, I opened the front door and before she could even get a peek at my digs, my mother, desperate to be positive, yelped in delight, "Oh, it's fabulous!" I had to say, "Um . . . don't you want to actually come in and *see* it first?" They then stepped inside. My mother stayed silent. So did my father—for about half a second. Then he said, in as supportive and enthusiastic a voice as he could manage, "Oh my god. What a shithole!"

ONE YEAR LATER, I'd finished writing my first novel, which I was certain would turn me into the next F. Scott Fitzgerald. That didn't quite materialize, although it was published by a real publisher and earned me enough money to order a steak once or twice when I went out to dinner—okay, just once, but it was a very satisfying cut of meat. I had also managed to fall in love. Cindy lived in L.A. but had come to New York on October 1, 1975. The reason I remember the exact date is that it was the start of the Red Sox/ Reds World Series, the one with the Carlton Fisk home run, which caused me to become a baseball fanatic again after five or six hippie-ish years ignoring the game. She arrived with a girlfriend and they wound up staying with me after a long-distance introduction from a mutual friend. I don't remember the girlfriend's name and paid little attention to her but I fell hard for Cindy.

By the time she left to return home to L.A., I was a goner. There

The Rat Apartment, 2016, now a men's spa. But still a shithole, with the same lovely view from the windows . . .

were stars in my eyes, and the combination of infatuation, lust, and distance was causing a somewhat painful and continual ache in the pit of my stomach. So I did what any red-blooded twenty-two-year-old boy would do: I immediately called my parents and lied to them.

I told them I was missing them and would love to visit them for Christmas and wouldn't they like to pay for me to come home for a week or so. It turned out, they would. My dad said he'd send me a check and I could buy my long-before-e-ticket plane fare.

I then waited a week or two before deciding it was appropriate to raise a new topic. I phoned the folks and chatted for a bit. Then I let it drop that I kind of had this new girlfriend and she was kind of in L.A. and I was really kind of looking forward to their meeting her and, uh, oh yeah, she was kind of going to be staying at their house with me for the week I was there.

Whatever the opposite of a shrinking violet is, that was my dad, particularly by this point in his life. My cousin Jon once compared

PHOTO BY MICHAEL LUPPINO

. . . and the same revolting stairway my parents descended many years ago.

him to Hugh Griffith in the movie *Tom Jones*. The gist of his
instant retort was: "Over my dead body . . ." "Keep dreaming . . ."
"Nice try . . ." and . . . "Not a chance."

Although his acting career had ended when I was three or four
years old, he still had an actor's theatricality. His favorite role was
that of "father"—he liked being a dad and playing a dad and he
took the role very seriously. He was a valuable sounding board for
me, personally, professionally, and morally. However, I didn't take
too kindly to his instant door-slamming reaction to my staying-at-
their-house-with-girlfriend bombshell. I didn't laugh at it, the way
I did with a lot of his moral bombast, and I couldn't ignore it. At
twenty-two, it's almost impossible to laugh at or ignore anything
that stands in the way of sex and romance.

What I did instead was start whining that I was really coming
out to see Cindy—inadvertently torpedoing my whole "I'm dying
to see you" strategy that got me the plane ticket in the first place.
My dad countered with, "Then stay at her place."

I had to admit that I couldn't because . . . um . . . she lived with
her mother.

He took that as a triumphant end to the conversation and hung
up. My mom lingered long enough for me to whine another minute
or two and for her to say, somewhat sympathetically, "You know
your father."

I did indeed. But despite that knowledge, somewhere around
three in the morning, after a night of boilermakers and more than
a few tokes, I sprawled on my perpetually damp and chilly water-
bed sheets and wrote the most pretentious, arrogant, annoying
letter in the history of father/son relationships.

I pointed out, in long-winded and very specific detail, his
hypocrisy—his recently divorced friend Edward was, as I scribbled,
staying in my parents' house with his new, much younger girlfriend!—as well as his nineteenth-century values and fake morality,
and, in a particularly nice vein of attack, how out of touch he was
with real life because he was so old.

I was so pumped up, I finished the letter in twenty minutes or so, stuck it in an envelope, went out into the predawn, late-autumn Village streets, and, with a satisfied and smug smile, shoved the letter into a stumpy corner mailbox.

As the paper left my fingertips, the smug satisfaction instantly turned into genuine panic. Reality set in with the subtle impact of a shiv in my shoulder blades. An angry father equaled no airfare. No airfare equaled no Cindy for Christmas. No Cindy for Christmas, in my suddenly addled brain, equaled a lonely, female-free, sexless future for the rest of my downtrodden, miserable life. *What had I been thinking?* I grabbed wildly for the letter but could only feel the air as the envelope floated downward and nestled into the heap of other less self-destructive letters left by other less desperate sons.

Gathering myself as best I could, I ran back to my rat hole and called my brother in L.A. (we were still on good and close terms). Waking him up, I said, "Okay, don't ask questions. I need you to go to Mom and Dad's tomorrow, camp out by their mailbox at the end of the driveway, and wait there until you see a letter from me."

"What?"

"When you see the letter, take it out, don't read it, burn it. Totally destroy it. Immediately."

"Who is this?"

"Seriously, you have to make sure Dad doesn't see it."

"I'm going back to sleep now."

"Really. Eric, I'm serious. Name your price!"

"Bye-bye now."

"Oh, come on . . ."

"Byyyyyyye."

This was the kind of situation my brother loved and it was hard to blame him. I was the one who, for a change, had done the totally moronic thing. I was the one about to face the wrath of God or, in this instance, our father, which was way worse because I actually believed in the wrath of our father.

Starting that morning, I called my parents every day from work. The first three days, all was fine. The usual chitchat. On day four, my dad answered and when I said, "Hey," there was a pause of about one one-hundredth of a second before he said, "I'll put your mother on the phone." His voice was so icy, I was surprised the telephone wires didn't freeze from coast to coast.

Moments later, my mom picked up. "So," I said, as nonchalantly as I could manage, "did Dad get my letter?"

"He did."

"So . . . um . . . what did he think?"

"He's already mailed you his response."

"Do you want to give me a hint?"

"You'll get it when you read what he sent."

"Can I talk to him?"

"He doesn't want to talk."

"Are you still paying for me to come out there?"

"You'll have to read his note."

"Mom, seriously, can't you just—"

But she couldn't just do anything. I sensed that my dear, dear mother, who always took my side and always offered total support, was enjoying this. I'd made a major blunder and I could visualize the same smile on her face that she used to have when I was a teenager and it was raining and she'd tell me to take an umbrella but I'd refuse, telling her I hated umbrellas. She wouldn't argue, she let me go out and get drenched. The smile would come the next day when I would wake up with a cold and she'd tell me that perhaps I'd learned my lesson—but since it was my own stupidity that led to my sneezing and runny nose, I had to get up out of my warm, comfy bed and go to school. Now!

It took three more days for my dad's letter to arrive. My hands were trembling just a tad and my stomach was churning as I tore open the envelope. Inside, to my relief, was the check so I could buy my plane ticket. Along with the check was this note, which I have saved and framed and still have hanging on a wall of my apartment:

It's putting it mildly to say I felt like the biggest shmuck in the world.

I called home. My mom picked up and heard me say a down-trodden "hello" and then ask to speak to my dad.

"I'm an idiot," I said when he got on.

"Yup," he agreed. He didn't gloat; he simply savored my resignation.

"That was an excellent response."

"I'm a writer. I have a way with words."

I didn't really have anything else to say. I'd lost, outboxed by a master.

"Do you want a real answer?" he asked. And when I mumbled a clever assent along the lines of, "Okay," he said, "It's my house. I'm too old to be uncomfortable in my house. It's not a question of morality or judging what you're doing. I'll feel uncomfortable if my son is sleeping here with some young woman I've never met. You can stay somewhere else and you're welcome to come here for breakfast, lunch, and dinner or any other time except sleeping. Or what you'll most likely be doing instead of sleeping."

I managed to get out the words: "That seems fair."

"Good. I'm looking forward to seeing you and meeting her. And, by the way, a lot of work went into tracing my hand. I hope you appreciate the effort."

A couple of weeks later, I was in L.A., staying at my best friend Paul's house, about a mile from my parents' home. Paul's mother had died when we were seniors in college and he and his dad had been playing Felix and Oscar, living together since then. But the dad had recently met a woman and had just gotten remarried, moving into the new wife's place, so Paul had the run of his parents' house until it was sold. Cindy and I got to use one of Paul's now-married sisters' bedrooms while Paul and his brand-new girlfriend, Laurie, stayed in his old bedroom, the one in which he and I used to race slot cars when we were ten years old.

Cindy and I got the parent test out of the way quickly and Cindy passed with flying colors (despite a fairly severe attack of nerves when I made the mistake of telling her the story about my dad and the letter). One night we had a lovely, trauma-free dinner with them at the forbidden house and, over dessert, my mom said that she wanted to take Cindy and me out to lunch the next day.

That turned out to be my mom's LC Day—Life-Changing Day.

My dad, being a serious restaurant guy, loved going out to hot new places and this place, my mom said, was their new favorite.

They'd been going two or three times a week. My dad liked it because it was becoming a big show business hangout. My mom loved it, she said, because the food was incredible. When she spoke about eating there, I noticed that something new and interesting flashed across her face. I wasn't sure exactly what it was, although I was able to put a name to it later: passion.

The restaurant, she told me, was called Ma Maison. And there was a new baby chef who she thought was brilliant. His name, she said, was Wolfgang Puck.

So the next day, my mom picked Cindy and me up—the proximity of Paul's house to mine was convenient when we were childhood buds and just as convenient now, since my parents had forbidden any carnal acts in my old room (when I actually lived there as a teenager, they never had to—the size of my Adam's apple and Jewfro pretty much took care of that all by themselves).

The restaurant was at the corner of Melrose and La Cienega in West Hollywood. On the surface, it wasn't anything special. There was an outdoor patio with cheesy-looking plastic chairs and an ugly plastic tarp that could be pulled over the roof to protect patrons from too much L.A. sun or the dreaded and greatly feared L.A. rain. Inside there were several rooms, all of which were so casually decorated, the restaurant had the feel of being in someone's long-lived-in house (thus the name, *Ma Maison*, I suppose). There was an upstairs room with a fireplace and a downstairs room that featured a beautiful bar. The atmosphere as well as the service felt informal and friendly and remarkably new. The crowd as well as the staff were young; a good time was being had by all. I suspect that everyone—from the owner, Patrick Terrail, to the young chef, Wolfgang, to the various sous-chefs, to the goofy, charming waiters—was stunned that they were at the epicenter of the hippest, most successful, most talked about restaurant on the West Coast of the United States.

We sat out on the patio—that was *the* place to sit, despite all the plastic—surrounded by Orson Welles (I'm trying very hard not

The beautiful Ma Maison menu

to say that he would have surrounded us if he'd been there all by
himself), Ed McMahon (who conceivably and depressingly was
more famous than Orson Welles in 1975; I later learned from the
inside guys at Ma Maison that Johnny Carson's sidekick used to
have private parties at the restaurant and get them to pour cheap
wine into empty expensive wine bottles so his guests would be
impressed but he didn't have to fork over the money for the actual
good stuff), Sammy Davis Jr., and a bunch of people who, judging
by the white belts and sweaters expertly and offhandedly strung
around their necks, I assumed ran TV networks, movie studios,
talent agencies, and record companies.

Forty years later I remember exactly what I ate: fish soup was
my starter, followed by warm lobster salad. Those were the two
most glamorous things on the menu, in my mind. Fish soup was

something I thought was only available in France, the country I most fantasized about living in. The first taste of that soup was so potent and fragrant and thick and fine, it instantly transported me to the Left Bank of Paris and a tiny divey restaurant where I'd first spooned the stuff into my mouth when I'd gone there at the age of seventeen.

Ordering the lobster was a less complicated choice; that simply was, to me, the fanciest, most expensive food on the planet Earth. Mixing a warm, expensive thing in a cool mélange of lettuce and onions and tomatoes and vinaigrette seemed unimaginably creative to me, as well as deeply satisfying. I don't remember being transported by that dish but I do recall with great precision the chewy texture and the trace of vinaigrette lingering on the lobster meat as it slid down my throat. I'm reasonably certain that my mother had Wolf's legendary Poulet à la Moutarde, which was deglazed with port, had a bit of cream, and was finished off with mustard, and I absolutely do recall that I begged Cindy to get the Croque-Monsieur, because that was also so French and exotic (how a grilled cheese sandwich can be made to seem exotic I didn't and to this day don't understand, but it was and still is). She obliged and was knocked out by it. Going purely French all the way, I ended with the Crepes Surprise, which I'm pretty sure had chocolate and some form of chestnut puree. Two espressos were the sublime finishing touch. I could have had a double but the dainty, tiny cups also seemed the more sophisticated way to go in my unsophisticated vision of coffee drinking, so I downed one, then another, rather than just taking the same thing in a larger, less interesting vessel.

The food was mind-blowing, but what happened during the crepe eating and the espresso sipping was the game changer.

Patrick Terrail, the owner—with slicked-back, Pat Riley–ish hair pre–Pat Riley, a fleshy but handsome face, and a manner that emanated a strange combination of welcoming, eager-to-please host and distancing, I-don't-have-to-please-anyone-because-my-joint-is-so-successful arrogance—came over to join us because my mom was such a regular customer. He pulled up a chair, sat, and began chatting. After a few minutes, my mother touched his arm and said, "I'd like to become a good French cook. What do you think I should do?"

I believe my mother had something short-term and fairly dilettantish in mind, as in going to France for a few weeks and taking some cooking lessons. Instead, without missing a beat, Patrick said, "Come to work in our kitchen three times a week. We won't pay you and you'll basically be our slave, but after a year you'll be a real French cook."

I remember thinking, *Yeah, right, that'll really happen,* but I didn't have a chance to say anything because my mom responded instantly.

"Okay," she said. And that was all she said. Just: "Okay."

I still remember her inflection on that one word. Her voice trailed upward, as if surprised that the word had come out of her mouth. The lilt in her voice carried a definite sense of jubilation.

I smiled and said something eloquent along the lines of, "Wow, this is very cool." I didn't want to get too excited. I figured her jubilation wouldn't last much past the moment when she told my dad she was going to work.

I could not have been more wrong.

My father's response was instant and unwavering: he thought it was a wonderful idea.

My dad, as I've said, was a fantastic guy and I loved him dearly. But he was used to being catered to. Everyone was surprised how quickly he acquiesced to this new situation. My sense is that if he had said no, my mother would have stayed home. I'm not positive about that—and she's not sure, even to this day, if that's true—but I suspect I'm right. He didn't just say yes, however; he was wildly enthusiastic. And as my mother's love for her new world and her satisfaction in her success in that world grew in leaps and bounds, he was even more wildly proud. And boastful. At some point, two or three years later, the food world in L.A., at Wolfgang's instigation, began calling him "Mr. Judy Gethers." His face lit up every time those words were uttered. Before too long, we'd show up for dinner at a restaurant, my dad would go up to the host and say, "Mr. Judy Gethers for four," and we'd be led to our seats. Eventually, Wolf and his then-girlfriend, later wife, still later ex-wife, Barbara Lazaroff, gave my dad a birthday present: a chef's apron on which was printed, in large block letters, MR. JUDY GETHERS.

I recently told my mom how everyone was surprised that he was so instantly supportive. "I know," she said. I asked if she'd been surprised. "Oh yes!" was her answer. "I was shocked."

We shouldn't have been so startled. My dad was wise enough to see what no one else could see about my mother at that time, including my mother: she was restless. She was ready to evolve. It was time, at the age of fifty-three, for her to become a different person. My dad loved the person she'd been for her first fifty-three years. He was secure enough, comfortable enough in his own skin, and confident enough in my mother that he knew he would also love whoever she became for the rest of their time together. And that the new Judy would love him right back.

My mother went to work at Ma Maison as soon as the New Year began. She cooked two nights—late nights—and one full day per week. It quickly became an all-consuming passion and her life soon revolved around crème caramels and salmon mousse and various foods en croute, and she had a new family, comprised of chefs (well, mostly Wolf, with whom she quickly developed a mother/son–like bond), sous-chefs, waiters, busboys, and just about anyone who spent time in the back of the restaurant.

There was, unquestionably, a new kind of exhilaration to my mother's life. She had, in a sense, been set free. Every day was a new learning experience, either technically in the kitchen or in the way she was now dealing with her new family of restaurant workers. She was suddenly the go-to person when wisdom needed dispensing. She could discuss the ups and downs of marriage from the role of observer as well as participant. My father had always been the storyteller and teacher in our family, but now, with relative strangers, my mom assumed that role. And the lessons she conveyed were not always the same as her beloved husband's. She would recount a tale from their past and realize that she had her own completely separate interpretation and perspective.

She liked coming home (or calling me in New York or going out to lunch with a new friend) and discussing her own experiences instead of having to listen and comment upon the experiences of others. For the first time in her life, she became the center of attention and she was surprised as well as delighted when she realized that she was worthy of that attention. At the same time, she remained remarkably without ego and never minded *not* being the center of attention. She could empathize with almost anyone's hurt or confusion but she also developed enough confidence in her point of view that she was now able to say to people, "You're wrong." Those two words coming from my mother were never said harshly, nor were they meant to stop someone in his or her tracks. They were spoken with kindness, and my mother's intention was always to help someone evaluate the path being taken before that path became irreversible.

In the kitchen, she was learning from experts (in the case of Wolf, an actual genius) and it thrilled her. As an extra bonus, I think my mother's new career probably gave my dad the courage—or at least the impetus—to move to a new level in his own work world. He started directing—two-hour TV movies and miniseries—and went back to his first love: playwriting.

Many years of being the calm center of many family storms stood my mom in good stead in the midst of the insanity and turmoil in one of the hottest kitchens in the country. There were divorces, feuds, and rampant jealousy (both personal and professional). There was even a murder (Dominick Dunne's daughter, Dominique, was strangled by one of the sous-chefs in the Ma Maison kitchen!).

My mother wound up with a whole cadre of new friends and,

in particular, gay friends, because she was completely nonjudgmental (a few years hence, after Wolf opened the original Spago, the manager, Johnny, a wonderful guy and as gay as it is possible to be, said to my mom, "I want you to think of me as the daughter you never had"). People talked to her because they knew she was responding to them and their issues, not projecting from her own past or her own prejudices. In fact, she had no prejudices. If a person could relate to food, my mother could relate to him or her.

Above all, my mom learned to cook.

Really cook.

A couple of years after my mother had taken her plunge into Patrick and Wolf's world, I went to L.A. on a business trip. My mom was in her kitchen fooling around with a small blowtorch.

"What the hell?" I said. "Are you welding now?"

She explained that using this particular tool was the only way one could get the crust exactly right on a crème brûlée.

Of course it was.

I got one as a gift the next Christmas, one of the very few people of the Hebraic persuasion to ever get a fire-breathing tool as a present from his mom.

She talked about food constantly. And her palate, which had always been good, stepped up to a whole other level. My family would have what we thought was a superb dinner at a restaurant and we'd all be raving about it, then we'd look at my mother and because of the slight frown of disapproval on her face one of us would ask, "You didn't like it?" My mom would more often than not say, "It was okay." And then we'd get a dissection of what was actually wrong: too much salt, too dry, too wet, overcooked, undercooked, the sauce was too runny, the crust was too doughy, the olive oil in which it was cooked was obviously not fresh enough, something that should have been fresh was frozen. My mom didn't have an ounce of pretension to her; this was not a question of putting on airs. She simply knew more than we did and she no longer felt the need to keep that knowledge to herself.

For many years before he died, I got to edit books written by the brilliant Robert Hughes. Known as a fierce art and cultural critic, he wrote a book about the one thing he loved uncritically: fishing. In his opening to the book, Hughes wrote about how fishing put him on the road to becoming an art critic. When one put a rod in the water, he explained, one was penetrating a calm, still exterior. It was necessary, however, to try to visualize the turmoil, the movement, all the things that were roiling underneath the stillness. One had to try to understand exactly what was beneath that which could only be seen. Exactly what an art critic must do, he explained.

Exactly what my mother was now capable of doing with food. She could bite into something and taste every ingredient. She could deconstruct almost any dish—after tasting it, she could re-create it from scratch.

Everyone in our family responded in different ways to my mother's remarkable transformation.

My father embraced it joyously. He had spent years building her confidence, quietly urging her to be more independent, and now she was flowering. He particularly enjoyed the fact that my mother now swore. Not often, not inappropriately, and not with the vulgarity of the proverbial longshoreman, but when she did curse, her point was made. Until I was in my mid-twenties, my mom never swore. She seemed incapable of doing so. If she hit her finger with a hammer while hanging a picture—my mom was the only one in the family who would ever dare take up a hammer and nail and try to actually do something with it—she would stutter out a "Shoot." She just could not bring herself to use bad language.

The change came after she began working at Ma Maison. Suddenly, if she broke a nail or screwed up some puffed pastry, she'd let loose with a "Shit!" Or she'd be talking about someone who did something nasty to my dad or to Wolf and she'd quietly go, "Fuck him." Then she'd smile proudly. Her cursing was both shocking and wonderful, and the frequency of it seemed to rise along with her fortitude. My mom had always been quietly steely, but now her unbending will expressed itself much more vociferously. She stood up to my dad more. She stood up to *everyone* more. My dad started telling everyone: "Oh . . . she used to be Sweet Judy. Now she's an animal." He began calling her "the Animal." And they both loved it.

As my mother got older, I think she came to see her cursing as a sign of her inner strength. Even at age ninety-three, she'll mutter "Shit" if something goes wrong and I'll say to her, "I still can't believe you're such an animal." She'll look at me, nod, and—her aphasia on temporary hold—say, "Fuckin' A" or "You bet your ass." She always laughs, but there is a sense of pride behind the laughter. It's her way of letting the world know she is no one to be trifled with.

I was on the other side of the continent during the years when these major changes were developing in my mom. But I followed her development closely. Even though I didn't see my parents all that often—I'd go to L.A. two or three times a year; they'd come to New York about the same—my mom and I grew closer. By this point, she fully accepted me as an adult but I was also able to accept and deal with her as one. She wasn't just my mother anymore. She was a person with a real life and real accomplishments. Sometimes she came to New York on her own and we'd have dinner. We could talk about all sorts of things that we never really discussed before: her family; the mistakes she felt she'd made with my brother and me; her relationship with my dad; her regrets; even, to a degree . . . gulp . . . her sex life. She told me that my father was the only man she had ever been with and that, at times, she wished she'd had more experience. I managed to survive that particular conversation without passing out.

I was fascinated by my mother's gradual alteration. Just as I loved my dad, saw his flaws, drew from his strengths, and enjoyed both the limits and the boundaries of our relationship, I was able to enjoy new and surprising dimensions in my relationship with my mom. She was now my equal in some ways, my superior in others, my friend in many ways, and my mother in all the ways that counted.

Each of her siblings dealt with the new Judy in his or her own fashion. Her brother Hy was condescending, acting as if he ran a real restaurant while Wolf and the rest of my mom's chef crowd were involved in something ethereal and a little bit fake. Lil took my mother more seriously but still treated her as a little sister. I'm not sure Natalie ever quite figured out what the hell was going on. Belle, not surprisingly, relished my mom's ascension. She began coming to L.A. more often and loved hanging with the chefs and the staff. Wolf and Barbara were crazy about Belle: whenever she walked into Spago, day or night, there was always a bottle of scotch waiting for her.

Both my brother and I, as adults, connected to my mom, in some ways, through food. Not only did I begin to edit cookbooks and produce food-related TV shows, I began to cook and, much to my surprise, I enjoyed all aspects of it—the preparation, the creativity, the giving of pleasure.

Eric began cooking, too, and he was a far better cook than I was right from the start. He had a real flair for it. He made delicacies that were much more difficult to prepare than anything I attempted. He was able to be more precise and was far more disciplined (he's also a terrific musician and very good with languages, and I think there must be a connection, since I'm a total washout in both of those areas). To me, however, my brother's culinary attempts seemed to lack some kind of core. I cooked solely for the fun of it. I sensed Eric's adventures in the kitchen were a way to try to reconnect to the family, from whom he'd slowly been moving away.

I don't think food is a tool that can be manipulated to bring people together. I think food is usually an extension of the person preparing it. People connect to other people. Food is the pleasurable bridge upon which both sides cross.

My mother's food has always been exactly like my mother: appealing, comforting, genuine, unpretentious, at times whimsical, always elegant. And always with a certain unknowable complexity.

WOLFGANG PUCK'S SALMON COULIBIAC

This was the very first dish that Wolf ever taught my mother to make, the first thing she learned to cook at Ma Maison. Of everything on her list of dishes that are important to her, this is perhaps the most important.

My mom loves Wolfgang Puck. I don't mean she likes him a lot, I mean she loves him.

Their relationship was special right from the start. Like a lot of European chefs, Wolf had left home as a teenager to start work in a professional kitchen. He trained throughout Europe in restaurants in his native Austria and France and, in 1975, became the chef at Ma Maison when he was twenty-five. The restaurant had been open for two years by then without causing much of a splash. Wolf got rid of the dishes that used canned sardines and packaged vegetables and began buying his food fresh every morning at San Diego's Chino Farm, which was a two-hour drive from L.A. Patrick Terrail was a great host and he wooed the stars and big shots from the movie and television industry. As a result of Patrick's odd but seductive charm, the A-list crowd, and, above all, Wolf's brilliant and innovative food, Ma Maison quickly went from being a kitschy outdoor café to become L.A.'s first great, world-class restaurant. In many ways, Wolf is the inventor of what has come to be known as California Cuisine and, along with Alice Waters, brought that cuisine to the world. Ma Maison became so insanely popular that, at some point, Patrick actually unlisted its phone number. Think about it: a restaurant so popular that unless you were a regular, you couldn't even call to book a table!

My mom and Wolf connected just as Wolf's star began to shine. Because he'd left home at such a young age, my mom quickly fell into the role of his surrogate mother. He talked to her about women, about his complicated relationship with Patrick, about his career. Simultaneously, he recognized her love for this new world and her desire to soak up everything she could about that world. She helped keep him grounded. He helped lift her off that ground.

My dad was also crazy about Wolf, and that affection was mutual. Wolf gives my father credit for helping to shape his sense of humor—and to Americanize it. My dad was often gruff with his jokes and he was a master of deadpan delivery. At Ma Maison, when Wolf was just beginning his rise, a waiter would ask how the food was and my dad would say, "Terrible." Wolf would hear about it in the kitchen and come out to see who had insulted his soup or his veal or the delicate sauce on his fish. His first response was to get angry, but then my dad would indicate his plate, which had been licked clean, and point out that he'd eaten there three times that week, and Wolf would realize that he needed to both toughen up and lighten up. He lightened up considerably and became a great practical joker. My parents became so fond of the young chef that they began going on vacation with Wolf and Barbara and another couple, the legendary dessert chef Maida Heatter and her husband, Ralph Daniels. They became a tight sixsome.

A year after my mother started working in the restaurant kitchen, Patrick erected a new building on the restaurant's parking lot and opened Ma Cuisine, Ma Maison's cooking school. My mother became its first manager and main teacher. She was now cooking and teaching alongside Julia Child and Paula Wolfert and her new friend Maida, the stars of that era's food universe, as well as with the new generation of great California chefs: Jonathan Waxman, Nancy Silverton, Mark Peel, and so many others. My mom became good friends with all of them and a surrogate mother to many of them.

Part of the new job description: giving cooking lessons to celebrities and L.A. power brokers and the wives or girlfriends of L.A. celebrities and power brokers. It was crazy. I went out to L.A. on business periodically and would always try to time my visits to the school to coincide with the end of my mom's cooking lessons because after each lesson everyone would sit around and eat the food they'd just learned how to make. I popped in there once to find my mom wrapping up a session showing Sammy Davis Jr. how to roll pastry dough.

My mom wasn't one of those people who left her work behind at the office. Cooking was not just her job now, it was her all-consuming passion. The dinner parties she threw became more and more elaborate and quickly became legendary. And that is not an exaggeration. Olivia Goldsmith, the bestselling author of *The First Wives Club*, wrote a novel in the '90s, *Flavor of the Month*, in which one of her fictional characters is "lucky" enough to be invited to the home of the Hollywood couple known to throw the best dinner parties in town: Steve and Judy Gethers. In the novel, Goldsmith provides a vivid description of my parents' home and the elaborate food my mom served. An iconic mention in a trashy popular novel: it doesn't get much more legendary than that.

Ma Maison was a phenomenon—culturally and from a cuisine standpoint—and stayed that way until 1982, when Patrick and Wolf went through a nasty professional divorce. In the wake of the unpleasantness, Wolf decided to open up his own restaurant, Spago. A lot of people at the time thought he was crazy. Even my mom was concerned about the gamble. Leaving Ma Maison to open what the Wolf was describing as a "pizza place"? The move turned out not to be so insane. It was an instant and enormous success. I think that the original Spago, with its offbeat waiters and gorgeous view and its reinvention of Italian food with such unheard-of dishes as smoked salmon pizza, was perhaps the greatest restaurant experience ever, anywhere in the world. The food was spectacular and it was just so damn much fun. There was a playfulness to that restaurant that is almost impossible to describe and is absolutely impossible to re-create.

And Spago was hardly a fluke. Three decades later, Wolf has probably become the most successful chef and restaurateur in the history of the planet Earth. I won't attempt to count the number of restaurants he now has around the world because by the time I try to list them, several more will have opened. He led the way for big-name chefs to open in Vegas and Singapore and other cities that are now food meccas. He opened Spago cafés in airports around the world. He's on the Home Shopping Network with an extensive line of cooking utensils. And he's got frozen foods. Unlike my uncle Hy's foray into the frozen blintz business, Wolf's frozen pizza is actually good. I was recently in Tokyo and, wandering the streets one afternoon, walked right by a large sign with a photo of Wolf on it, hanging outside his Tokyo restaurant. I took a photo with my phone and e-mailed it instantly to my mom.

The A-list followed Wolf to his original Spago, deserting Ma Maison almost immediately. And my mom, too, moved on from Patrick's cooking school. She pushed Wolf to write his first cook-book and helped him with it. She tested recipes for Nancy Silverton and Mark Peel's first cookbook. And then, years after writing the Ratner's cookbook with her niece, she began writing her own. *The Fabulous Gourmet Food Processor Cookbook* came out soon after Cuisinarts and similar contraptions became the rage. She followed that with what I think is her best work, *Italian Country Cooking*. For research, she drove around Italy with a friend, Joan Hoian, for three weeks, talked her way into family kitchens, used Wolf's references to observe in restaurant kitchens, and just stumbled into whatever interesting food she could find. My dad, against his wishes, was made to stay home: my mom wasn't allowed to stand by his side while he was directing; he couldn't be demanding her attention while she was learning to make a perfect minestrone soup or bread salad. It was clearly a good call on her part. The book is superb. I've yet to find a better pesto recipe anywhere else.

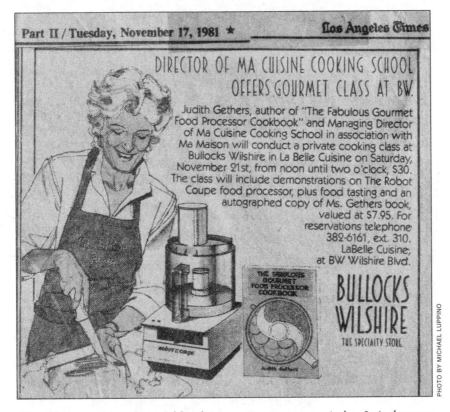

An ad for a cooking class and book promotion—my mom in her L.A. doyenne period

After that she published *The Sandwich Book*, which was simple and lovely. And then came two books she wrote with Mary Bergin, the second pastry chef at Spago: *Spago Desserts* and *Spago Chocolate*. The chocolate book was picked by *Food and Wine* magazine as the best cookbook of the year.

In time, my mother became the doyenne of the L.A. food world. The waiters she was nice to became maître d's at other restaurants and then managers and even owners. The young chefs she mentored went on to open restaurants all over the world and to write cookbooks and to spread some of the wisdom they had learned from my mother, in and out of the kitchen. Her active involvement in the food world lasted into the early part of the twenty-first century, when she was in her eighties; up until the time she had her stroke in 2007, she was still teaching and writing, sometimes formally, sometimes informally.

For those thirty years, my mom enjoyed a great rarity: an extraordinary second act to her life. But despite all the successes and all the wonderful accomplishments, I don't think she ever experienced the same exhilaration, the same sense of pure, unfettered enjoyment that she had that first year at Ma Maison and those first few years at Ma Cuisine.

Wolfgang Puck's Salmon Coulibiac Recipe

———————

In Wolf's book *Modern French Cooking for the American Kitchen*, the recipe calls for pike instead of salmon and crayfish instead of shrimp. But my mom, at her dinner parties, made it with salmon and shrimp, and that's what you're going to get here. Wolf does specify that shrimp make a fine crayfish substitute, and he makes it clear that salmon works just as well as pike, so I figure I'm on safe ground.

Yield: 6 to 8 servings

INGREDIENTS:

1 recipe brioche dough (**NOTE FROM AUTHOR: DON'T PANIC, I'M GIVING YOU THAT RECIPE, TOO; IT FOLLOWS SOON ENOUGH.**)

2 pounds boneless salmon fillets

1 teaspoon salt

½ teaspoon freshly ground black pepper

¼ teaspoon cayenne pepper

2 eggs

1½ cups heavy cream

1½ cups white wine

2 shallots, minced

1 tablespoon minced fresh tarragon

6 tarragon stems

1 recipe court bouillon (AUTHOR'S NOTE: NO NEED TO PANIC AGAIN, I'M
    GOT YOU COVERED HERE, TOO.)

24 rock shrimp (ME AGAIN: THE RECIPE CALLS FOR 24 LIVE CRAYFISH.
    GOOD LUCK FINDING THAT IF YOU DON'T LIVE IN NEW ORLEANS OR
    ELSEWHERE ON THE GULF COAST. ROCK SHRIMP—THE TINY ONES THEY
    USE FOR POPCORN SHRIMP—WORK JUST FINE. THEY'RE ABOUT THE
    SAME SIZE AS CRAYFISH SO I FIGURED I'D USE THE SAME NUMBER. I WAS
    CORRECT.)

8 to 12 stalks asparagus, cooked until al dente

1 bunch basil leaves (FINAL AUTHOR'S NOTE FOR THIS PART OF THE RECIPE:
    FOR SOME WEIRD REASON, WHEN I WAS SHOPPING FOR ALL OF THIS
    STUFF I COULDN'T FIND BASIL ANYWHERE. I HESITATED, MEDITATED ON
    WHAT TO DO, AND TOOK THE PLUNGE, GRABBING A HANDFUL OF MINT
    INSTEAD. A FEW MINUTES AFTER MY CAREFULLY CONSIDERED CHOICE I
    PANICKED AND CALLED JANIS. I ASKED HER WHAT SHE WOULD DO IF SHE
    HAD TO SUBSTITUTE SOMETHING FOR BASIL, BUT I DIDN'T GIVE HER ANY
    OF THE CHOICES I HAD. SHE PONDERED FOR A MOMENT THEN SAID,
    "MINT?" I LOVE VALIDATION.)

½ pound (2 sticks) unsalted butter, cut into small pieces

Lemon juice

DIRECTIONS:

1. Prepare the brioche dough a day in advance (through step 5).

2. Slice 1 pound of salmon into small pieces. In the bowl of a food processor,
   puree the salmon with the salt, pepper, cayenne, and 1 egg. Transfer the
   mixture to a chilled bowl.

3. Whip 1¼ cups cream to a soft Chantilly. Over ice, fold the cream into the salmon mixture. Test the mousse for taste and consistency in simmering water (to do this, poach a spoonful of the mousse in simmering water for 4 or 5 minutes. Remove the mousse from the water and taste) and correct the seasoning as necessary. Refrigerate until needed. (AUTHOR'S NOTE: NO WAY DID I BOTHER TO TEST THIS.)

4. Marinate the remaining 1 pound salmon fillets in a mixture of ½ cup wine, 1 shallot, and the tarragon.

5. Bring the court bouillon to a boil. Add the crayfish and return to a boil. Remove the crayfish and, when cool, shell twelve of them and reserve the other twelve whole. (NOTE: JUST REMINDING YOU THAT I DIDN'T USE CRAYFISH, I USED SHRIMP, AND EVEN THOUGH THEY WEREN'T ALIVE, I STILL BOILED THEM EXACTLY AS INSTRUCTED ABOVE. IT ALL WORKED FINE.)

6. Preheat oven to 400 degrees F. (NOTE FROM AUTHOR TO COMPUTER KEYBOARD DESIGNERS: WHY THE HELL DON'T YOU HAVE ONE OF THOSE LITTLE CIRCLE SYMBOLS THAT SYMBOLIZE "DEGREES" ON YOUR KEYBOARDS? I HATE HAVING TO WRITE OUT THE WORD "DEGREE" EVERY TIME. COME ON! SHAPE UP!)

7. Divide the brioche dough in half and roll out one piece ⅜-inch thick on a baking sheet. Spread half of the fish mousse down the center. Arrange half of the salmon fillets over the mousse, top with the asparagus, and spread the remaining mousse over the asparagus. Finally, arrange the remaining fillets over the mousse.

8. Lightly beat the remaining egg for an egg wash and brush all around the edges of the dough. Roll out the remaining piece of brioche, large enough to cover the fish. Press the edges together and trim. Brush with egg wash. Decorate with strips of dough and poke a vent in the top. Bake for 40 minutes.

9. While the fish is baking, reduce 1 cup wine, the remaining shallot, the tarragon stems, and ¼ cup cream until one-third of the liquid remains or until the bubbles are thick.

10. Using the food processor, puree the basil leaves. Add the butter and process until well blended.

11. Slowly add the basil butter to the reduced wine. Strain and correct the seasonings, adding a bit of lemon juice if desired. Add the shelled crayfish (**SHRIMP!**) to the sauce, just before serving.

PRESENTATION: Using an electric knife (or a very sharp chef's knife), slice the coulibiac into six or eight slices. Nap each plate with the sauce and arrange the whole crayfish (**SHRIMP**) decoratively on the plate. Center a slice of coulibiac in the plate.

BRIOCHE RECIPE

INGREDIENTS:

To make 2 large brioches or 16 to 18 individual ones

1 pound 2 ounces all-purpose flour

2 tablespoons sugar

1 tablespoon salt

2 tablespoons dry yeast

½ cup milk

6 eggs

10 ounces unsalted butter, at room temperature

1 egg, lightly beaten, saved aside for egg wash

DIRECTIONS:

If brioche dough is allowed to rise in too warm a spot, the yeast will be killed and an odor will develop. This recipe should give you perfect results; smaller proportions will not be as successful.

1. In the bowl of an electric mixer, using the paddle, combine the flour, sugar, salt, and yeast. Add enough of the milk to make a stiff dough that pulls away from the side of the bowl.

2. Add the 6 eggs, one at a time, beating thoroughly after each addition. Continue to beat until the dough is elastic.

3. If your machine has a dough hook, substitute it for the paddle and add the softened butter, a small amount at a time, until it is well incorporated and the dough pulls away from the sides of the bowl.

4. Transfer the dough to another bowl, cover with a damp cloth, and allow to rise at room temperature for approximately 1 hour, until double its original size.

5. Punch down the dough, cover again with the damp cloth, and allow to rise overnight in the refrigerator. Be sure to cover the bowl with a plate weighted with a brick (or other heavy object) to prevent the dough from over-rising and over-fermenting.

6. Form the dough into two large brioches and place them in lightly buttered 6-cup molds. Allow to rise until double in size.

7. Preheat oven to 350 degrees F. (AGAIN: WOULDN'T IT BE NICE TO HAVE ONE OF THOSE LITTLE CIRCLE SYMBOLS?)

8. When the brioches have risen and are ready to bake, brush with the egg wash and bake for 20 minutes. Reduce the heat to 350 degrees F (NEED I SAY IT?) and continue to bake for 30 minutes more, or until a skewer inserted in the center comes out clean. The baking time will be shorter for smaller brioches. (AUTHOR'S NOTE: I DIDN'T REALLY HAVE TO INCLUDE STEPS 6 THROUGH 8 BECAUSE FOR THE SALMON COULIBIAC, WE ONLY NEEDED TO FOCUS ON STEPS 1 THROUGH 5. BUT I PUT IN THE WHOLE RECIPE FOR TWO REASONS: 1) I JUST LIKE BEING THOROUGH, AND 2) THERE'S AN ACTUAL MISTAKE! I TYPED THE RECIPE EXACTLY AS IT IS IN WOLF'S *MODERN FRENCH COOKING* BOOK AND, IN CASE YOU MISSED IT, IT SAYS "PREHEAT THE OVEN TO 350 DEGREES" AND THEN, IN THE VERY NEXT STEP, IT SAYS TO TURN THE OVEN DOWN TO 350. I AM NOT SAYING ALL THIS TO ADMONISH WOLF. I AM POINTING THIS OUT TO SHOW THAT ANYONE CAN MAKE A MISTAKE. AS YOU WILL SEE IF YOU KEEP READING.)

COURT BOUILLON RECIPE

2 medium carrots

2 stalks celery

1 leek, thoroughly washed

1 sprig fresh thyme or pinch dried thyme

1 bay leaf

1 teaspoon salt

½ teaspoon freshly ground black pepper

2 quarts water

2 cups dry white wine

DIRECTIONS:

1. Slice the carrots, celery, and leek into ¼-inch pieces. Put them in a saucepan.

2. Add the remaining ingredients and bring to a boil. Continue boiling for 20 minutes, until the liquid is flavorful.

Okay . . . the first thing I did when I finished studying this recipe was to get borderline hysterical. I almost dozed off twice while reading, at some point had to get up and walk around my apartment, and after finally wending my way to the end, all I wanted to do was have a shot of bourbon and smoke a cigarette, even though I've never smoked an entire cigarette in my life. You should be getting the point by now: I was unnerved. A brioche? A mousse? Sauce? Several machines? What was I thinking? At the very beginning of this process, I thought that by learning how to do all this and eventually putting together the perfect dinner for my mother, I'd come to some understanding of her and her entire philosophy of life. What I was thinking after going through this recipe is that I was way out of my league and had no shot of pulling this off. Matzo brei was one thing. This coulibiac extravaganza was another.

Eventually, without benefit of either alcohol or tobacco, I calmed down and read through the directions carefully. If I took it step-by-step, this was doable. It might not be good, but making it was doable. The only thing that worried me was the brioche. Bread scared me. I'd tried baking it several times before and hadn't done well. But I knew someone who *wasn't* afraid of bread. A close friend. Close enough that I decided I could test the limits of that friendship. I called my pal Abby Levine.

The conversation went better than I thought it would. I played upon his parental sympathies ("Abby, I'm doing this for my mom. It will mean so much to her") and our years of being buds and fellow Martini Brothers ("Come on, it'll be fun. We'll hang out, we'll cook, we'll talk politics, sports, and women. C'monnnnnn"). And I closed the deal with bribery ("I'll make superb cocktails, I'll buy you lunch, and I'll have doughnuts waiting"). He said yes.

I e-mailed him the recipe and we discussed it over the phone. We concluded that this was a two-day job: one day to go through steps 1 through 5, one day for all the rest. We set a date, several weeks in advance, and I decided to ramp up the stakes: I invited a few people over for dinner that second night, including Abby's wife, Micheline, with whom I've been close friends since before she married Abby, who is a finicky eater and loves to give me a hard time. The pressure was on.

The first cooking day was a Friday. Abby came over at about one p.m. As promised, I had doughnuts stacked on a plate—coconut cream, vanilla icing, and a cinnamon—and take-out Middle Eastern food from a great place called Mamoun's, down the block from my apartment. As the pièce de résistance, I also had a cocktail shaker full of boulevardiers, the bourbon version of a Negroni: equal parts bourbon (whereas a Negroni is gin), Campari, and sweet vermouth. I did it up right, crushed ice and everything. Before we started in on the coulibiac, we put ourselves in the mood. We started with the doughnuts, of course. Then had a boulevardier each, then went for the hummus, pita bread, falafel, spinach pie, baba ghanoush, and grilled lamb kebabs. We debated having a second boulevardier, decided it couldn't hurt, so we poured, sipped, then decided we were ready to tackle the brioche. It was now two p.m.

I'd bought all the ingredients earlier that morning except for the yeast, which Abby, as a regular baker of bread, had plenty of. The first step involved mixing flour, sugar, salt, yeast, and some milk. This was a no-brainer, especially because I was an old hand with my electric mixer. My KitchenAid is my favorite food-related possession. I am comfortable using it, and I even am reasonably sure which of the various attachments is a paddle.

So we set up the mixer, poured in the ingredients, and . . . watched in horror at the disaster spinning right before our eyes. We saw no evidence of a stiff dough pulling away from the side of the bowl. Abby was particularly critical of the mixture and exhibited signs of panic. I insisted we pour in more milk. Abby thought that was a loser move. I did it anyway. Still nothing.

Stymied, I suggested another boulevardier and we agreed that maybe we should only have half a glass each this time. We did, keeping an eye on the whirling KitchenAid. By the time we were on our second sip, the dough was kind of stiff and sort of pulling away from the sides of the bowl. Despite our amazement that we'd somehow screwed up the easiest stage of the entire recipe, we moved on. Eggs were added. We beat until elastic (the mixture, not us). We then spent a few minutes trying to decide which of the remaining attachments was a dough hook. We finally picked one that seemed right and replaced the paddle. We added the butter as instructed and, once again, waited for the dough to pull away from the sides of the bowl. At some point, Abby said, "The dough's not even *on* the sides of the bowl. How can it pull away?" I decided that meant it was ready. So we transferred the dough to another bowl, covered it with a damp cloth, and waited an hour for it to double in size. That hour was quite productive: we polished off the remaining doughnuts, finished our third boulevardiers, and solved most of the world's problems. When we checked, despite all that extra milk, the dough had, in fact, risen to double its original size.

Abby allowed me to punch the dough—and really, that's what you do, you punch the dough as if it's a speed bag at a gym—and then prepared to put it in the fridge. I ventured an opinion that I didn't really need to weigh the dough down with a brick equivalent, but Abby explained to me that I was an idiot and that if I didn't, the mixture might take over my entire refrigerator. Yielding to his greater experience—and having seen *The Blob* when I was a mere lad—I found a heavy trivet, put that on a plate, put them both on top of the mixture in the bowl, and stashed the thing in the fridge. Abby and I congratulated ourselves on a job well done, although he still insisted it would fail because of all the extra milk. We finished the last dough-nut and decided we'd meet again at noon the next day.

In anticipation of the work we had to do on Day Two, I had looked up the word "coulibiac" to see what it actually was. I'd always assumed it was French through and through, since Wolf taught my mom how to make it in the kitchen of a French restaurant and the only other place I'd ever had it was at Lutèce, for many years New York's best old-fashioned French restaurant. It turns out those pesky Frogs had appropriated the dish from the Russians. Although the French had probably added the fancy sauce as an accompani-ment, unexpectedly I was, once again, delving into my roots.

Lunch was ready when Abby arrived—Chinese takeout. He was appreciative but said he'd been thinking about it and decided I was still an idiot for adding so much milk to the brioche dough.

"Oh yeah?" I said, and stepping over to the fridge, I took the trivet-and-plate-covered bowl out with a flourish and revealed a perfect brioche dough.

Pressing my luck, I staggered Abby just a tad when I revealed that I had also decided to make another of my mother's favorite dishes for dinner that night. We were going to have the coulibiac as an appetizer and, for a main course, I was making tournedos of beef with a black truffle cream sauce. He covered his surprise with a shrug and an almost imperceptible eye roll and, after boulevardier number one of the day, we were ready to start making the inside of the coulibiac.

The guests were coming at 7:30. We started cooking around two. We were finished and ready for company at 7:29. This thing is definitely work-intensive.

The surprise was that none of the work on Day Two was all that difficult. Everything required precision and exactness and those equate to time-consuming. I will say that this also proved to me the value of a real chef having a "line." There is no way in hell I could have done this by myself. There were too many choices, too many steps happening simultaneously; it was all just too much. Even for the two of us, it was a little overwhelming. Every hour on the hour we would look at each other and decide we would probably be dining around midnight.

One reason I needed Abby is that he's mechanical. He can actually fix things that have wires attached to them and put things together by looking at nonsensical line drawings on so-called instruction sheets. The coulibiac recipe called for the use of a Cuisinart and, although I had one, I'd never used it. I had no idea how to attach the blades or feed food into it. If left on my own, I'd be food processor–less (and this from someone whose mother wrote a food processor cookbook!). I'm not sure how I'd managed to avoid the confounded machine for so long, but I had. Abby heard my confession and forgave me for my sins. He handled the Cuisinart like a pro, set it up easily, and allowed me to feed the salmon into the whirling blade. The experience was surprisingly satisfying in a *Fargo*-like way.

I worked on the mousse and the fillets while Abby whipped up the court bouillon.

All the separate elements looked good, so we split the brioche dough and spread half of it on the roasting pan. I layered the various elements—the mousse, the fillets, the asparagus—over that bottom half. We covered the top of the mixture with the remaining

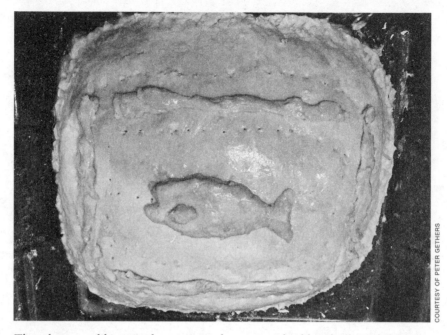

COURTESY OF PETER GETHERS

The salmon coulibiac, ready to go into the oven, with Abby's brilliant fish tracing

dough. Pleased and surprised, I said to Abby that our version looked much the way my mom's coulibiac looked when she used to make it in L.A. But Abby held up his hand, could no longer hide his self-satisfied smirk, and pulled out a line drawing of a fish that he'd been carrying around all day. He placed the drawing on top of a leftover piece of dough and, using a knife, traced the fish drawing. Then he placed the little fish of dough on top of the coulibiac.

It turned our cooperative effort into a work of art. Perhaps not a Picasso or a Matisse but definitely a Puck or a Boulud.

Into the oven it went. Now, all that remained was to prepare the sauce. A breeze. The only question being: Would mint work as a basil substitute? The answer, from all the guests, was a resounding yes. Even Micheline, who, when she walked into my apartment, announced that she hated salmon and wouldn't even taste it, consumed a fairly hefty piece after hearing all the oohs and ahhs and the praise heaped upon us.

Was it as I remembered from thirty-five years ago? Yes, it actually was.

Was it as good? I'm not sure. Would my mother have thought so? Probably not.

But if she'd been there that night for this tryout, I'm certain she would have agreed with my ultimate assessment and appreciated the language with which it was expressed: it was pretty fucking satisfying.

SOLFERINO'S STEAK WITH
TRUFFLE CREAM SAUCE

Twenty-five years ago, not too long after Janis and I became romantically involved, I wrote a book about my amazing and very handsome Scottish Fold cat, Norton. The publisher felt confident that the book—called *The Cat Who Went to Paris*—was going to be a success, so before it was even published I agreed to write a sequel. I knew exactly what the sequel should be and happily the publisher agreed, so Janis, Norton, and I went off to the south of France for a year so I could write about my further adventures with my brilliant feline.

I had, in my twenties and early thirties, found ways to spend a fair amount of time in Paris and the French countryside—writing a couple of films there, working with authors who lived there, doing business with French publishers. I'd come to love the country, the cuisine, and the culture and was determined that someday I would live in France, specifically Provence. Not surprisingly, it was my mother and her connection to Wolf that led me there.

Wolf and Barbara got married in 1982 at a hotel and restaurant called Oustau de Baumanière, in the magnificent town of Les Baux. My mom flew over for the wedding (my dad was working and couldn't make it) and the owner, Jean-André Charrial, treated her like a treasured guest. He even let her do some work in the kitchen, which was my mother's idea of a perfect vacation. When she returned, she created a picture of the Oustau that I couldn't get out of my mind, and it quickly settled into my brain as my fantasy retreat.

A year or so after the Puck/Lazaroff wedding, Jean-André visited Los Angeles and stayed at my parents' house for a week, cementing the connection. A few years after that, I managed to go to Provence and stay at Jean-André's hotel for a couple of days—the place was more beautiful and the food far beyond what I'd imagined. So when it came time to head off to write the second Norton book, I knew I wanted to be somewhere near Les Baux. Amazingly enough, I found the exact house I had pictured and hoped for in the perfect town of Goult, in the Luberon.

During this year abroad, my mother came over for a three-week visit. In the course of that visit, the four of us—my mom, Janis, Norton, and I—drove to Italy, with the express purpose of seeing the town of Lucca, where my brother had recently lived for a couple of years.

Lucca was as beautiful as Eric had said it was. We stayed in a lovely old hotel for one night and, using our guidebook, booked a dinner reservation at what seemed to be an excellent restaurant. In the afternoon, after strolling around the walled city, we struck up a conversation with the hotel owner. He didn't speak English and none of us spoke a word of Italian, so the conversation was composed of incorrect but understandable French on both sides and a lot of hand signals. He asked if we were serious about food and we said we definitely were. I told him my mother was a famous chef, which got my mother's usual instant response: "I'm not a chef, I'm a cook. Wolf is a chef." That got my usual response, which was: "Mom, it doesn't make any difference. No one cares." And in this particular instance, I tacked on: "And he doesn't understand what I'm saying, anyway." But he did understand and he was impressed enough to tell us that the restaurant we'd chosen for dinner that night wasn't very good and asked if he could recommend another place. We said sure. He then asked if we liked truffles.

I had discovered truffles while living in the Luberon. I'd read about them and had been desperate to try them and as soon as I arrived in Goult, I sought them out. You could buy them much the way people bought marijuana in Washington Square Park back in New York: from shady-looking characters who would go "Pssst" as you walked by. Farmers sold truffles under the table so they didn't have to pay the astronomical taxes. If you knew the right street corners in almost every Provençal town, there'd be a guy in an overcoat, loitering suspiciously, and if you said the magic words, "Avez-vous des truffes, Monsieur?" he'd open his coat to reveal several pounds of truffles, layered into different pockets, cut into different sizes. Once you got over the overpowering odor, it was quite a magnificent spectacle. In the town of Apt, not far from Goult, I began to rendezvous regularly with the local truffle dealer and Janis and I had become addicted to the stuff, although we doled the nuggets out carefully to ourselves and our new friends since, even when purchased on the black market, they were quite expensive.

Which is why the immediate answer to our hotel owner was, "Yes, we love truffles." Without saying another word, he picked up the phone, called a restaurant, and spoke rapidly in Italian. The only things we managed to catch were "famous chef" and "truffle dinner." That was enough for me. We were there.

The restaurant, Solferino, was located in an old house; its various rooms were each used as small and separate dining rooms. Before we ordered, Janis said that my mom had been treating us to everything on this trip so she insisted on paying for dinner that night. That was okay by the three of us—my mom, Norton, and me. Norton was not big on picking up checks, although in a very real way, he was paying for the entire year abroad.

Soon after we were seated, the owner of the restaurant appeared before us, made a fuss over my mother, and said we didn't have to order—we were being served their special truffle dinner. Over the next several hours, he proceeded to bring out a six-course truffle-laden meal. I can't remember everything we ate but I know it included truffled eggs, three separate pastas with three different truffle sauces, and a truffle-stuffed Cornish game hen. About halfway through the meal I leaned over to Janis and said, "I have some bad news. You chose the wrong night to pick up the check since this meal is going to cost about ten thousand dollars." She nodded, steeling herself for what had to be an astronomical bill.

Just when we all thought the meal had ended—and by this point we were grateful because we could barely move or breathe— we were served small filet mignons that were topped with gener- ous portions of truffle cream sauce. The sauce dripped over onto the sides of the steaks and onto the plate and contained chunks of black and white truffles the size of small dice. It was a magnificent sight and, although we thought it was impossible, we polished off every last bite. My mother, who weighed a hundred and ten pounds on her heaviest day but could outeat a horse, proclaimed this steak the best she had ever tasted. The sauce was not at all cloying or heavy and the truffles exploded with scent and taste.

At some point during the meal, we had an extended conversa- tion with the owner. It turned out he knew many of the chefs my mom worked with: Wolf and Nancy Silverton and a few others (we later found out that Nancy knew Solferino well and had even cooked with the owner). After our steaks, he led us into the kitchen, intro- duced us to his mother, who looked pretty frail but was clearly the one who had done all the cooking that night. She was thrilled to meet us, we were thrilled to meet her, we were presented with a bottle of homemade grappa as a gift to take with us, and then, back at our table, we were served dessert against our wishes—individual chocolate bombes with tiny American flags stuck in them—and yes, we ate every last bite.

Then we gulped and asked for the check.

Janis held out her hand, was given the bill . . . and discovered that all we'd been charged for was the two bottles of red wine that we'd downed with dinner. The whole meal came to about sixty bucks. When we protested, the owner—and his mother, who emerged from the kitchen to take part in the discussion—shooed us away and said that they were honored to have such a well-known chef dining with them and that they wouldn't think of charging us. I practically had to cover my mom's mouth with my hand to stop her from saying, "I'm not a chef. I'm a cook."

The next morning, while driving back to France, we all started sniffing, wondering what the odd smell could be that was filling the car. At some point, Janis realized that it was the smell of truffles: our epic dinner was emanating from our pores.

Before returning to Goult, we stopped off for lunch at one of the ritzy towns on the French Riviera. A friend of ours was visiting someone with a house in Villefranche-sur-Mer and, knowing of our travels, invited us to stop by for lunch on our way home. The house was tasteful and elegant with a view of the Mediterranean, the hostess was gracious, and she and her two guests—my friend Nina and an elderly woman who was a legendary Parisian book editor—prepared a perfect lunch of cold roast chicken, roast beef, French cheeses, salad, and, of course, good wine. We donated our freebie bottle of grappa, which was a big hit.

As we ate, we regaled the three women with detailed descriptions of every meal we'd eaten on the other side of the French/Italian border. We focused particularly on every magnificent morsel we had downed at our truffle dinner. At one point, the book editor, who smoked continuously and had a deep, throaty voice, said, "Congratulations."

We all turned to her, waiting to see whom she was congratulating and why. She nodded at me and Janis.

"You are now officially French," she proclaimed. "You are eating one superb meal while spending the entire time talking about another one."

Solferino's Steak with Truffle Cream Sauce Recipe

⅓ cup heavy cream

2 egg yolks, lightly beaten

1 tablespoon freshly squeezed lemon juice

⅓ cup extra-virgin olive oil

Thinly shaved fresh truffles, to taste

DIRECTIONS:

Whisk together the cream and the egg yolks until thoroughly mixed. Place in a medium saucepan over low heat. Add the lemon juice and olive oil gradually, whisking as you add. Add the shaved truffles. Stir gently for about 5 minutes.

Serve hot.

STEAK PREPARATION

1 small tournedos of beef per person

Preheat oven to 400 degrees F.

Over high heat, with a bit of olive oil, char each side of the beef. Don't cook through, just brown each side.

Put the tournedos in the oven and cook for exactly 15 minutes (although check after 10, just to be safe). This should leave you with perfect, medium-rare tournedos for everyone.

This is remarkably easy to prepare. Good thing, since this is the dish I'd decided to make at the last minute as a follow-up to Abby and Peter's two-day salmon coulibiac fantasia. I didn't think things could get any better than the coulibiac appetizer, but the people at the dinner party looked and sounded almost orgasmic when they bit into this follow-up dish. I think their response was largely due to the fact that people are rarely served truffles at a home-cooked meal.

I have only a few comments about how best to prepare this baby.

Normally, tournedos (a.k.a. filet mignon) is my least favorite cut of beef. I love skirt steak, sirloin, rib eye, you name it, but although tournedos might be the most expensive of them all, I've always found it somewhat tasteless and I've never loved the texture. To be totally snobby, I always thought that people who order filet mignon do so because it's expensive and they don't really know what they're doing. Um . . .

I'm wrong. When topped with this truffle sauce, these steaks were amazing. I tried this sauce with a couple of different and usually preferred cuts of meat and, yes, they were all good—what could be bad?—but nowhere near *as* good. I have no idea why this is so, but it is.

The only other thing you need to know is that truffles are insanely expensive. A little rock of white truffle can go for five hundred smackers. The black ones are less costly but they ain't cheap. I wouldn't tell this to too many people, but you can supplement the real thing with a canned version of a truffle cream sauce. Try Urbani Truffle Thrills, Cream and Truffles. Each 6.1 ounce can costs about ten dollars on Urbani.com, and you might need more than one can, depending on how many steaks you're serving. But this sauce has real truffles (almost all the versions of bottled truffle oil are chemical re-creations with no real truffles in there). Most people won't know the difference. I wouldn't use it *instead* of fresh truffles, but as a way of saving a few bucks, go ahead and use it *with* at least one fresh truffle to make more sauce. Real truffles are worth it. I swear.

A few years ago, I was in Tuscany and went on a truffle hunt. My small group and I trudged a few miles through a lot of dirt and mud, led by two dogs, a human guide, and the farmer who owned the land. By the time I got back to the hotel, I basically looked like a five-year-old boy who'd spent the day making mud pies. I was covered in the stuff.

But it, too, was worth it.

Here's what I learned on my hunt.

—Most farmers use truffle dogs rather than truffle pigs to find these goodies. Dogs are smaller and more agile and can find truffles in spots pigs can't get to.

—They train puppies to be truffle dogs by putting bits of truffles in their dog food, developing their taste for the delicacy. Oh, to be a truffle puppy in my next life.

—White truffles and black truffles do not grow separately at vastly different locations or times of the year or different climates. They just grow at slightly different elevations and require slightly different amounts of water. We found both white and black ones on our hike.

—There is a huge illegal fake-truffle scam throughout France and Italy. These fake truffles are being created in Eastern Europe and smuggled over the border into legitimate truffle-growing countries, where they are sold for an indecent profit to unsuspecting and not-so-discerning foodies and importers. This news shook me to my very core.

After our search was over, we repaired to a small stone cottage next to the farmer's main house. There, his wife served us red and white wines that they had made from their own grapes (very good), toast (from their homemade bread—*so* good) topped with olive oil (made from their own olives—scrumptious), *and* butter (yes, of course, churned themselves from the cream that came from their cows). And on top of it all were fingernail-size flakes of black and white truffles, shaved and placed to completely cover each slice of toast.

Worth it. Definitely worth it.

MY ALMOST-MADE-UP FAVA BEAN PUREE

If the coulibiac is the most important dish to my mother on an emotional level, and if the steak/truffle concoction is at or near the top of her taste chart, this side dish is probably the least important recipe on her list. It is here because she insisted that her perfect dinner had to have a vegetable, she settled on fava beans as her favorite green vegetable, and she really likes the backstory to this recipe. My mother has a wide range of things that make her laugh. But I think she laughs the hardest at stories that reveal me to be your basic dolt.

I made a fava bean puree for the very first grown-up dinner party I ever threw. I don't know why I picked it. At this point in my life, I'm not sure I'd ever even tasted a fava bean. I just know that I got it in my head to do it, I found a recipe, and I was off to the races.

The reason for this particular dinner party was that Cindy— the girlfriend who drew me back to L.A. and was with me and my mother the day she decided to go to work at Ma Maison and who changed my life and career by giving me my Scottish Fold cat Norton—wound up moving to New York to be with me.

Cindy was relatively easygoing and had a very good heart. She also had a mother who was not to be believed: sour, mean, and nasty—and those were her best traits. My mom used to love hearing about Cindy's mom because my mom came out looking so good in comparison. I would tell her some nightmare story about Cindy's mother and my mom would just smile and raise an eyebrow. I'd go, "I know, I know, you don't have to say anything," and mostly she wouldn't, although sometimes she'd mumble something about how lucky I was.

Not too long after I enticed Cindy eastward, her mom decided to pay her daughter a visit and see what all the fuss was about when it came to the new boyfriend. Cindy was a wreck, since her mother's favorite sport was tearing down Cindy's self-confidence. She'd say things like, "Oh, are you actually wearing that dress to go out?" or "Is that really the way you want your hair to look?"

Understandably, Cindy was a bit fragile around her mother, and always on edge. I decided I'd be the perfect boyfriend and give my pseudo- and horrid mom-in-law the time of her life. I was twenty-four years old, an assistant editor at a publishing company, and my first novel had just been published to limited sales (like, to my parents and their friends), so I wasn't exactly rolling in dough. Nonetheless, I took the two women—making it clear it was my treat—to the fanciest and nicest French restaurant I knew of in the Village. I don't remember what we ate but I do remember I ordered the best bottle of wine that was in my price range and that the entire dinner for three cost more than I earned in one week's paycheck. What the hell: I was doing this for my beloved.

Dinner was reasonably pleasant. Then I called for the check, as suavely as I knew how, and paid it with my credit card, trying my best not to look ashen or tremble even minutely as I added a tip and signed my name. When it was all done, I lifted my glass to take the final sip of wine before we left, told Cindy's mom how glad I was to get to know her, and posed the following innocent question: "So . . . did you enjoy your dinner?"

To this day, decades later, the words that came out of her mouth resonate inside my head as if spoken mere seconds ago. I can hear her distinctive, scratchy voice and hear her whiny, dismissive tone and see the not so subtle sneer on her face as she said:

"All food tastes like cold, gray lumps of clay to me. I'd be happy if I never had to eat again."

I knew several things at that exact moment. First: that Cindy and I were doomed because if there was even a 1 percent chance that she was going to evolve—or devolve—into her mother as she got older, I would most likely wind up in prison after I drowned her in our bathtub (assuming that at some point in the future, I'd be able to afford a place with an actual bathtub). Next: that I could live to be 150 years old and never understand why Cindy's mom hadn't mentioned her aversion to all solid food *before* I'd spent my entire bank account on dinner. And finally: that I'd made a huge mistake by insisting Cindy and I have a dinner party two nights hence so Cindy's mom could meet some of our friends.

I was out of the rat apartment by this time. Thank God for that because Cindy's mom's potential response to that place is beyond anything my fertile imagination could conceive. My new apartment was hardly fancy or luxurious, but it was at least rodent free with no visible garbage outside the window. I don't remember the full meal that I prepared on that Saturday night. I'm sure it was something simple like a roast that I stuck in the oven and a salad (my idea of cooking back then was to make my own salad dressing, using oil and vinegar and a dash of mustard instead of buying a bottle of premade Italian dressing). But for some unknown reason, I had it in my head that I had to make a fava bean puree.

Somewhere, I found a recipe and it didn't seem all that difficult. It was basically boiling a bunch of fava beans, mashing them up with butter and a few herbs, and voilà, a delicacy was born. So I bought whatever amount of beans the recipe called for and got up earlier than usual that Saturday morn, just to make sure nothing could be left to chance. I made myself a cup of coffee, read the paper, relaxed and confident, even though this was my first time preparing a real dinner for real company. Deciding it was never too soon to start, I turned to the recipe for fava bean puree and read the first instruction: "Shell the fava beans."

No problem. I'd helped my mom shell peas before. I figured this was the same level of work. I took one fava out of the bag and began shelling. Five minutes later, I was still trying to get the bean out of the hard shell. I checked the recipe. Yup, the beans were supposed to be shelled *before* they were cooked. I squeezed, I cut, I squeezed some more. Cindy woke up about an hour later, came into the kitchen/living room area, and I greeted her with the words: "Look! I've been doing this for almost an hour and I've shelled five beans. Five! There's thousands of the fuckers! It's going to take me three weeks to shell all these fucking beans!"

It didn't actually take three weeks. But it did take most of the afternoon. What no one tells you is that to properly shell fava beans, you either need Superman's strength and stamina or about a hundred people working for you who don't mind spending a good chunk of their healthy adult years trying to get little green beans out of hard green pods.

The beans were shelled by four o'clock in the afternoon. I was a sweaty, nervous, exhausted, bloody (well, just around my fingernails) mess by the time I got to step 2 of the recipe. I called my friends to tell them to come at eight instead of seven and begged Cindy to tell her mother that I was dead and she should just go home now to L.A. so Cindy wouldn't have to deal with the dinner's unpleasant aftermath. Cindy talked me down and we did our best to actually cook the dinner in time to eat before the chimes of midnight struck.

It must have turned out okay in the end. I don't remember anything particularly disturbing that came out of Cindy's mom's mouth. My friends insisted everything was delicious and I'm pretty sure I got drunk.

Cindy and I did break up a few years afterward. She dumped me on Valentine's Day. I always figured her mother would have thought that was a nice touch.

What follows is not the recipe I made for Cindy's mom. It is, however, a recipe I have made since. One of the joys of living in the twentieth-first century in Manhattan is that it is now possible to buy fresh fava beans that have been pre-shelled. It's a life changer.

Fava Bean Puree Recipe

Yield: 1½ cups

Total time: About 1 hour (from Chowhound, adapted from *Chez Panisse Vegetables*)

INGREDIENTS:

3 cups fava beans, removed from their pods (from about 3 to 4 pounds of favas in their pods)

6 tablespoons extra-virgin olive oil, plus more for drizzling

2 medium garlic cloves, minced

¾ cup water

1 medium thyme sprig

1 (6-inch) rosemary sprig

2 tablespoons freshly squeezed lemon juice

freshly ground black pepper

salt

DIRECTIONS:

1. Prepare an ice water bath by filling a large bowl halfway with ice and water; set aside.

2. Bring a large pot of generously salted water to a boil. Add the shelled favas and boil until the bean inside the outer skin is bright green and firm but not hard, about 1 to 2 minutes. Drain the favas and immediately place them in the ice water bath until cool. Peel the light green skin from each bean to reveal two bright green inner halves. Discard the skins and place the beans in a medium bowl.

3. Heat 4 tablespoons of the olive oil in a large frying pan over medium heat until shimmering. Add the garlic, season with the salt, and cook,

stirring occasionally, until fragrant, about 30 seconds. Add the favas and stir to coat with oil. Add the water, thyme, and rosemary and bring to a boil. Reduce the heat to low, cover, and simmer for 10 minutes more. (Add more water as needed, a tablespoon at a time, to keep the beans from sticking to the pan.)

4. Remove and discard the thyme and rosemary sprigs. Transfer the fava mixture to a blender and blend on low until coarsely chopped. Transfer a third of the chopped fava mixture to a small bowl. Continue to blend until the remaining fava mixture is finely pureed. If the puree is too thick, add water a tablespoon at a time to reach the desired consistency. Transfer the puree to the bowl with the reserved chopped favas. Stir in the lemon juice and the remaining 2 tablespoons oil. Season with salt and pepper and drizzle with additional olive oil if desired. Serve warm or at room temperature.

CHAPTER SEVEN

––––––––––––

I had my first great bottle of wine the day my father died.

When my mother was in her fifties and sixties, a period when many people start winding down and preparing for retirement, she went in the opposite direction, immersing herself in the food world, working at a level and pace she had never reached or even attempted to reach before. My dad relished her labors and took enormous enjoyment from her success; his pride was palpable. He also matched her culinary skills with his taste in wines. He had inherent good taste in many things: he always found wonderful and eccentric houses; he had an eye for antique furniture; he had a decorator's visual sense (which certainly aided his directorial efforts); and he was the snazziest dresser I knew. But most of all, he reveled in his taste for and knowledge of wine.

In the 1960s and early 1970s, most people in America were not drinking French wines. But my dad built a small wine cellar in our basement and stocked it mainly with Bordeaux, Burgundies, and Rhônes. He was buying Latours and Petrus for ten and twelve dollars a bottle. He also developed a taste for good Spanish wines, which were all of six or eight bucks. During my teenage years, my parents were drinking Château d'Yquem as their nightly dessert wine. It was under ten dollars a bottle, but my dad wasn't really conscious of the price—he went with what he liked. It just so happened that what he liked was quite good and, at that time, cheap. As the years went by, the prices went up. Château d'Yquem can now sell for thousands of dollars a bottle. A bottle of Petrus, if you can get it at all, won't go for less than seven or eight hundred dollars. My dad was not afraid of spending money on the things he liked and he would really splurge when he could share. Not to show off—he just wanted people to love what he loved.

My parents had a rather perfect decade after my mom began her career in food. My father became an even more successful director as well as screenwriter and producer and he enjoyed that leap as much as my mother enjoyed hers. He shot a TV movie in Paris and a miniseries in England and my mom went with him for both shoots. They also traveled for fun. One time they spent a week on a river barge going through Burgundy, stopping at various vineyards for *dégustations* (tastings) as often as they wished, going into country restaurants for dinner where, even in those small villages, my mom would drop a name or two that resulted in star treatment—this was my father's idea of heaven.

The decade became less than ideal, however, when, in 1986, my dad discovered he had lung cancer.

He had been a compulsive addict of a smoker. When I was a child, he used to smoke five packs a day, usually lighting one cigarette with another before the first one was out, so he never had to miss a moment of blissful inhalation. He would wake up in the middle of the night just to smoke a cigarette or two before going back to sleep.

When I was around seven years old, television commercials began running that warned of the dangers that tobacco engendered. Because I saw how much my dad smoked, these commercials scared me. Before my eighth birthday, my dad asked me what I might be thinking about as a present. I said that I wanted him to stop smoking—that would be the perfect gift. So on my eighth birthday, my dad stopped cold. He never had another cigarette for the remaining twenty-eight years of his life. But the damage had been done.

Soon after the cancer was discovered, he had part of a lung removed and seemed well on the road to recovery. But there was a huge difference between the way my mother and my father dealt with illness. My mother has had thyroid cancer, breast cancer, and cancer of the uterus, all of them life threatening, and she sloughed them all off. She didn't even bother taking painkillers after her mastectomy! When diagnosed with a melanoma and told she wouldn't live out the year, she absolutely refused to accept it. After her recovery, having spent months in bed, she would never so much as take a nap in a bed again, refusing to acknowledge any potential weakness. My mom had two strokes and after the second one was told she wouldn't walk or speak again. She believed none of that, fought against everything with a fierceness that came from within and that I had never seen and never expect to see again in anyone else, and she triumphed over all of it.

My dad, when told he had cancer, immediately decided that he was dying.

I saw him reasonably often during the period after his lung was operated on and before the cancer came back with a roar. There was a frenetic quality to his behavior after that initial diagnosis. He threw money around even more generously than he ever had before. He bought me things I didn't really want. There was a kind of desperation to his behavior as he tried to cram a lifetime's worth of activity into whatever time he had left.

During this period, the thing that probably brought him the most joy was that Eric and his wife had a son, Morgan. My dad went wild over his grandson. He lavished affection on him, made up songs about him, bought him piles of gifts. Some of his manic indulgence and over-the-top behavior was due to my dad's conviction that he was dying—and dying quickly. To some extent, his behavior stemmed from his guilt and complicated emotions about his relationship with Eric. He once said to me, "Having grandchildren is God's gift to us for not killing our own children."

We had several long talks during this period. He wanted to inhabit his role as a father as fully as possible and jam as much fatherly wisdom into my head as he could. He talked to me at great length about my mother.

During one of these conversations, I found out exactly why he had been so supportive of her new career and her new life that came with it.

"It'll make it much easier for her when I'm gone," he told me. "She has a whole new circle of friends. She has a whole new family," he said, "a whole separate world now, a lot of people who love her and who will look after her. And whom she loves in return. I know your mother. I knew that as soon as she started working at Ma Maison, she'd carve out a separate existence for herself. It's why I loved to see it happen and pushed her so hard to make it happen. She'll be fine without me and that's the most important thing to me."

It was a strange and emotional conversation to have because I knew he was right. My mom, who everyone thought was so dependent on my father, would be fine. If things were reversed, if my mom had died before my dad, I don't think *he* would have been fine. He was too dependent on her quiet strength and support.

Despite the successful first operation, the cancer did indeed come back, riddling his entire body, cracking bones as if they were eggshells. By November 1989, my dad was in Cedars-Sinai Medical Center in Los Angeles, loaded with morphine and waiting to die.

I flew out from New York. Eric was living in L.A. and, along with my mother, had absorbed most of the burden of the final few weeks. When I got there, my dad had a few moments of lucidity but not many. He marveled over the wonderful, psychedelic colors that were on the walls of his hospital room (the walls were completely white; Eric and I told him we were happy he could finally appreciate the reason we used to take drugs back in the sixties and seventies) and he got all excited that Pete Maravich was playing basketball in his hospital hallway (Pistol Pete had died the year before; we said nothing about that to my dad, but Eric pointed out to me that it couldn't be a positive sign).

It was at Cedars-Sinai that I saw the indelible image of my dad, half awake, half in a morphine stupor, desperately sucking in an icy root beer through a straw, the cold sweetness of his favorite nonalcoholic drink reassuring him that he was still alive.

While my father drifted in and out of lucidity, my mom, Eric, and I could do very little but wait. And try to provide as much solace as we could to each other.

On Thanksgiving Day, Wolfgang came to my parents' house and prepared a Thanksgiving turkey, with all the trimmings, for my mom, Eric, and me. We ate it at the massive eighteenth-century Spanish wooden table that dominated my parents' dining room. It was a tasty, if joyless, celebration. The empty seat at the head of the table was impossible to ignore, although Wolf's effort to provide some holiday cheer was a huge comfort to my mom.

Over the two or so weeks I was there, I made a lot of runs from my parents' house to Spago to pick up take-out food. Or a small truck would arrive at the house, Wolf and Barbara regularly sending pizzas, pastas, and desserts. Food became not just their way of sharing our grief, it was their way of helping us—and them—to overcome the sadness.

Food had always been their way of communicating with my family, and it was a language my mother understood better than most.

In the hospital, at the end of November, the doctor approached the three of us and said that although we were not officially having this conversation, all we had to do was to let him know when we wanted him to increase the morphine drip and end my dad's

life. He made it clear that my father was not going to get better
and the only thing he really had to look forward to was pain. My
mother and brother both said they were not capable of making
that decision; they could not accept the responsibility for ending
my dad's time here on earth. I said that I could and would make
that call. I would have no remorse and no guilt. I would want someone to do that for me. I did not believe in an afterlife, but I also did
not believe in unremitting pain. My dad was no longer my dad. I
could pull the plug.

I didn't have to. My father had made it very, very clear that he
did not want to die in a hospital. He wanted to die at home. He
was vehement about that. So, not long after the doctor let us know
that the end was near, we brought him back to the house he loved,
set him up in home hospice care, and waited.

The hospice nurse was quite wonderful. She explained to all of
us, in great detail, what would happen, preparing us for my father's
death. She told us death was not to be feared. She told us what would
physically happen to him the moment he died and the moments
afterward. She encouraged us not to be afraid to touch him.

On December 4, 1989, my father died at the age of sixty-seven.
He and my mother had been married forty-six years and had been
together for fifty-four, counting their teenage courtship at camp.

Janis had flown out for my dad's final days and she, Eric, my
mother, and I gathered at the long bar in my parents' house. I went
down to my dad's wine cellar in the basement, rummaged around—
something I'd never really done; choosing wine was my dad's
job—and I emerged with what I suspected would be a great bottle
of red. I'd never tasted La Tâche but I'd heard my dad talk about
it. I decided this is what he'd want us to do. And it was definitely
what *I* wanted to do.

I later learned that the bottle's vintage, 1962, was one of the
best for La Tâche, which I have come to believe is the greatest red
wine in the world.

I poured four glasses and we began drinking and crying. The next half hour or so was spent pretty much like this:

I would cry and say something about what a wonderful man my dad was. Then I'd take a sip of La Tâche, my tears would dry up, and I'd say, "Wow! This is really good!"

My mom would cry and try to say something about my dad but really couldn't manage to get out more than a word without more crying. Then she'd take a sip of the wine and her head would lift up and she'd say, "Your dad would be very happy we were drinking this."

Eric would cry, tell a story about our father, then: "Oh my God! This wine is unbelievable!"

And Janis, who was being strong for all of us, but obviously shared in the emotional drain, mostly kept patting my mother's hand, telling her she'd be all right, and then saying, "I've never tasted anything like this in my entire life!"

I have never experienced a more perfect definition of mixed emotions.

My dad's body was picked up and taken to the crematorium, and a few days later we had my dad's memorial service at my parents' house. It was made clear that the evening was meant to be a celebration of his life, not any kind of religious ceremony or even anything filled with sadness or regret. A celebration is what we wanted and a celebration is what we got.

Wolf catered the evening, so the food was extraordinary (he didn't come himself—he was too emotional and couldn't handle it). My dad's wine group, WOW, took care of the refreshments. Each of them brought one or two bottles of superb wine, something so good even my dad couldn't have criticized it. There were a few La Tâches and Romanée-Contis and Grands-Échezeaux, spectacular Burgundies all. But my dad was a Bordeaux guy at heart so there were some incredible Latours and Margaux and Mouton Rothschilds and Haut-Brions and, my dad's all-time favorite, Petrus.

People drank a lot and marveled at the food and told stories about my dad that had me roaring with laughter. Even my mom was laughing through her tears. Really laughing. Not just with relief but with gusto.

I stayed around a few more days but then, as happens, I had to return to real life: my job, my friends, my relationship. I had to return to the living.

Before I left, though, my mom and I went out to lunch. We were driving down Melrose Avenue and we were talking about my dad. It was a sunny day and things seemed to have started to return to normal. Suddenly, my mother burst into tears. She began pouring her heart out about the relationship she'd had with my dad.

"Your father loved me so much that he put my life ahead of his. No one ever realized that but I knew it. He told me that was his definition of true love: that he valued my happiness more than he valued his own."

"I know he did," I said. "He told me, too. He also told me that he knew you'd be all right."

"I will," she said. "I *will* be all right. I think that's why I'm crying right now. I know I'll be okay. And that seems so sad to me. And not really fair."

I joined her with a few tears of my own—I'm a serious crier—and then we just started laughing hysterically. Laughing at our emotions, laughing at our fears, laughing because we both felt silly crying and because laughing seemed to be the right thing to do.

Then we went to lunch.

LA TÂCHE AND BÂTARD-MONTRACHET

My father was a Bordeaux lover. He also drank a lot of Rhône wines—he was a huge fan of Châteauneuf-du-Pape. My dad was not subtle, in his life or his tastes, so he liked big, hearty wines that could overwhelm. But he also appreciated Burgundies. If they never quite claimed his heart, he admired them and respected their quiet superiority.

He preferred red wine but he would happily sip a good white. He drank Loire whites quite often—Sancerre and Muscadet were the everyday whites—but here he preferred white Burgundies. He liked cold Chablis and we always had bottles of Puligny-Montrachet and various other Montrachets. When I was in high school, my dad opened a bottle of Bâtard-Montrachet before dinner one night and he gave me a sip. I remember being struck by how smooth and silky it was. My dad was pleased that I liked it. He said it was the Moby Dick of wines—it was the Great White.

When I started drinking wine—not the gallon jugs of Gallo and Almaden I swigged in college, but as my taste became more sophisticated and I began to understand the real pleasure inherent in good wine—I started drinking Bordeaux because that's what I knew. I bought relatively cheap vintages. Of course, I couldn't afford Petrus (I couldn't even afford a glass of Petrus, never mind a whole bottle), but I found second-, third-, and fourth-tier vintners and began to discern different levels in tastes. Around the same time, I began cooking, too, enjoying the sensation of making my own meals and feeding others. I also had an actual girlfriend, Cindy, so it was fun to play at being domestic. I liked to make a reasonably fancy dinner—no salmon coulibiac yet but a good roast chicken, perhaps, and even a cake—and open up a real bottle of wine, a Chianti, always a fail-safe red, or a bottle of nonvintage Château Palmer. My taste level at that time was basically to go for anything that had a label with a nice drawing of a French château on it.

I have never developed a great palate, which drives me a little crazy because now I actually know a decent amount about wine; it's one of the few things I have the patience to study. I can discourse too long on the best years and different types of grapes. But

I don't have the ability to fully grasp all of the complex levels of tastes. I've gone to wine-tasting classes and the teacher will say things like, "Okay, what do you feel on your tongue? And what do you taste as it hits the back of your throat?" People will say things like "dirt, it's very earthy at the start" or "cherries" or "jasmine" or "it goes from blackberry at first to almost rose-like" and he'll be nodding, pleased, while I'm sitting there thinking, "I taste wine. How the fuck is anyone tasting jasmine?"

I appreciate a wine's nose, though. I'm decent at sensing the change in smell that occurs. It's one of my favorite things about wine, in fact, the way it changes. The aroma can be huge when the bottle is opened, then it can die down quickly, then reemerge the longer it is exposed to air, then disappear completely. So, too, can the taste of a great bottle of wine change during the course of drinking it: it can start strong and weaken the longer it's not drunk. Or it can start very small, even bland, and then fifteen minutes later the taste is enormous, exciting, as if the wine is fighting to show you it deserves to be imbibed.

Over the years, I have made a few wine-tasting trips with a small group of friends who are serious wine people. One of them, Don Zacharia, a.k.a. Zachy, sells wine for a living; I'd go so far as to say he's a legend in the wine business. Another of them, Len Riggio, has a world-class cellar; much of what I have learned of the great, great wines—the wines that normal people like me almost never get a chance to drink—comes from his generosity.

Ten or so years ago, we had a little foray to Bordeaux and Burgundy—the two wine experts and their wives, Christina and Louise, Janis, and me. We got to experience things that were once-in-a-lifetime opportunities for wine lovers: a private dinner at Château Margaux (with liveried footmen!); a hearty lunch with the grape pickers in the Petrus fields; a private tasting at Latour. That tasting was in a glass building, in the middle of the vineyards. Six glasses were put in front of each of us and we were told that we were having a surprise, blind tasting. It turned out that they had obtained all of our birth dates from our passports and thus knew how old everyone was. We were served wine from each of our birth years, most of which happened to be great vintages. It was unreal. Zachy was born in 1931 and the owner of Latour said that they only had two bottles of that vintage and no one at the vineyard had ever tasted it before.

In Burgundy, we had a private tasting at Romanée-Conti, sampling ancient vintages of La Tâche—I was swooning.

We had a remarkable afternoon at Domaine Ponsot, one of the great, small Burgundy wine producers. The winery is in the town of Morey-Saint-Denis and they began producing wine in 1934. Laurent Ponsot arranged for us to have lunch in his *cave*. He told us a bit of history about his farm and regaled us with an amazing story about his role in an FBI sting—the domaine's wines were counterfeited (a Ponsot vintage was being sold at auction for a lot of money—only it was a year in which they did not produce any wine!) and Laurent showed up at the auction, in person, to denounce the sale and help the FBI capture the counterfeiter. Sipping his extraordinary Ponsot Clos de la Roche and Clos Saint-Denis, wolfing down cold chicken and cheese and warm baguettes and olives, I made a silent toast to my dad. He is the only person I've ever met who would have enjoyed the experience even more than I did.

Something happens almost every day of my life that makes me realize that I miss my father. It is never the sense that I need him; it is never when anything bad is happening. I miss him at moments like when I'm sitting in Monsieur Ponsot's cave, laughing and marveling at the wine I'm sipping.

Admittedly, sometimes I do well up with tears at those times, but these moments are never sad for me. They are moments that make me appreciate the pleasures in my life. And they make me appreciate even more that my parents prepared me so well to understand and grab the opportunity to partake of those pleasures.

ÉPOISSES, THE GREATEST CHEESE
ON EARTH

In the early 1980s, when my parents came back from their barge trip in Burgundy, my mother tried to describe the taste to me of a cheese she had sampled. It was called Époisses and she said she had never had anything like it.

The cheese was not available in the States at that time and wouldn't be for quite a while. Then, Janis and I were invited, maybe fifteen years ago, to a friend's apartment for dinner. The friend is a French woman, Jeannette Seaver, who has the annoying, inherently French ability to effortlessly make a perfect meal. That night, she called around five p.m., said she had just decided to make dinner, and were we free? We were. We got there at seven thirty to find that she had prepared a cold soup, a roast duck, a tarte tatin, and several other courses that would have taken me a week to prepare properly. I kept saying, "Seriously? You really started cooking at five?" Jeannette pooh-poohed me and said, "Of course not, that's just when I called you. I started at five thirty."

After the meal and before the tarte, she brought out a plate of cheese and a baguette. The cheese, she said, was Burgundian and it was called Époisses. It took me a moment, but I recalled my mother's excitement when she tried to describe the taste of Époisses to me more than a decade earlier. Before I took my first bite, I wondered if this food could possibly live up to its hype. It's like going to see *Hamilton* after everyone in the world tells you it's the greatest play in the history of Broadway. It has to be disappointing, doesn't it?

No, it doesn't.

Époisses is the *Hamilton* of cheeses.

It must be served when ripe, which means starting to ooze onto the plate on which it sits. It has a medium-thick rind and when you cut past that rind—and the rind is to be eaten, do not think of dis-

CHAPTER EIGHT

One of the things that happens, which people rarely want to admit, is that when a parent or a spouse dies there is, along with the sadness and the ache of loss, a liberating kind of freedom. For the rest of one's life, the question becomes how one deals with that freedom.

My dad's death did not unmoor me, it only made me aware that I had to be a bit more vigilant in my life choices since I had lost 50 percent of the moral overview I greatly valued.

My brother felt true sorrow. But he also could now throw off what he felt to be a somewhat oppressive and restraining yoke. He was free to do what he wanted to do, not what he felt my father wanted him to do.

My mom grieved and lived with a layer of sadness that never truly left her—but she also leapt into an independent life where she was now her own key decision maker.

She and I grew closer. Our relationship became one of deep affection and mutual respect and we spent even more time together because we wanted to, not because we had to. In the same way she carding it—inside is a creamy, runny, very, very strong-smelling delight that I might go so far as to say is the best single food I can think of. It is perfect when slathered on a piece of thick bread—that is probably where it is at its best—but it also is delicious if, say, dripped over a cauliflower and then baked. Or, without over-indulging, used in an omelet with bits of ham or onion. Or try it—again, don't use a crazy amount—if you want to have the absolutely perfect grilled cheese sandwich. Just keep in mind: it is potent.

After my mother had her stroke, I will sometimes bring her a ripe Époisses from Citarella. It is not the neatest food to eat, even with two good hands and full motor skills. But my mother slaps it on bread as best she can, and after every bite looks as if she has been let into heaven.

On one trip to Burgundy, I stopped into a small roadside café—it was Christmas week so not many places were open—and one item on the menu was a thin steak that they said was topped with Époisses. This was irresistible. I ordered it, picturing a steak with a butter-size pat of the strong cheese on top. Wrong. Out came a steak—the same cut used in a real French steak-frites—*swimming* in melted Époisses. The cheese was actually dripping over the side of the plate onto the tablecloth. I don't know whether I'd recommend this to too many people. All I can say is that some people fall asleep fantasizing about Penelope Cruz or Emily Ratajkowski or, if you're of a certain age, Jane Fonda in her Barbarella costume. I'm a bit embarrassed to admit that, too often, I fall asleep dreaming about an Époisses-covered steak.

had once assumed a part-time father role, playing football and baseball with me when I was young, now she took up the mantle of moral checkpoint. She was far less vocal than my dad; rather than thundering, she tended to raise an eyebrow or perhaps say, "Is that the smart thing to do?" But her perspective was always clear and pointed.

Everyone told my mom not to make any rash decisions the first year of widowhood and she didn't. She remained in the large house, spent much time working in the kitchen at Spago (her preferred safe haven), wrote new cookbooks, did some teaching. But things changed around her. Some of her friends—at least people she thought of as friends—stopped calling. Mostly they were couples who valued the male part of the coupledom more than the female. But some were women, also widowed; many of them also stopped calling. I told my mom that some people simply didn't know how to deal with death. It made them uncomfortable and so they retreated. My mother, in full "animal" mode, had one response: "Fuck 'em." She never forgave those who carelessly or deliberately hurt her.

Increasingly, she struck out on her own. Some friends were carryovers—those who demonstrated that they were worth carrying over; my mom made it her choice rather than theirs—and many were new, people who met and valued my mother as an individual. Most of these newbies were connected to food: chefs or chefs' agents or restaurant owners or people selling cookware. Sometimes they were just food lovers: students of hers or regulars at Spago. My mom believed that an appreciation of food was a window into character and that became a shorthand method she used to open herself up to trust people.

She thought seriously about starting her own business—a cookie store; she made superb and unique cookies, thick and chewy as mini-brownies. However, the friend she was going to partner with died suddenly, in her sleep, and that put a damper on the new business. To a degree, my mom spent this period drifting. But this was the period in which she was allowing herself to drift, even being urged to drift.

Two years after my dad's death, a major earthquake hit L.A. My mom's house was up in the hills, and a big chunk of her hillside above Mulholland Drive disappeared in moments. She had no electricity for a week or two, which frightened her and made her feel trapped and vulnerable. She decided it was time to sell the house, which she did quickly, and she moved to an apartment that was walking distance from Spago. It was her first attempt to stop the drift.

She began to spend time away from Los Angeles, still mourning my dad but also appreciating her freedom. The first summer she was on her own, she rented a house in Sag Harbor, the town where I have a weekend house. It was great to have her there. She gave weekly cooking lessons to my friends and me: we learned how to make garlic soup and pie dough, and this was the first time I ever saw how to properly clean a mushroom by peeling off the top skin rather than trying to wash the pesky little things. Janis and I would also wake up in the morning and there would be fresh ginger scones that my mom had baked, sitting on the kitchen table, along with a jar of freshly made strawberry jam. It was a summer of homemade morning muffins and group dinners that honed my cooking skills and my palate and helped my mom come to stand on her own and begin to make peace with her new existence.

My mom had always loved to travel, and more and more she began to indulge her adventurous streak. For her first big trip, she went with her niece Beth to New Guinea, where they walked with natives in the jungle and slept in straw huts. In full Auntie Mame mode, and for some reason I could never quite fathom, she also bought native-made penis sheaths as gifts for many of her friends back home. After that, mostly with Beth, occasionally with her sister Belle or her sister Lil, over the next decade or so my mom went to London (several times), France, Hong Kong, Thailand, Taiwan, Bali, Prague, Budapest, Vienna, Salzburg, Kenya, Tanzania, the Netherlands, Morocco, Tuscany, Rome, Sicily, Russia, Poland, Germany, Spain, and southern India. I heard much about the food in all of those places (India might have been her favorite eating trip, although I think she was ready for a change by the time she and Beth returned home). And over the years, it never failed to tickle her when I would say, "I'd love to go to such-and-such" and she'd wave her hand dismissively and say, "Been there." She was proud of her adventurous spirit and enjoyed gloating about it.

After two years of L.A. apartment living, my mom decided it was time for another change. Despite the fact that it meant leaving many of her friends behind, she packed up and moved to New York. I found her a great apartment in the Village but she mysteriously resisted the idea of living downtown. She wouldn't explain her stubbornness but she moved into an apartment on the Upper East Side and slid into city living as if she hadn't been gone for thirty years.

New York City food and restaurant life was thriving in the early nineties. Many of my mother's L.A. disciples—waiters who were now restaurant managers, managers who were now owners, sous-chefs who were now kings of their own castles—had migrated east. It didn't take long for my mom to be as revered in the New York food scene as she was in Los Angeles.

One afternoon I came back from a business trip to London. I'd been gone for a couple of weeks and as I was going through my stacks of mail, I saw a postcard that announced the opening of a new restaurant on my block, two or three doors down from my apartment. It was called Blue Hill and the announcement proclaimed that they were open for a few weeks to just "friends and family." They made it clear that "family" included anyone who lived near the place. I immediately called my mom and said she should come downtown around seven thirty and we'd go try out the new restaurant. Without hesitating, she agreed.

After we'd had a martini, a bottle of wine, and the incredibly delicious fixed tasting menu—that was all they were serving during their six-week-long trial opening, so they could perfect both the cooking and the service—I told my mom I was going to go introduce myself to and praise the chef.

I made my way to the kitchen, introduced myself to the chef, who also happened to be the owner, and whose name was Dan Barber (now considered one of the major, most influential chefs in New York—Blue Hill is where Michelle Obama insisted she and her husband go on their first dinner date after he was elected president). We shook hands. I said that I practically lived next door, told him how great the dinner was and that I was his new best customer, and then told him my name.

He cocked his head and said, "Gethers? Are you any relation to Judy?"

I nodded and said that she was my mom.

His eyes widened and he said, "She's my idol."

I said, "Well, she's had a martini and some wine, so she's propped up by the front door, but I can go back and get her, if you want."

He very much wanted that. When my mom had made her way back to the kitchen, Dan told her that they'd met before—he had been on the line at Nancy Silverton and Mark Peel's L.A. restaurant, Campanile—and he said that my mom's Italian cookbook had been one of the things that inspired him to become a chef. He also talked about how everyone revered her in the L.A. cooking scene. My mom looked embarrassed—but thrilled—and told him how wonderful our meal was. Then she headed uptown and I went back to my apartment, still somewhat surprised by and pondering the fact that my mother was a great chef's idol.

That was not an isolated incident when going out and about with my mom. We'd go to one of Danny Meyer's restaurants and the server would bring a complimentary appetizer to the table, announcing, "Danny says you're the queen of the cooking world and he wants you to try this." Michael McCarty owns the eponymous Michael's on East 55th Street, the hot publishing and TV spot for lunch in midtown. I'd go in there and Michael, who goes back to the days of the Ma Cuisine cooking school, would come over and say, "Please bring your mom in! I love her! She's like my own mom!" She could get reservations instantly in restaurants that wouldn't take me for three weeks. Chefs would try out new dishes for her to taste. Sometimes meals were free or the final amount was half of what it should have been. My mom dismissed all this treatment. But she loved it. And although she never would admit it, she understood that she deserved it.

One day, my mother told me she wanted to go to Shopsin's. Kenny Shopsin, whom I've known for forty years, is legendary in New York City for many reasons: because he is one of the great short-order cooks of all time, because his various restaurants have all been tiny but he never has had less than a five-hundred-item menu, because he creates unique and extraordinary dishes like mac-and-cheese pancakes and an egg dish called Blisters on My Sisters. But his fame has largely spread because he terrifies his customers. He won't seat more than four people at a table. If you try to circumvent this rule and, say, sit with two of your friends at one table for three while two other friends sit at another, Kenny will throw you out of the restaurant. If you try to order a standard dish—one you've never tasted—but ask for him to, say, do it without the onions, he'll throw you out of the restaurant. If you just seem like the kind of person he doesn't like, he'll throw you out of the restaurant. Kenny's motto is "The customer is almost never right." I love Kenny Shopsin.

Kenny is quite a profound person, but without question he is also the most profane human being I've ever met—another reason he can make strong customers cower in fear. He cannot get through a complete sentence without using several nine- and ten-letter words that would make a sailor blush. He will say anything to anyone and not give it a second thought. So the idea of putting him together with my mom made me tremble just slightly. But I promised her we'd go. Before we went, however, I called Kenny.

"My mom's eighty-five years old," I said. "So try to be on your best behavior."

His comeback was: "I'm always on my best behavior."

True enough. That's what I was afraid of.

I took my mom down to Shopsin's and Kenny came over to join us. He knew my mom's food background and they discussed that for a bit. He was charming and friendly. I relaxed. Then my mom said, innocently, that she'd had dinner the night before at Daniel, Daniel Boulud's restaurant, which many people think is the best restaurant in New York. Kenny nodded politely and said, "Do you want to hear my theory about Daniel Boulud?"

I wanted to say, "No," but I was too late.

"I think he's a great chef. I don't have any argument with that. But my palate isn't nearly good enough to appreciate how fine he is. And I think most people are like that. They don't really understand how good his food is. They just go to his restaurants because they're famous, and everyone tells them they're great, and people are sheep, so they go to the place that has Michelin stars and they tell everyone they've eaten there. But they don't really have a clue about the food." My mom nodded, not disagreeing, and then Kenny made his final point. "It's like fucking a five-hundred-dollar hooker with a ten-cent dick, you know what I mean?"

There was a decent pause. I worked up the nerve to look at my mom. She was staring blankly ahead. Then she nodded and said, "Yes, I know exactly what you mean."

I THINK THE main reason my mother came back to NYC was to be near her sister Belle. The two of them had gotten even closer after my dad died. They enjoyed each other's company, could reveal things to each other that were deeply private and personal, and had fun together. My mother, although the younger sister, felt a certain pride that she had helped lift Belle out of the narrow life she had led for many years—bringing her into the more sophisticated world in which my mom thrived—and she liked the idea that, having moved back to Manhattan, she could keep Belle on a closer tether to that world. But soon after my mom's return, Belle was diagnosed with cancer and a year or so later, she died at the age of eighty-two.

I was asked to speak at her funeral and, although I humiliated myself by being unable to get through more than three or four consecutive words of the eulogy without bawling like a baby, I did manage to make one thought clear: Belle was a better, kinder, and more interesting person at eighty than she had been at forty.

My most rigid theory about people is that as we age we become more and more like our true selves. At first I thought that Belle had broken that mold. Then I realized she hadn't. She had fought for decades to tamp down her true self—partly out of familial duty, partly out of fear, partly because that's all she knew how to do. But with my parents' help—or more likely, with my parents as a kind of escape hatch—the older she got, the more she allowed that true self to emerge. By the time she died she was one of the funniest, sharpest, most interesting, most moral people I knew.

Belle's death was another blow to my mom, but she continued to amaze me with her resiliency. In Belle's absence, she grew closer to her sister Lil. As did I. Lil was as steely as my mom and Belle, possibly even more so, without the softer side. She was tough, tough, tough. But very smart and fascinating. She would tell stories about living in California as a young girl pre–World War I and talk about going to speakeasies in New York City (and drinking the psychedelic absinthe) during Prohibition. Well into her nineties, she could still tell you the exact address of her favorite 1920s speakeasy.

My mom also began traveling even more often. One of the places she now went, along with her niece Beth and one of my mom's oldest friends, Esther (Esther had been married to Albert, the frustrated garment exec/Dixieland drummer who played at

Arthur's in the West Village), was a restaurant in Sicily that had become near and dear to my heart: Gangivecchio.

In 1991, Janis and Norton the cat and I spent a week traveling around Sicily. Before we departed, we read a *New York Times* article by Mary Taylor Simeti about a place called Tenuta Gangivecchio. The intriguing elements in the article were: this was the best restaurant in Sicily, it was housed in a thirteenth-century abbey, and it was nearly impossible to find. Eating at Gangivecchio immediately became my quixotic quest.

Amazingly enough, considering my total lack of any sense of direction, we found Gangivecchio and had the best lunch imaginable: veal rollatini, pasta with five-nut pesto sauce, and, most memorably, small turnovers fried in lard and stuffed with warm lemon cream. Three days later we were in Agrigento and instead of spending the day among the magnificent Greek temples, I insisted we make the three-hour drive back to Gangivecchio so we could repeat our lunch. It was even better the second time around. The food was just as extraordinary but we also sat and talked with Wanda and Giovanna Tornabene, the mother-and-daughter team who owned the abbey and ran the restaurant. Wanda didn't speak a word of English, although she seemed to understand everything we said, and Giovanna spoke a lovely, fractured English that made me swoon. She was also brilliant, charming, and captivating. Wanda was mostly scary. She was like my aunt Belle on steroids—if Belle also had a shotgun and a history of fending off local mafiosi trying to collect protection money.

Wanda's and Giovanna's lives changed quite a bit as the result of our second lunch. I convinced them to write a cookbook, which they did, and then they wrote two more. Their first two books won James Beard Awards. They promoted the books throughout America, turned their stables into a lovely nine-room inn, and, as a result of their publishing success and ensuing publicity, people started to come from all over the world to eat and spend a few days there. My life changed as well.

I bought the renovated 150-year-old stone caretaker's cottage on the abbey's property after the six weeks I spent holing up there to finish writing my novel. My daily routine for those six weeks was: wake up early and go for a run in the mountains. Upon my return, Pepe—the man who did everything imaginable for the Tornabenes—would knock on my door and say one of the three phrases he knew in English, "Breakfast is ready." I'd have some strong espresso and fresh fruit, then write until one o'clock, at which time Pepe would again knock on my door and utter phrase number two in his English vocabulary: "Lunch is ready." After lunch, I'd write for a few more hours, then exercise like a lunatic because I knew what was coming, and then at around eight o'clock, I'd hear the final words of Pepe's trilogy: "Dinner is ready." I would then go to the abbey and, night after night, eat more than a pound of pasta. My pasta eating became somewhat legendary. Years later a friend stayed at the cottage, came back to New York and incredulously asked, "Did you really eat over a pound of pasta every night?" At first I denied it but, under pressure, was forced to capitulate. It was on the final day of that six-week writing and pasta-eating jag that I called Janis, who was in New York, and we agreed to buy the cottage.

My mom, Beth, and Esther spent a few days eating and cooking with Wanda and Giovanna. My mom fell in love with the place, as I had—the rusticity and occasional lack of heat and hot water in the cottage didn't faze her one bit—and she came back raving about one pasta dish in particular: Buccatini with Cauliflower, Pine Nuts, Currants, Anchovies, and Saffron. My mom was a pasta lover and she thought this was as good as it got.

I don't use this word lightly or flippantly, but my mom, as she approached eighty, was "cool." And I don't say this only because she was willing to rough it in the Sicilian cottage. She understood instinctively why, at the age of thirty-eight, I quit my relatively high-powered publishing job and took off for Provence. She appreciated nonconformity, didn't place much value on material possessions, didn't care what anyone's net worth was. She had long outgrown her Pollyanna-ish view of the world yet, with a remarkable lack of cynicism, saw life for what it was and people for who they were. She inherently understood people's actions. She knew immediately when someone was bullshitting her—a word she came to use more and more; she loved saying "bullshit"—and she had a real sense of whether someone was fake or genuine. She had an unerring radar when it came to assessing other people's motives. I think it was because hers were usually pure.

She had one absolute blind spot, to which she was entitled: her grandson. She never said no to Morgan, the product of my brother's second marriage. My mom loved him without equivocation and with no strings attached. He understood that from a very young age, grew to appreciate it and depend on it, and he never abused that love or took advantage of it. He was unfailingly polite to her, which was particularly sweet, and he not only took great interest in the things that interested her, he gently forced her to take interest in the minutiae of his own life. She was always attracted to young people and the immersion in his world and interests helped keep her young. My nephew—as I have told him many times—has done a lot of dumb things and things of which I've disapproved, but he never, not once, treated his grandma with anything but genuine love and respect.

Part of my mom's blinding love for Morgan was an extension of my dad's near-insane and manic captivation with him when Morgan was just a baby, a way of keeping my dad's feelings and wishes alive. But my mom's love was real and heartfelt, no question about it—and it stayed that way even as she began to also disapprove of some of his choices. But disapproval had nothing to do with how much she loved him and how much she supported his choices.

His parents divorced when he was young. During Morgan's teenage years my mother, approaching eighty, became his rock, the one thing he could count on and know would never disappoint him.

And when Morgan was twelve or thirteen years old, he became very interested in food and cooking. In college he took cooking lessons. My mom brought him to good restaurants on his New York visits and kvelled when he experimented with tastes and fearlessly tried the unknown. Morgan has inherent taste when it comes to food.

He has my mom's taste.

ON OCTOBER 5, 2008, a Sunday, a couple of months after my mother's eighty-sixth birthday, she, Janis, and I had lunch with some of my cousins (on my dad's side). My mom was in good spirits. She loved and enjoyed her nieces and nephews and the feelings were mutual. There were also plenty of great-nieces and great-nephews and my mom liked keeping tabs on them and knowing that she was, to a degree, a part of their lives.

After lunch, we had our usual taxi argument. The way it worked is that I'd hail a cab and my mother would insist that Janis and I take the first one. Even when it was snowing or pouring rain. Once when it was so windy we thought she might blow away if we didn't hold on to her arms and keep her feet on the ground. We'd explain that she was in her eighties, somewhat frail, and that she should take the first cab that came by. She'd shake her head and insist. I'd roll my eyes and insist back. She'd insist more vehemently. Finally, Janis would wind up saying, "Judy, get in the damn cab!" On this particular Sunday, we put her in the taxi around three in the afternoon and she headed uptown.

Around one o'clock the next afternoon, I got a call from my mother's close friend Jan (not to be confused with Janis). Even though she was thirty or so years younger than my mom, they were inseparable. Jan checked in with her every day and they saw each other constantly. On the phone, Jan told me the following:

Knowing my mom was a psychotically early riser (she refused to ever stay in bed much past six a.m.), she called my mother's apartment around eight. No answer. She assumed my mother was already out and around. By eleven in the morning, she was concerned that they hadn't yet connected, so she went over to my mom's building. The doormen let her up to the tenth floor and, stepping out of the elevator, she saw that my mom's newspaper was still in the hallway outside the door. She knew something had to be wrong—there was no way my mother could still be in bed at that hour. Jan had a key and let herself in. She found my mother on the floor of her den, unmoving, unable to speak, but alive.

Her bed had not been slept in so doctors later estimated that my mother had her stroke sometime between three thirty and nine p.m., which is when she might have normally turned in for the night, or at least gotten under the covers to watch TV. My mom did have one of those "Help, I've fallen and can't get up" things that she wore at home since she had her first stroke, but this attack came so suddenly and violently that she hadn't had time to press the button. Once down, she was paralyzed and couldn't move to reach it. She had been alone, overcome by the stroke, unable to budge, for at least fourteen hours, perhaps as many as nineteen. To recover from a stroke of this magnitude, the medical consensus is that the stroke victim must be discovered and treated within an hour of the attack, two at the most.

My mother was rushed by ambulance to Lenox Hill Hospital—conveniently one block from her apartment—and taken to the emergency room. I left my office, frantically hailed a cab, and met Jan there. Although she wasn't related and thus met some resistance from the hospital staff, she had refused to leave my mother's side.

My mother spent much of the afternoon lying on a mobile cot in the ER hallway. They were waiting for the right doctor; they were waiting for the MRI to become available; they were waiting to get her in the line for a CAT scan. She'd finally get one scan taken, then back she went to the hallway. No matter how much I yelled, insisted, or even tried to bribe, my mom spent at least eight more hours strapped to the gurney in the hall. Somewhere around nine p.m., she was finally under proper doctor's care and taken for more tests.

Jan and I went to a restaurant a block from the hospital. All I remember is that it was a French bistro and we both downed a decent amount of wine and neither of us ate much. Around ten o'clock, we went back to the hospital. It was difficult to attract anyone's attention or to get answers about my mother's condition. One of the attendants was absorbed in *Monday Night Football* on the TV at his desk and was loath to look away or respond to my badgering. Around midnight, we were told that she would not regain consciousness that night and there was no real reason for us to stick around. Quite a few of those hours at the hospital are blurry in my memory. I know that Janis joined me for a good part of the time, as did Beth. I know that it didn't occur to me to call or e-mail anyone else to reveal what was happening. I was able to focus on only one thing.

The next morning, I was back at the hospital, first thing. One of the doctors came over to tell me that there was too much swelling for them to be absolutely certain, but it looked like the stroke had been very powerful and had hit my mom in the worst possible spot, the dead center of her brain. As a result, it was likely that she would have locked-in syndrome—she would not be able to speak or move a muscle for the rest of her life.

The doctor told me I could see her and I found her in a curtained-off cubicle in the ER—she still had not been admitted to a real room in the real hospital. Her skin color was a faded and pasty green, her hair was sweat soaked and matted to her head. She looked to me as if she had died several hours ago. But when I stepped in, her eyes opened.

"Lookin' good, Mom," I said. And she rolled her eyes.

That roll said, "Don't be a smart ass." Her eyes also said: "How did this happen?" They showed humor and defiance. And utter exhaustion.

The next day, finally in a real room, she moved her left arm. The left arm they said would never move. Her finger crooked and made a slight motion that I should come closer. The finger they said would never move. And then she spoke, which they also said would never again happen. The words she spoke were: "What a lot of shit."

The next day my mother began physical and speech therapy—much to the shock of everyone in the hospital. They said that it was impossible for my mother to be doing what she was doing. I shrugged. I'd seen it before. The physical aspect was arduous and extraordinarily difficult. Straightening her head, aligning it with her spine, took a Herculean effort. Speech therapy was frustrating agony for my mother and fascinating for me. Her speech therapist was remarkably patient and gentle. She would start by asking my mom to fill in the blanks in a sentence. She would say, "I went to the store to get some _____ for my cereal." And my mother would say, "Cows." I couldn't help it, I'd laugh, and so would the therapist and so would my mom. But the therapist would explain that it was a good answer because it was close enough to one real and obvious answer—milk, and cows produced milk—to show that the brain functions were working.

Other sentences my mom tried to complete:

"For breakfast I had a glass of orange . . . beds."

"Two plus two equals . . . two." My mom immediately knew this answer was wrong, screwed up her face, nodded calmly, and gave what she was certain was the right answer: "One."

"Peanut butter and . . . red paint."

"All I want for Christmas are my two front . . . elephants."

Because I had explained a bit about my mother's past to the therapist, many of her questions were geared around food. Each time the therapist could explain the logic behind my mother's incorrect answers. She spent hours and hours explaining them to my mom, too, so she could slowly begin to untangle the twisted neurons misdirecting her language traffic.

Ten days after my mom's stroke, I was told that she had to leave the hospital in three days. I panicked.

"She can't move," I said. "She can barely speak. How can she go back to her apartment? What the hell am I supposed to do?"

The hospital social worker sat down with me. Reassuring and helpful, she explained that my mom needed to be moved to a rehabilitation center. Hopefully, after rehab she'd be able to return to her own home, with the proper live-in care. I was warned that I shouldn't count on that, however. The doctors suspected that she would be forced to live in an institution for the rest of her life.

She could not go back to the Rusk Institute, where she'd gone after her first stroke, because she was not advanced enough in her recovery to fit into their rigorous program. So I began scouring the city for nursing homes. The first one I went to was just a few blocks from my apartment—convenient from a travel time perspective if nothing else. And believe me, it was nothing else. Gorgeous on the outside, a landmark Greenwich Village building, inside it was a cross between the asylum in *One Flew over the Cuckoo's Nest* and the World War II Japanese POW camp in *The Bridge on the River Kwai*. I saw roaches scuttling around and the place was absolutely filthy. The guide showed me one room, the size of the smallest dorm room at the worst college imaginable. In it were two beds and one nightstand—there wasn't room for more. In one of the rooms was a person—I couldn't tell if it was a man or woman, and I don't think he or she could, either—who was hooked up to a few machines and wasn't moving. The other bed was empty. Indicating the body in the bed, the guide said, "This is Mrs. Johnson. She'll be a very good roommate for your mom because she's very quiet."

"That's because I'm pretty sure she's dead," I said.

I got out of there within seconds.

I looked at a few others and all I could think of was my mother saying to me, a few years ago, "If I ever wind up in a home with nothing but old, sick people, just smother me with a pillow and kill me."

After my tour of rehab homes, I was almost to the point of deciding that that was a reasonable and decent course of action.

Then my mother's wonderful doctor came through. He used his pull to get her into a lovely, humane rehab center, Amsterdam Nursing Home, on 114th Street and Amsterdam Avenue. I spent a lot of time there over the next few weeks and, if you're interested in some New York City sightseeing pointers, a couple of blocks from her rehab joint was the real-life diner they used as the George/Jerry/Kramer/Elaine hangout in *Seinfeld*. I had a lot of coffee and quick meals there and it always made me grin to step inside. I'm big on silver linings, especially if they involve pancakes or western omelets.

The day I learned that my mother could be moved into the Amsterdam home, I called my brother, who was living in France, to tell him what had happened. Eric called Morgan to fill him in and a few days later, both of them flew into New York.

My mom was thrilled to see them. Morgan stayed two or three days and my mom perked up every second he was around her. Same for Eric. He hung out at the rehab place, spent a lot of time talking to her and trying to do whatever could be done to help her. He said later that it was the first real quality time that he and my mom had spent together in years.

Now I began spreading the word, telling people what had occurred. My mom had an enormous and varied circle of friends, so Janis, who was amazing during this entire period, began sending out mass e-mails about the events of the past couple of weeks, regularly giving updates on my mom's condition. The first one gave a thorough overview and assured everyone that my mom was making progress. Then, over the next few weeks, there would be helpful tidbits: "Judy got out of bed and into a wheelchair!" "Judy moved her right hand!" "Great news: Judy took a shower and washed her hair and she looks beautiful!"

Everyone was, of course, concerned, and everyone was understanding and helpful, knowing just when to intrude and participate and when to step back.

Well, almost everyone. One of my mother's friends in Los Angeles called one night to find out what was happening and how my mother was doing. This was early on in the recovery process, so I was particularly stressed. I happened to be at the hospital, in my mom's room, when this woman called. My mom obviously couldn't talk on the phone, so I explained to her friend how we were handling the situation and I said that an e-mail would go out every few days for a while and then as often as there was something to report. The woman said, "That's not good enough." I explained that was the best that could be done because there were a lot of people who were concerned and with whom we needed to communicate. She then said, "No. I want you to call me every day to tell me exactly what's happening." I said, "Excuse me?" And she repeated it: "I want you to call me every day!" I guess she caught me at a somewhat fragile moment because my immediate and exact response was, "I don't think you do want that . . . because if I did, every single day, I'd tell you to go fuck yourself!" And I hung up the phone.

My mother, just a little startled, muttered something, which I understood to be, "Who was that?" When I told her, and repeated the conversation, my mother laughed for what must have been five minutes. Then she did her best to say something else, which I finally figured out was an admonishing, "You're terrible." Then she started laughing again.

After my mom had been in the nursing home for a week or so, Wolfgang called me to say he was coming to New York and would bring food to my mom. I told him that she was relearning how to eat. At first she could only sip liquids, and very slowly. Over the past few days she had progressed to soft food that didn't require real chewing. Wolf showed up two days later—it was a surprise to my mom—with a huge bowl of mushroom risotto. My mother was not the only one who was ecstatic. The entire nursing staff almost fainted when Wolfgang Puck—the one from the Home Shopping Network!—stepped out of the elevator to bring Mrs. Gethers food. She was golden from that day on.

Wolf's visit gave my mom a great boost. He was the first non-family member she allowed in to see her—my friend Paul and his wife Laurie counted as family—and eating his risotto made her realize that things could be normal again. Or reasonably so.

It wasn't long after Wolf's cameo that my mom spoke her first fully thought-out and complete sentence to me since she'd had her stroke: "Get me out of here!"

From that point on, the will of steel kicked in big time. She ate, she spoke better, she moved better. She walked, taking tentative baby steps, with a lot of aid. Because she was determined to get the hell out of there, she was an ideal patient, pushing her therapists to work her harder, doing everything by the rules except for one thing: she refused to take her meals in the common room with other patients. The nurses told me they thought it would be good for her to interact with other people. I told this to my mom.

"No," she said. "Don't like old, sick people."

"Mom . . . you're kind of an old, sick person yourself. So maybe it's not such a bad idea."

"I'm . . . getting . . . out . . . of . . . here."

And she did. She didn't make my favorite yearly tradition, Kathleen and Dominick's Thanksgiving Dinner, but she did make their annual Christmas party. Paul and I sprung her from Amsterdam for the night. She refused to go into Kathleen and Dominick's apartment sitting in her wheelchair. We helped her up, and she walked in on her own two legs (with a few helping hands) and ate her beloved croquembouche. After a couple of hours, Paul and I got her back to the nursing home.

Once again, my mom defied all the medical predictions. The head of the rehab center and her doctor told me that she was now able to return home. My mom was overjoyed. I was a bit nervous.

There were still so many things she couldn't do on her own. I didn't quite understand how all this would play out.

I interviewed several potential live-in aides. Again, the social worker at the nursing home was incredible, talking me through the process, explaining exactly what I needed to look for and how to go about it. She gave me a list of places to contact. I called a few and didn't feel the vibe. When I said to the director of one of the places that I would want to interview the candidates and so would my mom, she said, "We don't allow interviews. If you and your mother don't like them, we'll replace them as soon as we can." I said no they wouldn't because there was no chance in hell I was going to be using their services. After several more calls, I went with a company called SelectCare. When I said we wanted to interview the women who might be working and living with my mom, the head of the agency said, "Of course. We wouldn't let you hire anyone unless she got along with your mom." She then asked me to tell her a bit about my mother. When I was done, she said, "I think I have two perfect people. They both can cook. It sounds as if that's essential."

In early January 2009, my mother returned to her apartment.

And thus began the next stage of her life, probably the most impressive one yet.

SHE WAS STILL quite aphasic, she needed thrice-weekly sessions of physical and occupational therapy, she had to use a cane to get around (no walker or wheelchair for her), and she moved at a snail's pace. But as soon as she was home, my mother resumed her normal life.

She saw friends. Went to movies and to the theater. She went to restaurants all over the city. One day I called her up to say that friends had been to a brand-new restaurant and they thought we should try it.

"Already been there," my mother said.

"Mom, the place has only been open a week. You're almost ninety, you're stroke-ridden, and it takes you fifteen minutes to get to the elevator! How the hell do you still go to restaurants before I even hear about them?"

She just cackled.

It helped enormously that three of the kindest, most compassionate, most wonderful people I've ever met had come into my mother's life. They were her three aides from SelectCare: Jennifer, Janet, and Karlene. My mom kept her emotional distance from them at first, determined that she would eventually return to being self-sufficient and not need any live-in help. The doctors told me that would never happen, but doctors had used the word "never" many times before when it came to my mom. But this time they were right. The women rotated their shifts: Janet four or five days a week, Jenny on the weekends, Karlene whenever she was needed or as a vacation replacement. And over time my mom accepted them into her family and came to truly love them. In many ways they became more than family, they became friends.

Three other women also began to play an important part in my mom's recovery. This second stroke eliminated my mom's ability to cook—it took a long time for her right side to become even decently functional. She had to learn to write with her left hand and eat mostly with her left hand, two things I'd never be able to do. But cooking was too difficult. Her taste, however, remained. So one day, Janis suggested that an excellent birthday gift for my mom would be to hire a chef to come in and cook for her once a week and perhaps make meals that would last several days. My mom was thrilled by this idea and the first woman I hired was Jenny Cheng. Jenny's parents ran a Chinese restaurant and she had gone to cooking school to learn how to make other types of cuisines. When I hired her, she was working as a line cook at a Tribeca restaurant. She, too, was an instant hit. Jenny didn't just cook for my mom, they talked about food, which was terrific for my mother's mental acuity as well as great speech therapy. When Jenny outgrew the job, Joyce Huang replaced Jenny, and Joyce was eventually replaced by Cynthia Tomasini. They all learned a lot from my mom, and not just about food and cooking. They learned about spirit.

Sometimes I would bring Jenny and the other cooks ingredients that I knew my mom especially liked. Or I'd bring packaged food that my mom loved to eat. I'd bring her Époisses, which made her face light up like a neon sign. I suggested that Jenny cook out of the Ratner's book, so she made pirogen and blintzes for my mom (my mom gave both versions a C+—she was a tough customer). My mother told her chefs all about working at Spago on their special Passover dinners (my mom made the matzo balls) and helping Wolf prepare his Academy Award dinners. So I suggested they make dishes from Wolf's books that my mom used to help prepare. My mom was delighted to rediscover these tastes.

One other thing helped engage my mother, physically and mentally. I've never had children, but I do have two cats in the post-Norton era. When Norton moved on to the great Kibble Bowl in the Sky, it took me three years to work my way up to being owned by another cat. At that point, I went to a breeder intending to buy another cat just like Norton—a male Scottish Fold whose ears had folded (not all of their ears do). But the first little creature who crawled her way into my heart was a girl whose ears sat straight up. It was love at first sight with this five-week-old dark gray kitten, who soon became Harper. But I really wanted a boy with real Fold ears, so when her orange and white brother—I named him Hud—flopped his way over to me, I found myself saying, "Okay, I'll take them both." I had taken Norton everywhere with me, so there was rarely a need for anyone to look after him. But it's harder to travel with two of these guys, so now that my mom was in New York, she was recruited to be my cat sitter when I had to travel for any length of time.

The beautiful, regal Harper at age fourteen

She and Harper quickly bonded. My sweet girl cat would sleep next to my mom, my mom's fingers grazing the top of the furry little body all night long.

Hud died suddenly when he was six, which devastated me way more than I suppose it should have. He was my particular pal and I'm pretty sure he thought I was actually his dad. When he died, Harper mourned deeply. She didn't eat for weeks and she lost several pounds. She paced and cried and changed her personality from sweet and calm to nervous and cranky and unsure of the world. But she still loved going to my mom's if I had to take a trip. The cat took comfort from my mother and my mom took comfort from my lovely, loving cat.

When she was taking care of Harper, I'd call my mom every day I was away. We'd chat, I'd see how she was doing, how she felt, and then my mom would say, "Okay, you've done your job. You can ask." Sometimes I'd protest and say I was really calling to talk to her but she'd have none of it. "I know the truth," she always

Mitch as a kitten

. . . and as an adult

said. So then I'd ask, "Okay, how's Harper?" I'd get a detailed report and tell my mom that I'd talk to her the next day. "Just to talk to you," I'd say. And she'd go, "Uh huh." For years she'd ask if she could take care of Harper for a while—just to be sure I'd call her.

Five years ago, I got Mitchum. Harper, now fifteen, is as delightful and special as a cat can be. But Mitch is Norton-esque. He is crazy smart and extremely beguiling and he goes out of his way to seduce everyone he meets. He has yet to meet a human whose lap he can't be nestled into within fifteen minutes of the introduction.

My mom's companions love Harper and Mitch as much as she does. Janet, especially, is always saying to me, "When are you going away again so I can see my little boy?" My mom pretends to be somewhat indifferent, but she lights up when they show up. Harper ignores the aides and goes right to my mother's side. Mitch goes out of his way to say hello to and get petted by the aides, then hops on my mother's bed and makes himself comfortable, as if it's his bed and perhaps he'll let her join him for the night.

My MOM HAS two friends, Bill Chastain and Jean-Paul Desourdie, who are longtime partners. Bill is retired now from the movie business and JP is a caterer. I threw a surprise eightieth birthday for my mom at their apartment as well as a surprise eighty-fifth. Both times, but especially for the second bash, as the door opened and everyone yelled "Surprise!" it did occur to me that it might not be a great idea to give such a sudden shock to a woman of that age with a dicey medical history. But my mom took it all in stride and both parties were smash hits.

When my mom turned ninety we had one of the greatest parties ever. It wasn't done as a surprise and pretty much everyone she knew, on both coasts, was invited. Just about everyone came, too. We had sixty or seventy people at Bill and JP's apartment, the food was great, and, in essence, my mom got to witness her own laudatory memorial service because so many of her friends—young and old—got up and spoke. People talked about how much she meant to them, how strong she'd been for them at different points in their lives, and how strong she helped them become. They talked about the food she'd made and the lovely things she'd done to help them. It was a rare and moving outpouring of love.

One of my mother's oldest friends, Takayo Fischer, composed a song for her and sang it. Paul, who has known my mom almost as long as I have, and I prepared a PowerPoint presentation purportedly showing the complete arc of my mom's life. A lot of it was true and a lot of it was completely made up. Paul did the technical stuff and did it brilliantly, so dozens and dozens of photos popped up on the big white wall of the apartment as I narrated my mom's story. We had uncovered photos of my dad in a Camp Mohican show and a picture of my mom's camp bunkmates. My cousin Jon Korkes delivered to us a home movie of my mom and dad when they were in their early twenties, kissing and fooling around for the camera. I had a picture of my mom walking through the jungle in New Guinea with a studly native, explaining that this was my mom's wild period, when she ran away from my father to have her torrid affair. We had family photos from different eras and lots of photos of my mom at different ages. People laughed throughout—my mom most of all—but tears were flowing freely by the end.

I thought all of the speeches were completed, but my nephew Morgan suddenly raised his wineglass and made a toast.

"I want to say something about my grandma," he said. "I think she's the greatest person I've ever met." He then went on to talk about how much she meant to him and why. It was eloquent and moving and my mom, who rarely gets openly emotional, was definitely choked up to the point of repeatedly wiping her eyes.

After that toast, I told Morgan that he was now officially a mensch.

My mom stayed at the party until the very end. She ate, drank, and soaked up the love. When it was time to leave, I asked her if she'd had a good time.

"Oh yes," she said. "Oh yes." That was all she really had to say.

"You want my take on the whole party?" I asked. She nodded. "You have a lot of children," I said. "All the people here, they either think you're their mom or they wish you were their mom."

"And what's the lesson to learn from that?" she asked.

"You're lucky," I said.

And my mother said, with a triumphant smile, "No, you are."

THE TORNABENES' BUCCATINI WITH CAULIFLOWER, PINE NUTS, CURRANTS, ANCHOVIES, AND SAFFRON

Gangivecchio means "Old Gangi," which means that the town of Gangi that exists today is the *new* Gangi. The spot where the thirteenth-century abbey stands—now the inn and restaurant run by Giovanna Tornabene and her brother, Paolo—was the site of the original village. For six hundred or so years, monks ran the magnificent abbey. There are remnants of that period everywhere you look: the seventeenth-century chapel off the courtyard, sixteenth-century frescoes on the walls of Giovanna's apartment inside the magnificent walled structure. Several years ago, I participated in an archaeological dig on the grounds of the abbey and uncovered two-thirds of an ewer that the archaeologist from Palermo told me was from 300 BCE. Having discovered something that old and beautiful—and holding it gingerly in my palm—brought tears to my eyes. Wandering through the ruins of the abbey, I once stumbled upon a stack of beautiful terra-cotta tiles. When I showed them to Giovanna, she said, "Oh yes, those are seven hundred years old." She then offhandedly suggested that I should use the tiles to build the barbecue I wanted to erect outside the cottage, and that's where they now sit. Every time I spill grease from a sausage onto the ancient tiles, my stomach hurts a little bit.

Wanda Tornabene, the mother of Giovanna and Paolo, was an amazing woman. When I met her, in 1991, she was in her late sixties and she was no one to mess with. Like a lot of Sicilians, particularly after World War II, the Tornabenes were gentry who ran out of money. Even now, these Sicilian gentry have managed to have loyal servants and a certain regal carriage and an air that clearly conveys the belief that they are meant to lord over someone, somewhere. But at some point, they have all had to either go to work or face destitution. For many, being broke beats the humiliation of actually having to do real labor. Wanda was not one of those. When her husband was still alive, she put her foot down. She said that they were not going to sell off any more of the land they owned (once a thousand acres or so). Nor were they going to sell off any more antique furniture from the abbey. Instead, she said, they were going to open a restaurant. Enzo, her husband, was mortified. Cooking for, serving, and waiting on local people, whom they knew? People who should be working for Enzo and his family? No, this was not going to happen.

It happened. Because Wanda made it happen. Gangivecchio, over time, became the best restaurant in Sicily, and Wanda ran it the way a great general commands his (or her) troops. She gave orders, the people who worked for her as well as her family followed those orders, and somehow they all developed an appreciation for her passion and her talent. That appreciation developed into loyalty. And even love.

When Wanda's husband died, in the early 1980s, the restaurant is what kept her and her two children going. On the abbey's grounds were acres of superb vineyards and four hundred olive trees and cows and horses and chickens and cherry trees and almond trees, and although they could keep the land and its treasures alive, they could not mine them the way they should be mined. That was for a different era. What Wanda could control, what she could mine, was food. She was a magnificent cook and loved food fiercely. For my mother, food was a way to strengthen her identity. For Wanda, food was *part* of her. It was her blood.

The Tornabenes—Wanda, Giovanna, Paolo—sacrificed a lot to keep Gangivecchio in the family. Giovanna now says that Gangivecchio is her child: her purpose on earth is to keep it alive.

When she was in her mid-eighties, Wanda got sick. Eventually she went blind. But she would not leave Gangivecchio. She said she would die before she left Gangivecchio.

In 2012, when she was eighty-seven years old, Wanda stopped eating. Food is what gave her not just a way to live but also a reason to live. Food, literally and spiritually, had kept her alive. When she decided she did not want to keep going, she knew how to stop. She just pushed the food away. She removed her reason for living and she died.

MY MOTHER PICKED the Tornabenes' buccatini as her favorite pasta. It's mine as well.

When I was editing Wanda and Giovanna's first book, written with an American writer, Michelle Evans, who learned to speak fluent Italian just so she could do the book, the Tornabene women told me their secret to making great food: there should be no more than five main ingredients in any dish. This one just manages to squeeze itself in. Pasta is not an ingredient, in case you're wondering. As Giovanna would say, pasta is a member of the family.

I have made this pasta, over the years, perhaps more than any other. Recently, I cooked it standing alongside Giovanna in the kitchen at Gangivecchio's inn. The dish came out better when Giovanna was involved. I don't understand why that is, since I do it the exact same way at home. Perhaps her ingredients were better. Or perhaps she is actually something I'm not: a natural cook.

The same way I love wine but don't have the perfect palate, I don't have the magic cooking touch, either. I'm a good cook. I swear. I just don't have the magic. Giovanna has the same magic that Wanda had. She's a great cook and her Bucatini alla Palina, which is the real name of this dish as written in her first cookbook, tastes better than mine. But magic or no magic, you're going to like it.

I don't know why this dish works best with bucatini, but it definitely does. The pasta's thickness takes the sauce better than spaghetti and the length allows a bit more pasta on one's fork than, say, penne. But don't overanalyze. As Tom Stoppard once said about good writing: *It works because it works.*

INGREDIENTS:

Salt

1 small cauliflower, with florets cut into small pieces, approximately the same size

¾ cup olive oil

½ cup finely chopped shallots or onion

2 tablespoons minced anchovy fillets

¼ teaspoon powdered saffron

½ cup currants, soaked in hot water for 10 minutes and drained

¼ cup pine nuts

Freshly ground black pepper

1 pound bucatini, broken in half if need be

¾ cup toasted bread crumbs (see below)

DIRECTIONS:

Serves 6 as a first course or 4 as a main course

Bring 1½ quarts of water to a rolling boil in a large pot. Stir in 1 teaspoon salt and add the cauliflower. Cook at a slow boil for about 5 minutes. Using a slotted spoon, transfer the cauliflower to a bowl. Reserve 1 quart of the cooking water.

In a large saucepan, heat the olive oil and cook the shallots or onion and anchovies over medium heat for 5 minutes. Add ½ cup of the cauliflower water, saffron, currants, and pine nuts. Combine well and season to taste with salt and pepper. Simmer for 15 minutes. Add a bit more cauliflower water if you sense it's needed.

Meanwhile, combine 3 quarts of water and the reserved cauliflower cooking water and bring to a rolling boil in a large pot. Stir in 1½ tablespoons of salt and add the bucatini. Cook until al dente, or just tender, stirring often.

Reserve 1 cup of the pasta water, drain the pasta, and return it to the pot. Immediately add the sauce and gently toss. Add more pasta water, as needed, if a thinner sauce is preferred. Cover and let the pasta rest, off the heat, for 5 minutes. Toss again and serve with the toasted bread crumbs.

(AUTHOR'S NOTE: NOT TO KEEP LORDING IT OVER YOU, BUT WHEN I WAS MAK-ING THIS RECENTLY WITH GIOVANNA, SHE ADDED ONE FINAL INSTRUCTION AND I HIGHLY RECOMMEND IT. AFTER THE PASTA'S READY, PUT IT IN A BAKING DISH, WITH SOME OF THE BREAD CRUMBS—WHICH, IN HER LITTLE BOWL, SHE COMBINED WITH PARMESAN CHEESE, SO THEY WERE INSEPARABLE—AND PUT IT IN THE OVEN AT 400 DEGREES F FOR 10 MINUTES. MMMM-MMMM!)

BREAD CRUMBS FROM
LA CUCINA SICILIANA DI GANGIVECCHIO

Grate thoroughly dry two- or three-day-old firm Italian country bread—with or without the crust. (We always include the crust for the slight variety of colors it produces and, perhaps, a hint of extra flavor.)

One cup of bread crumbs is a sufficient amount for four servings of pasta. Heat 1½ tablespoons of olive oil in a frying pan and swirl it all over the bottom of the pan. Stir in the bread crumbs with a wooden spoon. Turn them repeatedly over medium-high heat, spreading them across the pan,

The final stage of the cauliflower, etc., pasta—about to go into the oven

until they blush a rosy golden-brown color. This takes only 2 to 3 minutes. (Double the amount of olive oil for 2 cups of bread crumbs.) Spread the toasted bread crumbs onto a plate, allowing them to cool, stirring once or twice before using them.

Serve toasted bread crumbs in a little bowl sitting on a saucer with a small spoon, or in a grated cheese dish with a spoon. Place the bowl on the table and pass it around so the bread crumbs can be sprinkled on top of the pasta as you would Parmesan cheese.

We have found that toasted bread crumbs keep well for only a day, so they must be made the same day they are used.

(AUTHOR'S NOTE: OR YOU CAN USE STORE-BOUGHT BREAD CRUMBS. NO, THEY'RE NOT AS GOOD, BUT THEY'RE FINE. AND IF YOU SERVE THEM IN A LITTLE BOWL WITH A SAUCER, PEOPLE WILL THINK THEY'RE BETTER THAN THEY ARE.)

TARTE TARTIN

I am a total Francophile. I have spent a lot of time in France, working, playing, living, eating, and drinking. Yes, yes, I know all the
flaws with the French—they think they're better than everyone
else, they think their culture is so superior, they lord their food and
wine over the rest of the world. Well . . . um . . . I tend to agree
with them. In quite a few ways, they are somewhat better than anyone else: they're stylish, educated, informed, involved, sophisticated, they drink the best wine, and when it comes to food, it has
always amazed me that almost any average, ordinary French person can throw a dinner party, organized at the last moment, and
provide a meal that is 100 percent satisfying. I'll admit the whole
capitulation-to-the-Nazis thing gives me pause. And so does the fact
that most of their culture—their architecture, literary output, and
music—over the past forty years is giggle-inducing. But, in one of
the greatest philosophical observations ever made, written by Billy
Wilder and spoken by Joe E. Brown at the end of *Some Like It Hot*:
"Nobody's perfect."

There is no question that my romantic view of the French has
been stoked by the books and films I've loved all my life: Fitzgerald writing about Paris in the twenties, the movies of Lelouch and
Truffaut. So yes, I tend to view French people and French life
through rosé-colored glasses.

I was once at the apartment of friends, Nikolas and Linda
Kaufman, who lived in Paris. She is American and he is very, very
French. Linda is an amazing home cook, one of the best I've ever
known, and she made a superb meal that night. But as is often the
case, the oohs and aahs came over the dessert, which was Nikolas's
domain. It was a tarte tatin and I was staggered by it. I told him I
would love to know how to make it. He responded that it was
quite easy. He said that there was a great French chef who wrote a
cookbook that contained the perfect tarte tatin recipe. He assured

me that if I followed it exactly, anyone who ate the tarte would swear it was made by an honest-to-goodness French person. He then led me back to their kitchen, pulled a cookbook from a shelf, and handed it to me. The great French dessert chef was Martha Stewart.

Martha Stewart's Tarte Tatin Recipe

INGREDIENTS:

5 to 6 medium apples, such as Braeburn

¾ cup granulated sugar

3 tablespoons water

4 tablespoons (½ stick) unsalted butter, cut into small pieces

1 lemon

½ recipe pâte brisée (recipe follows)

DIRECTIONS:

1. Peel, halve, and core apples. Set aside half of the apples. Quarter the remaining apples and transfer them to a large bowl. Squeeze a lemon over the apple slices and set aside.

2. Combine the sugar and water in a 9-inch cast-iron skillet. Bring the mixture to a boil over medium-high heat; immediately reduce the heat to medium and cook until the mixture begins to thicken and turn amber. Remove from the heat and stir in the butter.

3. Place the reserved apples in the center of the skillet. Decoratively arrange the remaining apple slices, cut side up, in the skillet around the reserved apples. Continue layering the slices until level with the top of the skillet. Cut any remaining apples into thick slices to fill in the gaps. If the fruit does not completely fill the pan, the tart will collapse when inverted.

4. Place the skillet over low heat and cook until the syrup thickens and is reduced by half, about 20 minutes. Do not let the syrup burn. Remove from the heat and let cool.

5. Preheat the oven to 375 degrees F. Line a baking sheet with parchment paper and set aside.

6. Roll out the pâte brisée to a 10- to 11-inch circle, about ⅛ inch thick; transfer to a baking sheet and chill until firm, about 30 minutes.

7. Place the pâte brisée over the apples and tuck the edges. Transfer the skillet to the prepared baking sheet; transfer the baking sheet to the oven, and bake until golden brown, about 35 minutes. Transfer to a wire rack and let cool for 15 to 20 minutes. Loosen the pastry from the skillet using a sharp knife. Place a rimmed platter over the skillet and quickly and carefully invert. Serve immediately.

RECIPE FOR PÂTE BRISÉE
(AUTHOR NOTE: FANCY WORD FOR PIE DOUGH)

Pâte brisée is the French version of classic pie or tart pastry. Pressing the dough into a disk rather than shaping it into a ball allows it to chill faster. This will also make the dough easier to roll out, and if you freeze it, it will thaw more quickly. (AUTHOR NOTE: I DON'T GET THIS WHOLE DISK VS. BALL THING. SMOOSHING IT INTO A BALL SEEMS TO WORK FINE.)

Makes 1 double-crust or 2 single-crust 9- to 10-inch pies

INGREDIENTS:

2½ cups all-purpose flour

1 teaspoon salt

1 teaspoon sugar

1 cup (2 sticks) unsalted butter, chilled and cut into small pieces

¼ to ½ cup ice water

DIRECTIONS:

1. In the bowl of a food processor, combine the flour, salt, and sugar. Add the butter and process until the mixture resembles coarse meal, up to 10 seconds.

2. With the machine running, add the ice water in a slow, steady stream through the feed tube. Pulse until the dough holds together without being wet or sticky; be careful not to process more than 30 seconds. To test, squeeze a small amount together: if it is crumbly, add more ice water, 1 tablespoon at a time.

3. Divide the dough into two equal balls. Flatten each ball into a disk and wrap in plastic. Transfer to the refrigerator and chill at least 1 hour. The dough may be stored, frozen, up to 1 month.

The last time I was at Gangivecchio I told Giovanna that I wanted to make a tarte tatin and she immediately said that we should prepare one together. I showed her the Martha Stewart recipe and she agreed to follow it. More or less. During the course of our baking, Giovanna showed me a few tricks to make Martha's recipe a bit simpler and even a bit better.

The following Sunday, she was having a luncheon for eleven people, so we went into the kitchen around ten o'clock and began to make the filling. Cooking with Giovanna is not a fully satisfying participatory experience. If you can keep up, great. If not, you better get the hell out of the way. Especially if ten guests are on their way to the *albergo*—hotel—for a meal. On many of these steps, I just got the hell out of the way.

We used her cast-iron skillet. It's not necessary, but it really does work best. If you don't have one, any frying pan will suffice. But you'll feel a lot more professional if you go for the cast-iron one.

We put the butter in, as Martha says to do, and melted it over low heat.

Next: time to core and peel the apples. Giovanna needed a large tarte, since so many guests were coming, so she decided we'd need fourteen apples. And this is where it started to get ugly. Giovanna has a lovely woman, Giuseppina, who helps her out from time to time, cleaning and cooking and waiting on tables. Giuseppina pushed half of the apples in my direction, she gave me a knife so I could start peeling, and she picked up her own knife at the same time. I did my best to visualize my knife skills class, got my confidence up, and began. I inserted the blade carefully under the skin, began slicing away, got maybe an inch of peel off. Satisfied that it looked good, I did the same thing again, and then again, carefully and precisely. When I finished with my first apple—cleanly peeled, looking very professional—I turned proudly to Giuseppina, who was staring at me with a confused expression. In addition to staring, she was also holding twelve perfectly peeled apples. Pride instantly evaporated and transformed into dismay. To make me feel worse, Giuseppina took the final apple and peeled it while I watched—she stuck the knife in and in less than five seconds the peel was off, with one continuous slice as if she were quickly unwrapping a small gift engulfed in tissue paper. Shaking her head, she handed me a different knife so I could start coring. But before I could move, Giovanna raced over, grabbed the knife out of my hand, and replaced it with an apple corer. She didn't have to say anything. I knew she didn't want to have to take me to the Gangi emergency room. Giuseppina stuck with her knife. I did manage to core more than one apple; I did four; she did the remaining ten. The process seemed easy enough when I started: an apple corer is inserted into the apple, directly over the core, and pushed straight down, then removed with the core in its grip. I'm not sure how I managed this, but the tip of my corer kept coming out the side of the apple instead of at the bottom. Each time, I had to insert the thing twice. All of the apples I cored looked as if some giant worm had managed to slither inside from a perfectly round third hole somewhere to the right or left of the core. My one tip on this step is:

although Giuseppina could peel and core her apples in the time it took the butter to melt in the pan, I suggest coring the apples *before* you turn the heat on under the butter.

Doing my best to ignore Giuseppina's look of bemusement, I moved over to the stove. The butter was just about melted. Giovanna said that she always added the sugar by eye. Her exact words were, "I have not a weight." So she mixed the sugar in and just did her best to make the correct distribution. The next instruction from her: "Don't touch." All you have to do at this point is let the sugar and butter caramelize over medium-low heat.

Next: Giovanna allowed me to squeeze a lemon over all the apples. This prevents them from turning brown and makes sure they're as beautiful as possible for the finished product. As Giovanna said about this process: "When you peel the apples, it's like the sun on your skin." The lemon works as sunblock on naked apples.

Remove from the heat when the mixture is caramelized. This is also done by sight: when the thing is bubbling and brown and looks kind of gooey, but before it's burnt, it's done.

Put the apples in the pan—and here is Giovanna's clever trick that differs just a bit from Martha's recipe: she cuts off the bottom of each apple so it's flat and she stands them all up in the pan rather than laying them down. First they go around the edge of the pan, forming a perfect circle, then you form another circle within that one, then another, until the pan is completely filled with upright apples. It's like a bunch of little apple soldiers standing at attention.

Turn the heat back on to medium. When the bottoms are brown, turn them over and brown the other side. Do it carefully, one apple at a time. When both sides are done—tops and bottoms should be nice and brown, but be careful not to burn them—remove the pan from the heat. The apples have to cool before you put the crust on or the crust will melt and sag into the mixture. That's a big no-no.

I get nervous making crust. Giovanna kept saying it was easy and for her it was. The crust has to be done in advance because it needs time in the refrigerator. You can do it two or three hours ahead of the filling, but it's probably better to do it the day before so you don't screw it up.

It's confession time: I didn't make the crust with Giovanna. She did it the day before and stuck it in the fridge. She wasn't worried about screwing it up, she was just too busy to do it the day of the luncheon. When I got home to New York, I did the Martha version just to make sure it's doable by people like me. It is. She's Martha Stewart—what did you expect?

When the apples are cool, cover them and the skillet with the dough, rolled out as Martha instructs. Then, in the oven it goes. Keep it in until the dough looks like a nice, brown crust.

COURTESY OF PETER GETHERS

Giovanna's Tarte Tatin. See what happens when you stand those apples up?

Take it out of the oven and let it cool. Eventually, you're going to turn the thing over so the crust is on the bottom. There are two ways this will fail: If the tarte isn't cool. Or if you don't have enough apples in the pan (think of them as columns holding up the crust when you do the inversion). You turn it over by putting a round platter tightly on top of the dough, take a deep breath, utter a quick prayer if you're a spiritually minded person, and flip. You should have a perfect tarte tatin: browned apples standing on a lovely crust.

Serve—whipped cream can be a nice addition—and take your bows.

NANCY SILVERTON'S CHALLAH AND BOULE

I have been lucky enough to work with several actual geniuses over the course of my career. Not just really smart people but geniuses. People who have a vision unlike others in their field; people who produce things on a different level from others in their field. I've edited books and written screenplays with Roman Polanski. Genius. I've edited books by Stephen Sondheim and worked with him on a show that I cocreated. Genius genius genius. I'd add Robert Hughes, whom I've also edited, to this short list. And if I can add the word "eccentric" before the word "genius," I would have to include Bill James of *Baseball Abstract* fame. And Nancy Silverton definitely belongs. She is a genius baker.

Because of my mother's friendship with Nancy, I've known her for ages and have watched her rise in the food world with considerable awe. She was the original pastry chef at Spago. The Los Angeles restaurant she ran with her then-husband Mark Peel, Campanile, was innovative and superb (never more so than when Nancy instituted Grilled Cheese Sandwich Night every Thursday). She now oversees three magnificent L.A. restaurants, all in the same building:

Osteria Mozza, Pizzeria Mozza, and Chi Spacca. But of all her successes, the one I found to be the most intoxicating was the La Brea Bakery, which she started in 1989. Nancy's bread baking is beyond compare. I still dream about the chocolate cherry bread she used to sell when the bakery was at the front of Campanile.

You can delve into the pleasures of Nancy writing about wheat and bread texture and all sorts of other doughy topics on your own if you read Nancy Silverton's *Breads from the La Brea Bakery*, which I believe is the best book ever written about bread and bread baking. But I'm only going to discuss her starter, as well as her boule and her challah, my mother's two favorite breads.

So about Nancy's starter: I find it absolutely impossible to make. Every time I've tried I've totally screwed it up. I consider this a major failing on my part.

Fortunately, good old Abby Levine, he of the successful salmon coulibiac preparation, really knows what he's doing when it comes to baking bread. He makes it all the time, although he tends to use the ingenious and almost fail-proof no-kneading method, perfected and made famous by Jim Lahey, founder of the Sullivan Street Bakery. For my mom, however, I told Abby that I needed serious support on the bread front and that I wanted to go old school and use Nancy's starter and recipes. Foolishly, he agreed.

You can make Lahey's great bread in one day. Start from scratch in the late afternoon and have it warm for dinner. Nancy's sourdough starter takes fourteen days! Two weeks! And that's before you even start baking. The upside to that is once your starter is grown, as long as you feed and maintain it, it will last the rest of your life. It's kind of like Audrey II in *Little Shop of Horrors* except not as funny and you eat it instead of vice versa.

DAY 1: GROWING THE CULTURE (FERMENTATION BEGINS)

(NOTE FROM ME, NOT NANCY: SO DO THE DRY SWEATS)

HAVE READY:

Cheesecloth

Scale

One 1-gallon plastic, ceramic, or glass container

Rubber spatula, optional

Plastic wrap, optional

Long-stemmed, instant-read cooking thermometer

Room thermometer

1 pound red or black grapes (pesticide free)

2 pounds (about 4 cups) lukewarm water, 78 degrees F

1 pound 3 ounces (about 3¾ cups) unbleached white bread flour

I am not going to go through every step of Nancy's recipe. For one thing, it wouldn't be fair to her to give away all her secrets. But I will tell you that, out of respect for Nancy, Abby and I followed the instructions perfectly. I was so excited during this process that I went out and purchased the same digital scale Abby uses and the same measuring cup, which has both American and European measurements on the side. I also bought the same digital thermometer, because I couldn't believe how cool it was to actually know that the water we were using was exactly seventy-eight degrees.

Working side by side in Abby's kitchen, we each made the starter. We did precisely the same thing at the same time. Then we sealed our starter into our gallon bowls at the exact same moment. I took my starter home. Abby kept his in his kitchen.

Nancy's book provides day-by-day instructions for the remaining thirteen days of growth. By the time I got home from Abby's, he had sent me an e-mail with those instructions, formatted to go into my e-calendar. So for the next many days, the first thing I did every day was check that calendar. Along with *8:00 a.m. gym* and *12:30 p.m. Lunch with President Obama* (okay, I made that one up, but I really do go to the gym) were such things as: *Day Two: You will notice a few tiny bubbles in the mixture, and the bag of grapes may have begun to inflate.* And: *Day Ten: Begin early today, because this is the day the culture becomes a starter—and the day you put it on a permanent feeding schedule.*

Abby and I swapped photos on our phones every day, sometimes several times a day. We compared the odors emanating from our respective one-gallon containers to the best of our descriptive abilities. We discussed the nature of bubbles in late-night texts. It was a little like starting a new romance, except, even on its best days, the object of my desire had a "distinct, unpleasant, alcohol-like smell" and "a yellowish liquid top layer." On Day Three, Abby was certain his had flopped. There were no bubbles and very little grape inflation. I, on the other hand, was brimming with confidence. My grapes were enormous—I boasted about them in several texts to Mr. Levine—and bubbles were aplenty. By Day Seven, my confidence had flagged substantially and Abby's was on the rise. By Day Eleven, I was certain I had bombed out big time. Abby was questioning his starter but hadn't lost all confidence.

On Day Fourteen, my starter was as dead as anything could possibly be. It was, as was I, a dismal failure. But Abby texted me a one-word verdict on his experiment: SUCCESS!

His starter lived to be baked another day.

On Day Fifteen, Abby sent me a photo of the boule he made from his starter. It was perfectly round and crusty and I could practically smell the enticing yeasty aroma through my phone.

Determined to succeed, I went back to the drawing board. I decided that it was the cab ride home from Abby's, with my starter in tow, that had done me in. So I began again, in my own kitchen. I got my pesticide-free grapes, used my scale with the precision of a Nobel Prize–winning scientist, and pointed my digital thermometer at seventy-eight-degree water. This starter was my Terra Nova Expedition to the South Pole and I was Roald Amundsen. That analogy turned out to be a bit flawed. I turned out to be Captain

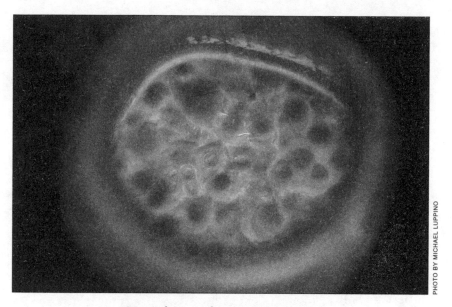

My pathetic and pretty gross starter

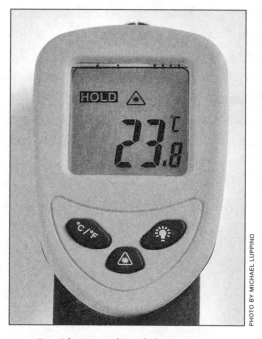

But I love my digital thermometer

Robert Scott rather than Amundsen. The South Pole won. On Day Eight, after watching it refuse to bubble, expand, smell wonderfully yeasty, or develop into anything remotely like what Nancy described in her book or what Abby had inserted into my daily calendar, I threw my starter in the garbage.

CHALLAH

Having proved a dismal failure with the starter, I was dependent on Abby to come through for my mom. I told her what we were doing—and was honest about our respective roles and successes and failures. Abby's boule was mom-worthy. But challah was a different challenge.

Even Nancy, who thinks that all baking is easy, says that challah is one of the hardest shapes to make. I accepted the fact that I was out of my league. Unwilling to face failure again, I went with Plan B: begging Abby to do it for me.

Remembering how deftly and artistically he'd added the fish shape to our coulibiac, I knew he could manage the challah's braid. I was correct: he made something that *looked* like the challah I used to get at Ratner's take-out counter. But the taste?

Solid.

Not incredible, but good.

He was more critical than I. But he could afford to be; he'd succeeded in making the damn thing and he could calculate what he needed to do next time to improve the texture, the design, and the taste.

Me?

I could only dream.

PART FIVE

AFTER-DINNER DRINK

My Mom's Favorite Dessert Wine:
Château d'Yquem

All sorrows are less with bread.

—Miguel de Cervantes Saavedra

And Château d'Yquem.

—Judy Gethers

CHAPTER NINE

_____

My intention, my sole goal while writing this book, was to cook with my mom, to share the breakfast and lunch menus with her as I went along, and to become proficient enough in the kitchen so I could make the dinner of her dreams. My plan for that dinner was to invite the people who were most important to her, and to whom she was important, and we would all share a dazzling sequence of marvelous dishes that had emotional resonance for many at the table. We would finish with a glass or two of d'Yquem. The evening would be spent enjoying and critiquing the food, as well as reminiscing about great meals, groundbreaking restaurants, and eccentric characters, laughing, crying, and celebrating a unique person and her extraordinary life.

I didn't quite make it.

On February 1, 2016, my mom died.

Her death, and the final several months of her life, could not have been much more perfect or inspiring. Strange to say, her final months were even great fun, for her and for those around her. I don't know how she made that happen but she did.

Many people assumed that my mother's post-stroke period, which lasted seven years, would be the ultimate testament to her strength and courage. But it wasn't. In some ways, it wasn't even close. Her final and most remarkable stage began on October 26, 2015.

That evening, I was invited to a screening of a documentary about Kareem Abdul-Jabbar. The theater was uptown, about sixty blocks from my apartment. After the movie, I went to dinner with friends, then took a taxi downtown. At 10:45, with the cab two blocks from my apartment, my cell phone rang. It was Carla, the woman who runs SelectCare. She told me that my mother had had some tests done earlier that day and that the lab just called; they thought the results of the tests warranted a call at this late hour. My mother's INR (internal normalized ratio) count—it measures degrees of anticoagulation—was insanely high. Normal was one or two. Three was high. My mother's count was fourteen. I asked Carla what this meant and she said that if the results were accurate, my mom was in serious danger of internal bleeding, which would be life threatening. She wanted my permission for the SelectCare aide to take my mom to the hospital immediately so the test could be re-administered. If the initial results were incorrect, then my mom would just come right home. If they were true, the hospital could treat it with medication and return the INR count to normal.

The cab pulled up in front of my apartment and I told Carla that I needed five minutes to think. I said I'd call her back.

I went upstairs and quickly fed my cats. Before I let Mitch gobble down his delicious bowl of Minced Turducken, however, I picked him up and hugged him tightly to my chest and cheek. Harper did not love being held and squeezed—she was much more of a cuddler, and then only at moments of her choosing. Mitchum was always happy to let me do whatever I wanted with him, so now I used him for fifteen seconds of much-needed comfort.

I needed those five minutes to think because, just as my father had done twenty-six years earlier, my mom had made one thing very clear to me: she did not want to die in the hospital.

About two years earlier, she'd fallen and broken her pelvis. She was rushed to the emergency room, where Dr. Lachs met us. He explained that my mother had suffered the most painful injury imaginable. But my mom refused to acknowledge the pain because she knew that if she did, she'd have to stay in the hospital. I had a choice: 1) force her to stay against her wishes; the surgeons weren't going to operate on someone so fragile but she might get some form of treatment and would probably spend another night in the hallway of the ER, or 2) get her the hell out of there and hope that she could survive and recuperate at home. I decided my mom was going home. I told her what was happening, promised she'd be leaving as soon as I could get an ambulance, and then, knowing that her pain tolerance was at a superhuman level, I said, "Okay, you're going home no matter what the real answer is, but let me put it to you this way. I know you keep saying that *you're* not in pain, but if it was me, would *I* be in pain?" She managed a thin smile and said, "Oh yes."

She went home, refused to even take her pain meds, and, once again, despite what the doctors told me would happen, she returned to normal in six weeks.

After that little episode, I knew that the only way she was ever going to the hospital at this stage of her life was if the choice was taken out of her hands.

That night in October, the choice was removed from both of our hands. As I paced in my apartment and wondered what the right thing to do was—get her to the hospital or let her stay at home and risk the likelihood that she would start bleeding and die—my cell rang again. It was Carla. My mother had started bleeding profusely from her anus. An ambulance was already rushing her to Lenox Hill Hospital.

I was back uptown by eleven thirty p.m. and stayed with my mom until four a.m. The first doctor who came by to see my mother

was a young woman—she looked to be about fourteen to me—
with tattoos and body piercings. I explained that I didn't want any
extreme measures performed that would keep my mother alive: no
machines, no invasive treatment. Expecting an argument, I got
none. The doctor said that she understood. I also said that if my
mother was dying, I did not want her dying in Lenox Hill. I wanted
her home. Again, the doctor said she understood. She calmly
explained that all they were going to do was give my mom an intra-
venous injection to try to get her INR level down to normal. By
that point, it was at eighteen.

I agreed to that treatment.

For the next few hours, my mom was in and out of consciousness. She seemed shriveled, small, and so weak, I imagined that a
deep exhalation of breath blown in her direction would knock her
out of bed. She was having excruciating abdominal pain—even my
mom had acknowledged the severity—and she seemed resigned, as
if she knew her time had come. Although I suspected she could hear
me and was only feigning sleep when I tried to speak to her two or
three times, she did not respond or acknowledge my presence in
any way.

At three a.m., she opened her eyes and spoke to me for the first
time. She said, "You look exhausted. You should go home."

I laughed and said I was staying. Then she said, "I want to go
home."

I said I knew she did. Then I carefully explained exactly what
was happening. I told her they had to lower her INR count, which
would take a few hours. As soon as that was done, I'd get her out
of there. I promised. No matter what. She nodded and went back
to sleep.

At four in the morning, I went home, managed a fitful three
hours of sleep, and went back to the hospital. Nothing had changed.

The head of palliative care came over and said that, in her opinion, my mother did not need curing, she needed relief from pain
and suffering. I told her that it wasn't just what my mom needed,

it's what she wanted. It's what I wanted for her as well. I was amazed that doctors, who for years had been trained to keep patients alive at any cost, were now committed to such a humane and dignified approach to the end of life.

During the night, the hospital had done an MRI. A new doctor appeared and told me that they'd found a large mass in my mother's stomach that was most likely cancer and that was most likely causing her intense pain.

After huddling with various doctors and surgeons, I made my decision: my mom was going home. The consensus was that she had just a short time to live, anywhere from a day or two to another week. She would go back to her beloved apartment, have home hospice care. Along with a decent supply of morphine and a hospice nurse, we would wait for the end. It was now about one in the afternoon on October 27.

My mother had not spoken or stirred since I'd returned to the hospital nearly five hours earlier. Now I went over to her, not sure if she could hear me or not, and said, "Mom, we're getting you out of here. You'll be home in about an hour."

My mom opened her eyes, lifted her head up, smiled brightly, and said, "Really?"

I laughed. Even the doctor who was standing nearby laughed. "Really," I told her.

She was home and in bed by two thirty. The hospice nurse arrived a short while later. My mother's wonderful aides—Janet, Jennifer, and Karlene—were still going to be there to take care of my mom, too. Karlene had been on duty when my mom was rushed to the hospital; she spent the night in the ER, staying even when I went home at four in the morning. At six a.m. she was supposed to be replaced by Janet, but when I got back there at seven thirty or so, they were both there. Karlene wouldn't leave. I knew my mom would want these women, whom she'd come to love and who had come to love her, to be nearby.

The hospice nurse, kindly but somewhat long-winded, explained to me what would happen: My mom didn't have much time. Because of the huge mass in her stomach, she would not be able to eat anything but ice chips. She would slowly—or possibly not so slowly—fade away. It would be peaceful.

I said that I understood and went into my mom's room. I wanted to talk to her but I also wanted to escape the nurse's ongoing lecture that wasn't comforting me quite as much as it was driving me crazy. My mom was awake, if a bit disoriented.

"Why am I here?" she asked.

At first I didn't understand her question. Eventually I realized she meant: why was she at home instead of in the hospital.

I told her the truth. I said it was because she'd made me promise she wouldn't die in the hospital. This was the endgame, I explained. And she would spend her remaining time, however long that would be, in her own room, in her own bed, in her own home. I said we were not going to do anything to try to revive her, if that situation came up. And I told her she was never, ever going back to the hospital, no matter what. She didn't say anything at first, so I took her hand and said, "Is that okay? Did I make the right choice?"

And she said: "That's wonderful."

I went into my mom's living room now to call Eric and tell him what had happened. He called Morgan to tell him the news. I also spoke to Morgan and said the same thing I'd explained to his father: I could not tell how long Mom/Grandma would last. It might be a day; it might be a week. But if they wanted to see her, they'd better come soon.

Morgan, now in his mid-twenties and recently married, flew to New York two days later. My mom was very weak, seemingly not aware of much that was going on, or at least not very responsive. But when Morgan and his wife, Stephanie, walked into her room, she certainly knew they were there and was extremely happy about it. Morgan and Stephanie stayed the weekend. On their last night in New York, they came to my apartment for dinner. It was the nicest few hours I'd ever spent with them. Morgan completely let down his guard—something that's very difficult for him—and talked a lot about his grandmother, although tears kept interrupting his conversation. He said that my mom had been the one person who had always loved him unconditionally. He said that she was his rock. He said that he could always call her whenever he felt bad. Or just call her whenever he felt good. He said he loved sharing things with her. Stephanie said that Morgan wasn't prepared for my mom to die. Morgan agreed—he didn't know if he could deal with what was about to happen. I said that he could, that it's what happens in life. I told him he was lucky because he was now happily married and that Stephanie would now become his rock. That's the way it works. I told him that my mother's biggest regret was that she hadn't been well enough to go to their wedding in Hawaii, but she had loved watching the videos they'd sent her and looking at the photos. Every time I went to my mom's apartment, she had their wedding photo in plain view, usually on her dinner table, so she could look at it when she ate. Now they both cried. And the next morning they went up to my mother's apartment, said good-bye to her, and left for the airport.

Eric came the day Morgan and Stephanie flew back to L.A. and he stayed a week. Even though her responses were still weak and she was barely able to speak, my mom was clearly very happy he was there.

My relationship with my brother had changed so much over the years. We'd gone through periods of great closeness, experienced a lot of anger on both sides, and had settled into a kind of distant wariness. He and I had dinner one night, the first time we'd done that in quite a while; my cousin Beth came, too, but it was still the most intimate we'd been in recent memory. He told a few stories about our dad and our mom, tales from the past. I thought he had rewritten history to form the picture he wanted to keep in his mind. But I didn't say anything. I didn't really care if his memories were real or not. I cared only that they gave him whatever comfort he could take from them.

During my brother's stay in New York, my mom was so frail, so weak. Neither of us thought she could last much longer. Then, on Eric's last night before he was returning to France, I came up to my mom's apartment with take-out Chinese food. It was for him and for my mom's nurses; my mom was not eating much other than ice chips, to keep her hydrated, and an occasional spoonful of ice cream. Eric took the Chinese food into our mom's room to eat it there. Within seconds, my mom lifted her head and said, "That smells good."

A bit incredulous, I asked, "You want some?"

Without hesitation, she said yes.

I asked the hospice nurse if it was okay. Confused, she said, "They told me she wouldn't eat."

"Well, can it hurt her?" I said.

"I don't see how, if she wants it," was the answer.

So I prepared a plate of Chinese food, gave it to my mom, and watched her eat an egg roll, sesame noodles, and moo shoo pork.

"I thought she had this big blockage," I said to Jennifer, one of my mother's beloved aides, who came in to watch my mom eat.

"What can I say?" was Jennifer's response. "Your mother's not like regular people."

Three or four days after Eric left, I called my mom's apartment to talk to her aide—it was Janet that day—and I asked how my mom was. Janet said she'd gotten out of bed.

"What do you mean 'out of bed'?"

"She spent a couple of hours in her wheelchair," Janet told me. "She was getting restless."

"They told me she wouldn't move again."

"It's your mom," Janet said. "Nobody knows what she'll do."

The next day, when I went to the apartment, my mom was back sitting in her wheelchair, in her bedroom. Janet had washed my mother's hair and brushed it and she looked . . . well . . . like she always looked. She had on lipstick and was wearing her favorite earrings and necklace. She didn't look sick.

I asked my mom if she'd been to the living room and she shook her head. Janet said no, she wasn't quite ready for that yet. My mother glanced at her and frowned.

The next day she went to the living room in her wheelchair.

The day after that she ate breakfast at her dining table.

The third day, I called in the afternoon and Janet told me that she and my mom had gone for a walk.

"Where?" I said.

"Outside," Janet told me. "Do you want to talk to her?"

"She can talk on the phone?"

"Oh yes."

I heard Janet ask my mother if she wanted her to hold the phone while my mom spoke to me and I heard my mom say, clear as day, "No, I can do it myself."

The next thing I knew, my mother was saying, "Hello." I asked her how she was feeling and she said, "Fine," as if she was surprised I'd even ask such a thing.

Over the next week, instead of fading, she seemed to grow stronger every day. Wolfgang came to New York and went up to see her. He brought her food and stayed for two hours. My mother was thrilled. Beyond thrilled.

"Do you know how busy he is? He was here for two hours!"

She said he had reminisced about Ma Maison and their trips with Maida Heatter and cooking together and, just like the old days, they had a personal, private talk. He filled her in on his life. She could not have been happier.

At first she didn't want anyone else to see her. But as she started feeling better, she began to welcome company. My cousin Jon went up a couple of times. So did other cousins. Beth visited every day; dutifully and happily, she was there to provide anything my mom wanted or needed. Barbara Lazaroff, Wolf's ex-wife, came to New York every few weeks and always made a point of spending time with my mother. She would bring gourmet chocolates and other goodies and my mom would invariably be a bit giddy after

Barbara left. My old buddy Paul and his wife, Laurie, went to the apartment several times and so did their kids (their children, Ben and Sara, always called my mom "Grandma" and my mom thought of them as her own grandchildren, too). Laurie went up alone one day and showed my mom pictures of the wedding dress that Ben's bride-to-be, Carolyn, had picked out. She said that my mom glowed. When I asked my mother about it, she said, "She's going to be so beautiful." When I said that she'd be able to judge for herself when September rolled around, my mom just said, "We'll see."

I went to see her almost every day. And I called at least once a day to either talk to my mom—whose speech actually seemed better than it had been in years—or to one of the aides. Janet, Jennifer, and Karlene were all overjoyed at the turn of events. But none of them seemed surprised.

The hospice nurse, however, was in a state of disbelief. She said to me, "I've never seen anything like this. Your mother is incredible."

Janis's group e-mails had been going out yet again, updating the throngs on my mom's condition. After telling everyone that my mom was on the verge of death, the e-mails now seemed as if they had been made up.

- "Judy went out for a walk today. And she ate two bowls of ice cream."

- "She has yet to take any morphine. She says she's in no pain."

- "Judy is eating full meals. Today she had pancakes and bacon for breakfast."

Her appetite hadn't just returned. It returned with a ferocity even I had trouble accepting. I called one day and when I asked to speak to her, Janet couldn't stop laughing.

"What's going on?" I said. "What's so funny?"

"We just got back from lunch."

"What do you mean?"

"Your mother insisted we go to a restaurant. The three of us went." The third person was the hospice nurse.

"That's impossible."

"I have photos," Janet said. "But that's not the most amazing part."

"It isn't?"

"No," she said. "Ask me what your mother ate."

"Okay. What did she eat?"

"A pastrami sandwich. With mustard. And pickles."

"How much did she eat?" I asked.

"Exactly what she usually eats: half a sandwich. And she insisted on bringing the other half home."

I spoke to my mother's doctor, Mark Lachs. He told me that the blockage had obviously disappeared.

"Does cancer just disappear?" I asked.

"It does not," he said. And then he said, "You do understand that what your mother's doing is actually impossible."

When I went up to see my mom the next day, I said to her, "You know, you have to be the only person in history who ever went out with her hospice nurse to get a pastrami sandwich."

She laughed.

And the next day she came to our traditional Thanksgiving Dinner. It was usually held at Kathleen and Dominick's, but this year, thanks to a gas leak and extensive renovation to their building, we had to switch the venue to my apartment.

I had suggested the idea to my mother a few days earlier.

"You're doing so well," I said. "If you're feeling strong on Thursday, I'll send a car to pick you up and you should come for an hour or two. And we won't tell anybody. You just show up—people will be shocked."

Over the previous few weeks, many of my friends had gone over to my mom's to say their good-byes. No one expected to see her at Thanksgiving. Hell, no one expected her to be *alive* for Thanksgiving. But even at her lowest ebb, my mom never lost her sense of humor. Kathleen and Dominick came over to see her one day. My mother was very weak and not particularly responsive. She was having great difficulty talking so Kathleen prattled on, taking the onus off my mom. She told my mom how much she loved my mother's shirt: she'd always loved that type of shirt, she could never find one for herself, it looked so good on my mom. My mother just smiled weakly and none of us were sure she was really listening. But when Kathleen and Dominick got up to leave, my mom put her hand out to stop Kathleen. With her good left hand, she grabbed her own shirt and said, "Relax, it's yours. I'll leave it to you."

Knowing that everyone thought she was done for, when I said she should make a guest appearance for the turkey dinner, she said, "I'm there."

At three p.m. on November 26, 2015, she got wheeled into my living room, all dolled up and grinning like a madwoman. She got a standing ovation—whistles, cheers, the whole shebang.

Laurie Eagle, who was like a daughter to my mom, was especially surprised to see her. She had called my mother that morning to say how sad she was that she wouldn't see her at dinner.

"I'm sad, too," my mom had said.

When Laurie saw her arrive for the meal a few hours later, she said to my mom, "You stinker! How could you do that to me?"

My mother said, "It was easy."

I had rarely seen her quite so proud of herself.

OVER THE NEXT four months, my mom and I had many long talks. All of them were sweet, interesting, inspiring, and truly funny—not a day went by that she didn't make me laugh. We discussed my dad. And Eric and Morgan. Things that had happened in the past—she never got tired of telling me how she refused to forgive my father's father for his slight when Eric was born. She finally told me why, when she moved back to New York after my dad died, she wouldn't live downtown. It was because her family lived downtown and she didn't want to be too close. Moving three thousand miles away from them was what had enabled her to find her confidence and her real identity. Even in her seventies, she still felt that, as the baby in the family, she would be overpowered by her siblings. You are what you start out as, I suppose. Or, more accurately, no matter your age, you too often run the risk of being what your family thinks you once were.

She talked about her many friendships—she reveled in all of them—but she saw everyone with a remarkably clear eye. At this point in her life, she saw everything with a clear eye. She was impossible to con or bullshit. Her brain was working 100 percent, even as her body was failing.

Sometimes we'd argue about something trivial. I'd say, "You told me that was happening on Tuesday" and she'd go, "I said Monday." We'd go back and forth and then suddenly something would spark my memory and I'd go, "Umm . . . I think you're right. I think you did tell me it was Monday." And she'd go, "Of course I did. I don't forget."

Many of our conversations were about death and her feelings about what was happening to her. She wanted to be cremated. She wanted certain people to get specific possessions. She wanted me to stop spending so much time taking care of her problems. As always, she was more concerned with others than she was with herself. I have never felt closer to my mother than during these conversations.

"Are you afraid?" I asked her once.

"No," she said.

"Really? Really and truly?"

"No," she said again. "I'm really not. I'm tired. I'm ready. I've had a good life."

In mid-January she began to fade. She was getting out of bed less frequently, no longer eager to go outside. And she was barely eating. She was back to milk shakes and root beer floats. I asked if she remembered how much my dad loved root beer; she just smiled and nodded.

On the morning of January 30, I rushed up to her apartment because Janet had phoned to tell me that my mom was up and having a full breakfast. Sure enough, when I got uptown, she was dressed to the nines, including her favorite earrings, sitting at the breakfast table eating eggs and toast. And happy about it.

When I said to her, "Mom, you are unbelievable," she glanced at me as if she didn't understand what all the fuss was about. Of course she was dressed and having breakfast. What else was she supposed to be doing?

By the time I left, though, an hour later, she was back in bed, exhausted. And I think the reality of her exhaustion hit her head-on.

"It's too hard now," she said.

"You've told me that before, you know, but it wasn't."

"It is now," she said. "It's very hard."

When I left a few minutes later, she was asleep.

On January 31 she didn't wake up when I went to see her. I sat by her bedside for a while, then took her hand. It was bony and weighed almost nothing; her fingers and palm had remarkably little flesh. She didn't react to my presence. I couldn't tell if she knew I was touching her.

"Mom," I said, "you don't have to keep fighting. You're unbelievably strong but it's okay to relax. You don't have to keep fighting for anyone's sake. It's okay if you let go. It's okay if it's too hard. I won't mind. No one's going to mind."

I don't know if she heard me. I don't think she did. But I was glad I'd said it.

The next morning, my phone rang at seven thirty. It woke me up although I was not in a deep sleep. It was Jennifer, the aide who'd been with my mom the longest and who is one of the gentlest souls I've ever encountered.

"I gave your mom a hot chocolate," she began. "That's her favorite and I knew that's what she wanted. She took three sips, then she let me know she'd had enough. I took the cup; she closed her eyes and died."

I took a few minutes to shower and dress and let the news sink in—to memorialize the moment, in a way—then called Janis to tell her what had happened and went uptown to my mom's apartment. I called Eric from the taxi. We both cried, separated by several thousand miles and a complicated past but connected by loss and grief. I also called Morgan. I did my best to be stoic but his sobs got my tears flowing again.

Janet, even though she was not scheduled to work, arrived at the apartment a few minutes after I did. I watched while she and Jennifer went into my mother's room and spoke to her. They both said they loved her and told her they knew she was in a better place. The words were lovely, but I did not think she was in a better place. I thought she'd just left a pretty great place. It was a place she cherished and that place now had a huge void.

The craziest thing happened that morning. My mother had many beautiful plants that flourished on the windowsills of her living room and dining room. The plants brought her a lot of pleasure and she and her aides tended to them with great care. Her favorite plant was a beautiful cactus that she kept in the living room, near the spot where she usually sat. The cactus had thrived for years, healthy and strong. Minutes after my mom died, Jennifer walked into the living room and saw that half of the cactus had suddenly drooped. One half was defiantly erect but the other had collapsed as if in mortal sadness.

DYING ON FEBRUARY 1 was the final considerate act of my mother's life. I had made a pledge to myself to have a dry January. I hadn't had a drink the entire month. But the night she died, Paul and Laurie and Kathleen and Dominick and Abby and Micheline and Janis convinced me that we should go out to dinner and get really drunk. Which I did.

Condolences began to pour in. People knew how close my mother and I had been and everyone was concerned that I would be overwhelmed by grief. The odd thing was, it was impossible to really grieve for my mom. Or be devastated by her death. She was ninety-three years old and she lived a life that was filled with all the things a life should be filled with. The only grief comes from the fact that the world is now a lesser place than it was when she was here.

What I was unprepared for, in some ways, was the amount of work that came in the aftermath of her death. Over the next few weeks and months, I made the arrangements for her cremation, canceled credit cards and store accounts and magazine subscriptions, began the process of selling her apartment—after spending many weeks with Janis, Beth, and others doing our best to clean it up and figure out what to do with the six food processors and four coffeemakers and the hundreds of pots and pans and the fishing rod in the hall closet. As part of this workload, I had possibly the most bizarre conversation I've ever had with my mother's mobile phone service provider. I called to pay her final bill and to cancel the account—and learned that I didn't have the authority to cancel the account. I asked who did have that authority and was told: the account holder. I explained that the account holder was dead but that didn't seem to solve the problem—if my dead mother didn't call them to say that she was dead, and thus didn't need phone service anymore, they'd keep her service active and they'd keep on sending monthly bills. I'm not kidding when I say that it took several conversations with various levels of management people before we worked out a deal: I would send them a copy of my mother's official death certificate along with my power of attorney document and they would let me cancel my mom's cell phone.

That was one more detail: I had to get fifteen copies of the death certificate because other companies and organizations also made it extremely difficult to use death as an excuse to cancel their services.

I waited a few months after her death to plan my mother's memorial. I needed a bit of emotional separation. Also, I knew that people would come from far and wide and I wanted to make sure everyone had enough preparation time.

The memorial became the special dinner I had been planning to prepare for her.

Her fantasy dinner with all her friends and loved ones.

We had the memorial feast at Jean-Paul and Bill's apartment, the site of her surprise parties and ninetieth birthday bash. It seemed only fitting.

Sixty people came. The youngest was thirteen, the oldest was eighty-six. Family, friends, people from the food world—everyone who came had loved my mom and everyone had, in some profound way, been affected by her.

I brought over several hundred photographs of my mother—with my dad, on exotic trips, eating and drinking with friends and family members, young and at camp, elderly in her wheelchair. I told everyone to take any photo that struck an emotional chord with them.

The menu for the memorial meal was all the food that my mother had selected for her perfect dinner. I made tournedos of beef with truffle cream sauce for the throngs. I also cooked a massive amount of the Gangivecchio cauliflower pasta. Cooking pasta sauce for sixty took almost all day—not being a professional chef, I don't own "Land of the Giant"–size pots and pans so I had to prepare the identical sauce three separate times. JP offered to make individual salmon coulibiacs but asked if he could use his own recipe (which substituted puff pastry for brioche crust and also used a tomato sauce) instead of Wolf's. I agreed and it was delicious. He also made the fava bean puree and, even using pre-shelled beans, became almost as frustrated by the dish as I had been nearly thirty years earlier. A couple of hours before the celebration began, he said these exact words: "I am never making this fucking thing again!" Happily, JP's third culinary contribution came off without a hitch: individual tartes tatin that were as delicious as they were beautiful.

Expedience required that I purchase the boule and challah rather than bake them myself (or bribe Abby to bake them). But I did hold up one of the two challahs that Abby and I had made a few nights prior to the memorial, allowing everyone to admire its beauty before setting it aside, since there wasn't enough for everyone.

We served white and red Burgundies and vodka martinis. During my toast—I can't quite bring myself to call it a eulogy—I did my best not to burst out sobbing. Whenever I got too choked up to continue speaking, I reached down for my glass and took a sip to wet my whistle and steady my nerves. The next day, talking to Janis, I congratulated myself on my composure. She said, "Well, you did have to stop and take a drink every three or four sentences. You must have gone through six big glasses of water."

"Water?" I said. "That wasn't water. Those were martinis."

I needed every sip, too.

Many people spoke that night. They didn't just talk about how much they liked or loved my mom. They talked about how extraordinary she was, about how strong she was, about what they learned from her. Jennifer, her aide, wrote a lovely speech that she delivered beautifully, bringing the entire group to tears. Janet, the other aide closest to my mom, then spoke extemporaneously for several minutes. Her toast was eloquent and precise and perfectly captured my mother's remarkable dignity.

The evening ended with fifteen or so people sitting around Bill and JP's dining table, surrounded by the remaining photos I'd brought, sipping Château d'Yquem, my mother's favorite libation. We were still laughing and crying, but everyone felt a bit exhausted by the emotion that had been expended over the course of the night. And then, around ten fifteen, something extraordinary happened.

JP and Bill's apartment is on Central Park West and it features a glorious view of the park. Apparently, there was a free concert in the park that night. And when the concert ended, fireworks went off. Not just one or two fireworks: this was the Fourth of July times ten. For half an hour the sky was filled with explosions of color. After a few minutes, someone turned to me and said, "Oh my God, did you *arrange* this?" I would have liked to take credit but I couldn't. Nor did I take the fireworks as any kind of spiritual sign. I took them for exactly what they were: a happy coincidence and proof that the world outside the apartment had a reason to celebrate. The fireworks were not celebrating *a* life, as we were within the apartment; they were celebrating life itself.

THIS IS WHAT I spoke about, in between gulps of martinis, in the toast I made at my mother's memorial:

I learned a lot about my mom, while cooking for her and learning to prepare the foods she loved, and talking to her about her life. I learned a lot about her after she died, too.

At her ninety-second birthday party, she told me that she'd saved all of the love letters my dad had written to her when he was in college, in the army during World War II, and after the army, when he was touring the country as a member of a theater company. She told me I should burn them without reading them. I nodded politely and said, "That isn't happening, Mom." She said, "I'm serious." And I said, "So am I. If you don't burn them yourself, I'm reading them." Not long before she died, she brought the subject up again. "Burn them and don't read them," she told me. "There is zero chance of that happening," I said. "It's my past, too." She sighed and reluctantly acquiesced.

She didn't destroy those letters. She said that she couldn't. At her memorial, I spoke a bit about the insights I'd gotten from them, insights into both of my parents, things I'd learned after my mom died:

My dad only went to one year of college at the University of Iowa (I knew he'd gone there but I never knew it was only for one year).

My mother graduated summa cum laude from NYU. My entire life I knew two things about my mom's education: that she'd spent some time at Beaver College in Pennsylvania (and as a thirteen-year-old boy, oh my God, did I love saying that my mom went to Beaver College) and that she spent some time at NYU after that. My mom never discussed her academic superiority because she never wanted to overshadow my dad. Wow.

My parents were . . . um . . . having sex before they were married. This is in the early 1940s. Kind of a big deal back then.

My dad's letters to her were extremely bawdy. Sometimes flat-out dirty. A lot of sexual references. When he knew he was coming home from the army, after three years away, he told her that their reunion might be difficult. He said they'd need a period of read-justment, which he was certain would be brief, and that their relationship would be better than ever. Then he referred to a "marriage manual" that he'd sent to her. He said that in their years apart he'd come to realize just how important a physical relationship was between husband and wife and he hoped she'd read the manual. He promised her that they'd study it together when he got home. By "study," it was very clear that what he really meant was: "We'll put it to good use."

My dad had a gambling problem when he was young. He lost way too much money playing poker in the army and my mother was constantly getting angry at him.

Some members of my mother's family put pressure on my mom not to get married. They thought she was too young and my dad's career as an actor might not be a stable one. My dad bulled right over them, told my mom that she was strong enough to pull away from their restraints. Clearly he was correct.

He called her "Cook" as in "Dear Cook." At first I thought that she had begun cooking even then, but no, after pouring through many more letters, I realized it was short for his term of endearment, "Cookie." He also called her Darling, Sugarbunch, Sugarpie, and Honeybabe. The only other person I ever heard use the word "honeybabe" was Bob Dylan.

When he was broke, he dreamed of buying her diamonds and fancy clothes. He demanded that she want those for herself because he wanted to provide them for her.

They loved each other for their entire lives, almost from the moment they met. My mom saved every Valentine's Day card he had given her, up until the last one he gave her before he died. All of them were funny and sweet and affectionate and, most of all, wildly romantic.

After my mother's death, I learned things from sources other than my dad's letters as well as from my own observations.

My mom was a hoarder. She didn't just keep everything husband-related, she kept every Mother's Day card Eric and I had sent her since we were young, and every letter I'd written to her from college and beyond. She saved plastic bags and empty jars and gallons of Purell antiseptic hand cream.

She had an insane amount of grandson-related things: report cards, hundreds of photos of Morgan in all stages of his life, even poems he wrote when he was five.

My mother kept all of her press clippings about her books and her cooking school and various interviews she'd given over the years. She also kept track of Wolf's career via dozens of press clippings. She had hundreds of recipes, many scribbled in her own hand, some saved in books, some just cut out from newspapers and magazines.

She had more kitchen equipment than any restaurant imaginable. I had always said that when I finished writing this book I'd buy myself a perfect set of knives. I didn't have to. The professional set of knives from my mother's kitchen are now proudly displayed and gleaming in my kitchen.

My mother showed her love for food by the things she left behind. But more than that, she proved her love for her family.

HERE'S WHAT I learned from cooking with my mother and talking to her and absorbing her wisdom. Here is what I learned in my search to find meaning in my mother's kitchen:

Food is not a be-all and end-all. It does not provide meaning, though it does provide pleasure. Nothing that provides pleasure can do so in a vacuum. It is sharing our pleasure that provides *real* pleasure.

The patience I learned from cooking all the recipes in this book will stand me in good stead for the rest of my life. But so will the ability to say "fuck it" to and about anyone or anything that demands *too* much patience. Plunging forward has its value, too. Instinctive behavior may not be neat and it may not always end happily, but it can lead to a delicious result.

Fear has no place in or out of the kitchen.

Neither does anger. You cannot get angry when something fails to bake, broil, or coalesce properly. Anger does not ever work when putting things together. It only works as *motivation* to try to put something together. Once anger has done its job, you have to let it go.

Love can fade. Families can break apart. Nothing you do in the kitchen can really alter that.

But love can also last. Friends and families and lovers can stay tied forever. When they do, they provide strength and comfort. And food can be used to celebrate and cement love and family, strength and comfort. It did for my mother. It does now for me.

The most wondrous thing I learned is that cooking can give us hope. Hope that by combining different ingredients we can somehow create something newer and better. Something magical. It gives us hope that if we try again, maybe we'll get it right.

I am definitely going to prepare Nancy Silverton's bread starter again. And I will make that perfect challah. I really will.

No one lives forever, of course. But I had almost come to believe that my mother might.

I have said this to many people since she died: There is a huge void and I am terribly sad. But her death was not tragic. It wasn't even depressing.

My mother died knowing who she was and she was comfortable with that knowledge. She went out on her own terms. In her own bed. Steps away from her own kitchen.

Drinking a hot chocolate.

I'll take it right now.

We all should.

CHÂTEAU D'YQUEM

Two of my closest friends, Len and Louise Riggio, decided they wanted to start the new millennium with an unforgettable night, so for New Year's Eve 1999 they rented the entire Four Seasons restaurant, at the time perhaps the most famous restaurant in New York. And they didn't just invite their own friends. They realized this was a day and a night—and a new century—when people should be with their loved ones. So they told each of their close friends that they would have their own table and could invite whoever they wanted to sit with them. Janis and I were lucky enough to qualify, and we invited those nearest and dearest to our hearts to celebrate with us. My mom, of course, made the cut.

She hobbled in on crutches—she had hurt her foot—and made her way to our table. In front of each place setting was a festive menu that listed the meal, course by course. As my mom perused the menu, her eyes lit up. The final item listed was Château d'Yquem.

Yquem is, without question, the greatest dessert wine on the planet. A Sauternes from the southern region of Bordeaux, in 1855 it was designated a Premier Cru Supérieur—Superior First Growth—acknowledging its superiority over all other wines of this type. It is the only Sauternes so honored. I am hardly an expert, but Yquem is far more complex than any sweet wine I have ever tasted. A sip seems to spread flavor from head to toe, filling the entire body with a combination of sweetness and depth that no other wine can achieve.

In the 1960s and early '70s, not too many people were imbibing Yquem, but my dad loved it and had cases of the stuff, at a cost of ten dollars a bottle. Today, you can probably find a bottle for seven or eight hundred dollars, although top vintages go for way more than that. I've seen bottles on sale for $15,000 and more. That's for *one* bottle. In 2011, at an auction, a bottle of 1811 Yquem was sold for $117,000! My mother, who was not a big drinker in those days, always went into raptures when sipping it. And her appreciation for Yquem never flagged, although she could no longer afford to buy it by the case.

When my mom saw that the Riggios were serving Yquem that epochal night, to say she got excited is a bit of an understatement. Somewhere around one a.m. the party was still going strong but Janis and I were exhausted. We told my mom we wanted to leave and that, since she was on crutches, we'd help get her home in a taxi. My mom said, "They haven't served the Yquem yet." I said, "I know, but we're tired." And she said, quite ferociously, "I'm not leaving until I get my Yquem!"

Bad foot and all, she made her way over to Louise Riggio to ask when the dessert wine might be coming. Louise, the perfect hostess, immediately went to check it out. On her way back, she passed our table, leaned in to me, and said, "Your mom *really* likes her Yquem." All I could do was shrug and say, "She's an animal."

We stuck around another hour or so until my mother had a glass of her beloved sweet wine. Or, rather, three or four glasses. We finally poured her into a cab and she went home soused but satisfied.

This led to another yearly ritual.

My mother's birthday and her sister Lil's birthday fell a couple of weeks apart: my mom's was on August 30 and Lil's was in mid-September. When Lil was about to turn ninety-four, we decided it was time to have a dual celebration. The Riggios have a close friend, Starr Boggs, who runs a wonderful eponymously named restaurant in Westhampton. So after some back-and-forth, we divvied up the responsibilities: Toward the end of August, I'd rent a stretch limo and take fifteen people to Starr's for my mom's birthday. Starr would prepare a major feast, I'd pay for the car and the dinner, and Len and Louise would bring the wine. The first year we did this, I'm sure prodded by their remembrance of my mother's obsession, Len and Louise brought two bottles of 1967 Yquem—one of the great vintages.

My mother was thrilled, of course, but my ninety-four-year-old auntie went berserk—she had never tasted this particular quaff before and couldn't believe how good it was. Len noted that night that one bottle would generally suffice for fifteen people or so, since Yquem is usually sipped slowly and savored appropriately. But these two old dames guzzled it like there was no tomorrow, and between them they probably drank half a bottle. Standing in the parking lot after dinner, my aunt Lil took my arm and told me how much she loved the dessert wine. "Peter," she said, "could I buy that on my own?" "You could," I told her, "but the bottles that Len brought tonight, if you bought them today, they'd probably cost a few thousand dollars."

For one brief moment, I thought I'd given my aunt a heart attack. But she recovered, staggered into the limo, and never again brought up the idea of buying a bottle on her own.

We repeated this ritual celebration for the next several years. It was always the same: the limo, the spectacular meal, the great wines, and the final presentation of two bottles of Yquem. Then, a few weeks before my aunt's ninety-eighth birthday, she went into the hospital with heart problems and had a fairly serious operation. I called her when she was still in the hospital and asked how she was feeling.

"I was really scared," she told me. "I thought this was it. But when I came out of the anesthesia, do you know the first thing I asked the doctor?"

"No," I said.

"I asked him if I'd be able to drink dessert wine in a couple of weeks. He said yes, thank God, so everything's okay."

That year's party, in August 2008, was as fun as always. The pastry chef at Starr's made a strawberry shortcake at my mother's request, and, as usual, Len and Louise brought the Yquem. Lil and my mom drank it happily, and they both even took a glassful with them to drink during the ride back to Sag Harbor. Lil died a few weeks later, not quite reaching the century mark but having lived long enough to, once again, have the pleasure of filling up on Yquem.

The annual birthday celebrations continued on. In August 2015, when my mom turned ninety-three, we once again got in the limo with our various guests, drove the forty-five minutes from Sag Harbor to Starr's restaurant, and had a wonderful celebration. My mother recalled that after the previous year's dinner she'd awakened the next morning with a major hangover, so she cut back on the red and white wine and saved most of her drinking for the Yquem.

While she sipped it, I did my best to make a toast. I tried to read from the opening pages of this book but it didn't go too well. I'd read a sentence, get choked up, start again, burst into tears, maybe get through a whole paragraph, have to stop. People seemed to be moved by my display of emotion; I just felt like an idiot because, while I had no trouble writing about my mom, I was unable to read this to her aloud.

Almost all of this book was written while my mother was alive, which is why I kept most of it in the present tense. It never felt right to use the past tense when writing or talking or thinking about my mom. Sadly, she didn't get to taste my salmon coulibiac or the truffle-covered filet mignons or the tarte tatin. She didn't get to taste the challah, either, although she was around to take great pleasure in my detailed description of my dismal attempts at making it.

At my mom's final birthday celebration, my emotions got the better of me and I didn't make it through the passages I intended to read. But my mom got the gist of it—and when, at last, I gave up and retreated to my seat—she raised her glass of Yquem. Her eyes shone with happiness and I could tell she was reveling in the love that was radiating from all of us around the table. And I knew what she was thinking:

You're lucky.

PHOTO BY MICHAEL LUPPINO

ACKNOWLEDGMENTS

All books, especially a book like this, need a lot of help from inception to bookshelf to living room. For these people, "help" is an understatement: Esther Newberg, John Sterling, Stephen Rubin, Maggie Richards, Pat Eisenman, Carolyn O'Keefe, Fiona Lowenstein, Michael Luppino, Loriel Olivier, Zoe Sandler. The same applies to Sandi Mendelson, who also lived through most of it. Jenna Brickley did a lot of . . . well . . . just plain stuff that was invaluable. And Jordan Rodman went above and beyond the call of duty. Thanks.

ABOUT THE AUTHOR

PETER GETHERS is an author, screenwriter, playwright, book editor, and film and television producer. His eleven previous books include *The Cat Who Went to Paris*, the first in a best-selling trilogy about his extraordinary cat, Norton. He is also the cocreator and coproducer of the hit off-Broadway play *Old Jews Telling Jokes*. He lives in New York City; Sag Harbor, New York; and, whenever possible, Sicily.